'PLAY AWAY PLEASE'

'PLAY AWAY PLEASE'

THE TALE OF THE SALE OF GOLF'S GREATEST ICON – THE ST ANDREWS OLD COURSE STARTER'S BOX

JOHN PETER HAGEN

MAINSTREAM
PUBLISHING

EDINBURGH AND LONDON

First published in Great Britain in 2010 by
MAINSTREAM PUBLISHING COMPANY
(EDINBURGH) LTD
7 Albany Street
Edinburgh EH1 3UG

ISBN 9781845966058

This book is a fictional account based on the life, experiences
and recollections of the author. In some cases, names of people,
sequences or detail of events have been changed to protect the
privacy of others, and some characters have been created for
artistic purposes. The author has stated to the publishers that,
except in such respects, the contents of this book are true

A catalogue record for this book is
available from the British Library

Typeset in Requiem and Sabon

Printed in Great Britain by
Clays Ltd, St Ives plc

1 3 5 7 9 10 8 6 4 2

http://www.mainstreampublishing.com
http://www.randomhouse.co.uk
http://www.playawayplease.com

This book is dedicated to
Jeannette Marx Geller
En coelo quies est
In heaven there is rest

ACKNOWLEDGEMENTS

I am grateful to many people who have given freely of their time and intelligence to keep me focused and help me make this book a reality. I offer specific mention to:

Alan McGregor, chief executive of the St Andrews Links Trust, and his management team, for granting me access to records and photographs, for their encouragement once the auction process had been completed and for their unqualified endorsement of public golf in St Andrews – the Home of the *Golff*.

Anita Clay Kornfeld, for her persistence, solid reasoning and belief in me and my passion.

Ann Buchwald, literary agent, and Frank Cooper, literary and theatrical agent, who encouraged and supported me early in my writing career.

Frank D. ('Sandy') Tatum Jr, for his wisdom, knowledge and introducing me to the business of ensuring golf's integrity will be maintained everywhere and by everyone who plays the game.

Lewine Mair, for being the consummate professional journalist and maintaining her resolve with me in the project.

Readers and supporters during the eight-year process of turning my journals into a cohesive whole: Roxanne Barnes, Malcolm Campbell, JoJo Capece-Osgood, Meryl Comer, Joyce Dash, David Joy, Mike Marix and Sally Witzky.

I also thank Karyn Millar, my editor, for her incisiveness, integrity and professionalism.

I thank my granddaughter Madelynn 'Maddie' and my grandson, Blair, for their humour and love in often difficult times.

Finally, I thank my mother, Gladys, now counting the days of her 100th year, for her love and for being my mother.

CONTENTS

Foreword by Jack Nicklaus *xi*

Preface *xiii*

CHAPTER 1   Holy Grail *1*

CHAPTER 2   Why? Why the Change? *9*

CHAPTER 3   Kitchen *14*

CHAPTER 4   Victorian Bathing Boxes *19*

CHAPTER 5   The Links and the St Andrews Links Trust *22*

CHAPTER 6   Three Columns *28*

CHAPTER 7   Timing and Luck *33*

CHAPTER 8   Jack Franks *37*

CHAPTER 9   The Auction *42*

CHAPTER 10   The First Visit After the Auction *50*

CHAPTER 11   Lunch with the Links Trust *55*

CHAPTER 12   European Tour Productions *61*

CHAPTER 13   Fisher Wives and Mozart *65*

CHAPTER 14   Ladies Lake and Tontine *69*

CHAPTER 15   The Passing of the Keys Ceremony and the Dutch Journalist *77*

CHAPTER 16   Iain Macfarlane Lowe *84*

CHAPTER 17   Pittenweem, Bugatti and Ferrari *90*

CHAPTER 18   Princes Street *94*

CHAPTER 19   Dunhill Links Championship *97*

CHAPTER 20   Jim Brown: Starter *99*

CHAPTER 21   Fraser Smart, Mike Horkan and Rob Donaldson *107*

CHAPTER 22	Ian Joy's Photography Shop	*111*
CHAPTER 23	Dunvegan Pub	*114*
CHAPTER 24	Will	*116*
CHAPTER 25	Lord Angus Locards	*120*
CHAPTER 26	California Banking	*131*
CHAPTER 27	Loch Leven and Golf Place	*134*
CHAPTER 28	'Play Away Please': the Final Round	*137*
CHAPTER 29	Kingsbarns	*143*
CHAPTER 30	Prince William	*145*
CHAPTER 31	Bricks, Flues and the Gang of Six	*150*
CHAPTER 32	Lunch at the Royal and Ancient Golf Club's Woollen Mill	*159*
CHAPTER 33	Saw Blades and Snakes	*163*
CHAPTER 34	The University Library and Mascara	*165*
CHAPTER 35	Ballet, Robots and Sleet	*174*
CHAPTER 36	British Golf Museum	*177*
CHAPTER 37	David Joy	*179*
CHAPTER 38	Snow Squalls and Rainbows	*182*
CHAPTER 39	Old Tom Morris	*186*
CHAPTER 40	The Good, the Bad and the Ugly	*188*
CHAPTER 41	Farewells	*193*
CHAPTER 42	Paris and Gallic Ambivalence	*202*
CHAPTER 43	US Customs	*204*
CHAPTER 44	Jack Franks – Reprise	*207*
CHAPTER 45	Nostalgia	*211*
	Epilogue	*214*
	Appendix: The Holes of the Old Course	*217*
	Glossary	*224*
	Bibliography	*233*

FOREWORD

My love affair with St Andrews and the Old Course began in 1964, and to this day, St Andrews remains one of my favourite places to visit and the Old Course is still among my favourite places in the world to play golf. Once you get there, meet the wonderful people and play golf, you understand what it is – one of the most beautiful places in the world. In this book, John Peter Hagen transports you to the magical lands through the eyes of golf's greatest icon – the Old Course Starter's Box – and gives a revealing portrait of the icon's sale, the town and a 'wee' bit of history and lore. Bob Jones often said that if a golfer is to be remembered, he must win the Open Championship at St Andrews. This book is a way of remembering the honesty and integrity the game of golf represents – and stirring the passion in every golfer to make the pilgrimage to St Andrews.

*Jack Nicklaus, Open Champion on
the Old Course 1970 and 1978*

PREFACE

I had a vision. I had a passion. They combined to create an uncertain odyssey that became littered with the detritus of near failure, misguided emotional detours and, finally – success.

This is not a history book, but it is a story of observation, recollection and place, and the people who live in that place – St Andrews, Kingdom of Fife, Scotland. It is also a personal account of patronage and my quest to assure golf's greatest icon – the Old Course Starter's Box – was preserved as a consummate symbol of integrity and fair play.

This is also an adventure story that will stir passions in every golfer to make the pilgrimage to Scotland and play the Old Course, whether on a balmy summer day with a whiff of salt and seaweed in the air, or in the early spring or late autumn when snow squalls often ride sideways in the wind.

I have travelled to many places, had many incredible adventures and overcome many obstacles. My journals attest to that. This experience was unique. Purchase of the Box at auction the day before 9/11 obviously contributed, but so did the inherent humanity of the Scots I met during the process – and the fact that it took me to places I would not have thought of going or, in a few instances, even dared to go.

Most important of all, my eight-year journey with the Starter's Box allowed me to open my eyes and laugh, and widen my gaze, and embrace that 'special' something that so often happens at the margin of everyday life – where everyone dreams of a better life and simple answers to life's fundamental questions.

John Peter Hagen
December 2009

CHAPTER 1

....

HOLY GRAIL

SUMMER OF YESTERYEAR 1992

When I first looked out in September 1954, it seemed like
heaven. All my imaginings were proved true. There before
me in the soft damp light of autumn lay this holy ground.
So wide and keen was that first hole, sharing with the last
the width of two cricket fields, and down at the end that
dark surface ribbon that indicates the narrow burn. And
over it, banking, the closer cut green with the flag straight
out in the wind.

Peter Thomson, five-times winner of the Open Championship.
His second win, in 1955, was on the Old Course

It was a warm August morning in the summer of 1992. The air
was filled with the wonderful smells of the salty sea and sandy turf
and the music of soaring gulls and fulmars.

Claudia and I were in Scotland's Kingdom of Fife, the heart of
our dream. We looked at each other with expectant smiles as I
turned our little car onto the infamous Grannie Clark's Wynd in St
Andrews. Her face was beaming and blooming with the intuition
our adventure was finally beginning. Suddenly it did, because there
in front of us, framed in the expansiveness of a deep-blue North
Sea sky, was golf's holy grail, the most enchanting and famous
vista in the world of sports.

My eyes scanned the panorama from the distant West Sands
– the beach featured in the motion picture *Chariots of Fire* – to
the Victorian architecture of the Caddie Pavilion and the stately,
foreboding Royal and Ancient Golf Club, sitting regally and
protecting the Starter's Box, then the vibrant green of the sparse,

Number of times Ben Hogan w on the Open Championship
(Carnoustie, 1953)

1

low-lying lands of the first and eighteenth fairways, and finally the menacingly shadowed Valley of Sin, fronting the eighteenth green of the 600-year-old Old Course Links.

'Stop the car!' Claudia's trilling words came out a command as she fought to unlock and open the car door. I slowed the car until the chattering diesel engine died, then gazed to the little elongated Roman-arched bridge on our left, a haunting bump over the Swilcan Burn. She hopped out, stopped for a moment to inhale the freshness of the air and ran towards the eighteenth fairway, her tall, curvy body bending and twisting in ecstasy as she raised her arms and hands to the heavens. When she reached the fairway, she fell to her knees and kissed its hallowed soil, her long dark hair falling from its bun and clouding her face.

'I am so ready for this, darling! We're here . . . at the Home of Golf and on the Old Course!' Her words rang out to the sky as she got back in the car, clapped her hands and laughed with an excited thunder more common to a megaphone-holding cheerleader than the 35-year-old respected cleric she was. Still laughing a few moments later, she reached for a tissue to wipe away her tears and the thick, red evidence of the solid kiss she had planted on the side of my mouth.

'I like the taste. Leave it, my dear. You're lucky you didn't get hit by a ball coming off the eighteenth tee.'

'Oh my God. I forgot this is a double fairway!'

'Let's play golf,' I deadpanned while taking in the wonderful odour of her perfume. We waited for a foursome walking down the first fairway to cross the Wynd before driving on and parking 'Roller Skate', as we had affectionately nicknamed our rental car. I collected another kiss as we unpacked our golf clubs and quickly walked to the Starter's Box and read the sign – the literal confirmation we had arrived – paid our fees and met our caddies.

'This is it, J.P. At last,' Claudia said in her soft, bendy Italian accent. She nudged me. 'It is so beautiful here – and *so* infectious! No wonder people want to keep coming back.' She paused and looked around and up at the facade of the Royal and Ancient Golf Club (or the R&A, as most refer to it). 'It *is* real.' Her words carried a tone of disbelief. 'After seeing all this on television and in books for so many years . . . and the Wynd . . . what a romantic word.'

My adrenalin was rising also as I told her Grannie Clark's Wynd was named after a Mrs Clark who ran a small inn alongside the

Number of times Jack Nicklaus won the US Amateur Championship (1959 and 1961)

Old Course in the early 1800s, and that in the beginning it was a simple dirt path that was used to transport the town's lifeboat across the Links to the beach.

'Look at everyone,' I chuckled. 'Standing here, nervous as hell, taking practice swings they hope will let them score the round of their lives . . .'

'Like us – you're right. Everyone is talking so quietly, almost reverently.' She took a deep breath and exhaled heavily as she tried to calm herself. 'Look at their faces,' she said as she touched my arm. 'Most of them look like they're crying with happiness.'

'Or with humility. Oh, the rush of adrenalin!'

I listened to the conversation of a family foursome of local residents standing politely next to the tee. It was a mother, father, teenage daughter and a relative, I guessed, without caddies, carrying their own golf bags. Claudia was right. I sensed that, even for them, teeing off on the Old Course was special and emotional, no matter how many times they had done it before – from the ages of the husband and wife, it had certainly been for decades.

Without warning, the deep resonating baritone of the starter broke the stillness as he bellowed the family's starting time over the tannoy. We watched them tee off as we chatted with some of the others who were also waiting to play. Instantly, a breeze began whipping the flagstick on the eighteenth green and the temperature began to drop. We each took a club from our bags and went behind the Starter's Box to stretch and take a couple of practice swings.

'I love you,' I said, as she raised a club above her head with both hands in an arching, seductive stretch of her back. 'You're still invigorating.'

'Why thank you, J.P. What a nice thought after all these years.' She followed her words with a long, deep half-smile.

'Hard work triumphs.'

A few minutes later, the starter's rich, practised voice pierced the stillness and bellowed, 'Will the 10.40 tee time . . . *play away please!*'

The words startled us. It was our tee time! We were being called to play the Old Course! We hugged gently, kissed each other and walked to the back of the first tee to stand alongside our caddies. The couple from Spain who were playing with us played first. It gave me time to study my caddie, who introduced himself as 'Davey'.

'Do you have a family name?' I asked.

'Davey is mor'n enough for t'day,' he said, dismissing me. Squint-eyed, he was focused on the wind direction.

I laughed. He could have been a character from Hollywood's Central Casting, with wind-burned reddish cheeks, searching eyes and a tweedy snap-brim cap from which long, wide, unkempt salt-and-pepper sideburns coursed below his ears. He wore a well-frayed, belted, grey-stained mackintosh with one epaulette. When I looked down at his feet, I shook my head. 'Davey, you're wearing two left shoes.'

'Aye.' A downcast, wary eye caught my smile. 'They fit.'

We couldn't stop giggling. Finally Claudia composed herself and casually teed her ball from the men's markers, surprising everyone, including the starter, I noticed. With but two practice swings, one a bit manufactured and slightly jerky, she swung her driver in a high, wide arc with a wonderfully orchestrated pace that produced a 'whacking' sound so solid, so sure, I knew the ball's path was high and on a drifting right-to-left trajectory from over the white fence line that defined the out-of-bounds to a landing in the centre of the fairway. She had played the stiffening wind blowing in off the sea perfectly as her ball stopped rolling 140 yards from the meandering Swilcan Burn, which guards the front of the first green.

Claudia looked at me, disbelieving, and made a small perfunctory curtsy to those who were applauding. Her long steely legs, the legs of a chorine, outlined themselves perfectly through her tailored burgundy trousers, held tight to her narrow waist by a silver-buckled blue alligator belt. 'All this is stopping my life in its tracks, sweetie, so don't ruin my mood. Your turn.' Her signature wide, crooked grin spread across her face almost mischievously as she passed her driver to her caddie and leaned into me a little.

I walked to the tee box, hoping my first swing on the Links would not be an embarrassment. I was more nervous, I think, than I had ever been over almost anything in my life. All I thought about was gripping my driver lightly and keeping the tension out of my shoulders. It wasn't very pretty, but I hit the ball well enough: it went straight but still stopped 20 yards behind Claudia's ball.

With catcalls and whistles following us down the fairway, I tried to slow my adrenalin rush by talking to Davey, who looked to be, well, elderly. Claudia? She was Claudia, which meant all 5 ft 9 in. of her strode the fairway with her usual confident, straight-spined gait, all complemented by a muted red-and-blue-diamond argyle cashmere sweater worn over a purple polo neck. The sight of her confirmed to me again that no matter what she wore, including the blousy gown when she was awarded her doctorate, or her habit during Sunday services, she personified the *bella figura* of her Italian heritage – the belief in substance and acting your best in everything in life. The near swagger and white golf glove hanging from her rear trouser pocket were the only signs she was also a consummate jock.

I smiled, acknowledging the borderline-crude gestures directed towards her by players passing on the eighteenth-hole side of the fairway. She was talking to Little Joe, her caddie, in a warm, interested voice and missed the innuendos.

When we came to my ball, she turned and half-skipped a couple of times, causing her mass of tied-back hair to billow in the breeze a full foot above Little Joe's slumping head. 'This is what life is all about,' she said to Little Joe. 'This is why we work, struggle and save money – even pray,' she added with a giggle. 'This is *joie de vivre*, an epiphany! There really are no other phrases for it.'

'Aye, words I dinnae ken or need tae ken, I think,' Little Joe answered seriously as he took off his cap, scratched his balding, scarred scalp and looked towards Davey with a serious frown. 'Wee bedtime dram o' whisky 'nuf o' life-livin' for me.'

Three and a half hours later, as we walked up the eighteenth fairway – with Claudia certain to make another par and shoot a respectable three-birdie, seventy-five – my smiling, voluble partner put her arm around me, jabbed me playfully with a pointy hip and rested her high-cheekboned head next to mine. 'There *is* a spiritual presence out here,' she said resolutely. 'This place – these lands – are packed with myth. Everything I've read and heard is true. We are not alone out here, J.P. These lands *are* mystical.' She lowered her head, pouted like a ten year old and spoke softly: 'When can we come back? There's a lot of sermon material here, daddy. When can we come back? Huh? Huh?' A passing kiss found my forehead while she giggled again and my roving hand reached down and grabbed her firm, tight buttock. The caddies, who for three hours had really said little aside from giving us local knowledge and green reads, smiled and applauded. Then they lifted our golf bags back on their shoulders, their faces became dour again and they returned to their job of giving us the slopes in the green and yardages to the top of the Valley of Sin, as the hole was cut just behind the rise.

'Where ye off tae now?' Davey said as we walked off the eighteenth green and I paid the caddie fees. 'Aye, earned a whisky the missus did . . . Fine round of scorin' for a first-time lass on the Old, an' a parson at that. Aye, a first.'

Claudia laughed at his seriousness. 'What, Davey?' she said. 'Is this the first time you've caddied for a preacher?'

'Aye. That I want to remember. An' the first time with a preacher, an' a lady preacher at that . . . for three hours 'tis.'

'My husband mostly calls me Doc, because of my divinity degrees, if that name makes you feel more comfortable,' she offered while she took off her glove and put it in a pocket of her golf bag.

'Doc? Better start for friendship, 'tis.'

I laughed. 'We're going to the Jigger, of course.'

'Aye,' he quickly retorted as his eyes squinted and searched the sky for something obtainable.

We drove to the Jigger pub, which lies alongside the stone wall abutting the seventeenth hole. Ales and ceremonial whiskies were quickly ordered, with the whiskies chosen because they had names we had never heard of and couldn't pronounce. One was Bunnahabhain and the other anCnoc of the Knockdhu distillery. In the case of the former, relish the smell of smoke followed by a rushing taste of unfamiliar nuts and spoiled fruit that lingers far too long; in the latter, think honey, lemon, vanilla and toffee, mixed together with the smell of wet, sweaty woollen mittens as they steam dry on a hut's warming kerosene-fuelled stove aside an ice-skating pond in the frigid winters of Minnesota.

'We must finish these, honey. They're expensive,' Doc laughed, almost slurring her words as she tried to get the whisky down between sips of lager. 'They're sus . . . spensive. More than we collect in loose bills in the plates on a slow summer Sunday.'

'Awful?' I answered, looking at my whisky glass. 'Bloody awful.' I took another sip of ale. '*Bloody* seems to be a convenient word here. Did you notice, with the caddies? Good and bad.'

Doc choked a bit as she tasted my anCnoc, winced and took a quick swallow from her water glass. 'Awful!'

'When you drove the ninth and made a good birdie, Little Joe said, "Bloody strong shot, that." When I made a bad bogey on the twelfth, he said, "Bloody awful swing – not to be remembered."'

Doc nodded, took a mirror from her purse and gazed at herself. The wind and an hour of rain that had started as we stood on the fourteenth tee had taken their toll. Her hair was knotted and her make-up barely a blur of colour. 'Why didn't you tell me I look like hell?' she asked as she retied her hair.

'You didn't ask,' I answered at once, knowing that I was damned if I did and damned if I didn't.

'Touché. When you mis-hit your ball in the Hell Bunker, Davey sighed and looked at me: "No bloody golf being played now."' Doc laughed and swept her hair back with open hands.

'I liked Little Joe's answer when you were standing at your ball on the seventeenth fairway. You asked him if you could reach the green with a five-iron.'

A wounded smirk crossed her face because Doc knew Little Joe's answer was one I would never forget.

I laughed. '"Eventually," he said, "eventually."'

We looked at each other, our eyes read each other's minds and we picked up the tumblers again for another volley of whisky. I caught sight of Davey and Little Joe out of the corner of my eyes, walking towards our table, caps off. Davey's cap was a weathered tartan with the remnants of a red pompom sprouting from the top.

'The lads,' I said cheerfully, the whisky 'n' ale well on their journey to my brain. 'What brings you here?'

'Aye, ye forgot these,' Davey answered with a studied meekness. He reached into his pocket and took out three tees, a twenty-pence coin I had been using as a ball marker and one of my golf balls.

Doc's eyes flickered as Davey eyed the lager glasses and she caught his look. 'Would you join us for a lager? As our guests, of course?'

'Why thank ye, mighty kind,' they answered quickly, Davey's hushed words following Little Joe's.

'Aye, many thanks. Nice to ask,' Davey added sincerely, his weather-beaten face glowing with a broad, appreciative smile.

The bartender nodded understandingly and began drawing the lagers and pouring the drams.

We toasted the day, Little Joe taking the dram in a single swallow. 'I thought you might have softened it with water after the toast,' Doc said innocently.

'Aye, whenever someone asks me if I want water with my whisky, I say I'm thirsty, not dirty.'

When the caddies left us an hour later, after four pints of ale, two wee drams of Bell's whisky, hamburger dinners and I don't know how many bags of crisps between them, the bartender came to our table. 'Welcome to Scotland,' he said with an apologetic smile as he wiped his hands on the flap of his apron. He told us the classic caddie ploy was to keep a few tees or a player's golf ball in his pocket after the round. Then, when they knew which pub the players were off to, they would follow under the guise, in true Scots honesty, ahem, of returning the equipment. In reality, it was for the certain ale and whisky and, if they were lucky, a hot meal.

We left the pub a little later and dashed to the car as the rain had become heavy and the wind was noisily gusting. On the way we tried kissing, but our noses and Claudia's wet hair kept getting in the way. When we were finally under the sure protection of the porte-cochère of our hotel, I looked back towards the town and a low, monotonous grey sky. The gulls were swirling now, with more urgency in their patterns of flight.

'What was the bill?' Doc asked as we walked along the corridor to our room. 'Or don't I want to know?'

'You don't want to know,' I said, stifling a burp. 'More than one collection plate's worth.' My mind was focusing on us, five hours before, and the fact it was the first time I recalled grabbing her buttock in public without being admonished.

'OK. No sense in ruining the trip.'

'You're not going to be doing much knitting this trip,' my loose tongue added as I reached into my pocket for our room key.

She looked at me with crinkled eyes. 'Hmm,' was her too quick answer.

Little was I to know that nearly less than a decade later I would be back in St Andrews and – as befits much of Scottish history, with its troubled propensity towards sieges, bloodshed, burnings at the stake and fierce battles (not to mention the fury of the Reformation) – I would be caught, figuratively speaking, in the nets of life with an archer's target on my back and a healthy percentage of the population aiming at the bull's eye. Unpleasant thoughts, if you understand some consider golf a slow form of death and archers are held as deities and heroes in several mythologies that emanate from the United Kingdom.

---

8 Number of golfers who played in the first Open Championship at Prestwick (three rounds on a twelve-hole course)

CHAPTER 2

....

WHY? WHY THE CHANGE?

EARLY AUGUST 2001

They christened their game golf because they were
Scottish and revelled in meaningless Celtic noises in the
back of the throat.

Stephen Fry

The *Los Angeles Times* sports columnist Tommy Bonk wrote an
early August 2001 column on the St Andrews Links Trust, which
manages the operations of the all-public Links on behalf of the
town, and the fact it had made the decision to auction the Old
Course Starter's Box on its website on 10 September.

I was shocked, to put it mildly, even after I read the column a
second time. Why would they sell this icon, I asked myself? Why
would the Links Trust sell a national treasure?

My mind flashed back to when Doc and I were living in
Minnesota and we drove out to our club on a particularly cold,
borderline snowy November Saturday, hoping to play a last
round of the year. It was not even eight in the morning when we
stood in the clubhouse with the other members – foolish enough
to think as we did – and waited for the greens to thaw. When
Jimmy, the club pro and a native Scotsman, realised a certain
level of gloom and boredom had settled in, he picked up the word
sportsman and, for who knows what reason, came up with the
suggestion of having a little contest, then and there. We were to
name the 'homes' of specific sports and decide which venue best
epitomised the spirit of sportsmanship – the homes of individual
teams such as the Boston Garden or Dodger Stadium, or Lord's
in London weren't to be included – and, as we all agreed, the

year-long betting pool would go to whoever came up with the best idea.

After a fair amount of argument and discussion, we concurred with Doc's suggestion that the venue which most famously epitomised sportsmanship was not one of the thousands of nameless arenas or stadium pitches that populate the world's major cities and double as rock concert and boxing venues. Instead, it was the Old Course vista with its ribbon of distinctive green boundary fencing and criss-cross of white slats – with Jimmy emphasising the Starter's Box because everyone who has played the course has checked in there and paid their fees. ''Tis the little building,' I remember him saying, 'the Starter's Box, golf's greatest icon. She's every golfer's celebrity icon.' It almost brought him to tears. 'For me, in me youth, checking in at the Box was the physical and emotional confirmation I was at the Home of Golf and about to play the Old Course Links.'

Doc collected the wager, most of which was wiped away by an order of Bloody Marys.

Curious, I logged on to the Trust's website, which took an eternity as the new dial-up Internet line in our house kept dropping the connection and downloads. The auction was already in progress with a posted bid of £7,000 (about $15,000 in 2001 US dollars). I remember spending most of the rest of the day recollecting our too few trips to Scotland and fantasising about owning such a treasure – and the Pandora's box that would surely be a part of the package.

The next morning I went on the website of the *Daily Mail*. A sports-page headline blazed: 'For Sale: a wee slice of our golf history'. I decided to call the Links Trust's chief executive, Alan McGregor. In a voice filled with richly defined enthusiasm, he told me the area around the first tee of the Old Course was to be reworked over the coming winter to accommodate a rebuilding and enlargement of the putting green as a concession to contestants in future Opens. 'At the same time,' he added, 'the R&A has scheduled an upgrade of its underground utility lines as a phase of its long-overdue clubhouse renovation. The lines either pass under or alongside the Box; no one is sure because the building has undergone many undocumented upgrades since its construction in 1854 . . . This means the Box has to be moved, perhaps five metres or so, and then moved back. In the end, when her perhaps fragile condition was factored in, our engineers said it was unrealistic and economically unfeasible to try to move the Box, and then move it back into place, without any damage occurring. Common sense tells us – unfortunately, perhaps – that we should demolish her and build a new box.'

'There must be other answers?' I asked weakly.

'Perhaps, but at the Trust's summer board meeting, the launch of the town's junior-golf programme and the Old Course's first-tee construction issues were on the agenda. Mind you, the cost of the junior-golf programme was going to be formidable. During the meeting, almost as an afterthought, a distinguished board member suggested selling the Hut at auction on the Trust's website instead of demolishing her. "Everything is selling on the Internet these days," he offered casually, "why not the Hut? Let someone else worry about moving it – on their money. Maybe there's a crazy, rich American lurking. The proceeds can help us kick-start junior golf."'

I said nothing for a moment. 'Hut?' I finally asked.

'Oh, yes. We sometimes call her the Hut.'

(Appropriately, all starter's boxes are feminine because they birth every round of golf played – and, in the case of the Old Course box, she has been the midwife to the round every golfer who has played the Links wants to boast about – plus, she *is* where you pay your green fees.)

I told him I was interested, though I had no idea what I meant, and said I would call him back in a few days.

Next, I called Doc. 'Hey preacher,' I blurted out excitedly before acknowledging her hello, 'I have a new intellectual challenge for you.'

'Hi, *J.P.*,' she countered, deadpan. 'What are you talking about? You must have called Scotland . . .'

Visualising her rolling her beautifully lustrous brown eyes, I didn't care if her use of the letters 'J.P.' this time referenced heathen, helpmate or one of the other nouns in her literary arsenal. (At least she didn't use the *Jonathan* word, which only showed its face when her Italian temper raged, or when she became introspective, which, I had noticed, was becoming more and more commonplace.)

'Ah, yes, you knew I would. I think I have uncovered a unique "marketing" opportunity for both of us. Think passion. Think an iconic symbol for living a better life. Think life-changing moments . . .'

'What?' She cut me off.

'I offer you fresh lessons from the Old Course on how to save the souls of mankind. Success, happiness, love, peace and whatever else you believe constitutes a just life is represented by the Starter's Box.'

'Huh?' Her question slid out of her mouth slowly, which was the giveaway her mind was focusing on the word *golf*. 'We've talked about how I often collect topics for sermons, or should I say observations on the human condition, on the golf course, but is this not a stretch?'

I ignored the question. 'All right,' I conceded, 'I don't know what I'm talking about yet because the potential of this opportunity has only been germinating a day or so; it's all been right brain ... but since it involves the Old Course and the Starter's Box ... as well as the words, I think, *global marketing*, *icons*, *passion*, *symbol of integrity*, *fair play* – and who knows what else – it has my attention.'

'J.P.,' she finally said, mockingly, in a fake Scots accent, ''Tis better for you to fall on your knees in gratitude before me than fall under the wrath and curse of this Box, even if it is under the control of Fife's golf gods.'

'I'll fall on my knees in front of you in gratitude any time,' I chuckled, taking advantage of the double-entendre opportunity. 'Think of the Starter's Box as an icon representing fresh directions in people's lives. After all, golf brought us together.'

Her sandy voice tone sounded hesitant as her mind absorbed my comment. 'As in ... beyond-the-box thinking?'

'You said it, I didn't. Bad pun.'

'I don't need you to lay parables on me that focus on mankind's longing for innocence or nostalgia, or give us illustrations that demonstrate how we can open our eyes ...'

'Really?'

'Yes, *really*.'

'Lighten up, honey.' I could imagine Doc in her patented pose of reflection, looking out of the window of her study, combing her hair with a hand and reworking her chignon with its combs, her furrowed, heavy eyebrows pinched in a tight focus on the landscape.

'Heavy rain from the monsoon in Mexico and possibly even tornados are forecast for later,' she answered. 'I would rather be

12 Number of people who have aced the sixteenth hole at Cypress Point Golf Club (one a w oman, Mhairi McKay)

trapped by the weather of Scotland. September in Scotland has a nice ring to it, don't you think?'

I paced the carpet with an occasional glance out to the picture-perfect wide expanse of the golf courses my office overlooked in Los Angeles. Storm clouds were gathering out in the Pacific Ocean. My brain had been spinning full-time with a myriad of intuitive and random musings on my eclectic business career: from practising architecture to creating a traditional real-estate development business and the promotion of World's Fair pavilions in Spain, Hungary and Japan, with Hughes Aircraft and Tokyo's Mitsubishi Corporation. All had been driven, in reality, by the marketing of singular ideas.

In the middle of it all, the thought hit me that the Box was presenting herself to me as another unique marketing opportunity, which my history had conditioned me to successfully exploit. This time the marketing opportunity was based on sportsmanship because what I remembered most after we left Scotland – and what still rises from my subconscious every time I go there, even now, all these years later – was that with the Links, including the Old Course, being absolutely public courses, the venue is certainly unique in the world of sports. Everyone, from high-handicap amateurs to professionals, regardless of age, class, race or gender, can play the Links on a near daily basis in a unified spirit of fair play.

Indeed, few amateurs will ever play tennis on Wimbledon's Centre Court or bat in Yankee Stadium in a Little League uniform, and few who spend a lifetime playing the piano will ever appear in concert on the stages of either Wigmore or Carnegie Hall. Who really remembers, except the fanatic, where any Super Bowl or NBA title or World Cup has been played?

CHAPTER 3

KITCHEN

MID-AUGUST 2001

The 'second sight' possessed by the Highlanders in Scotland
is actually a foreknowledge of future events. I believe they
possess this gift because they don't wear trousers.

G.C. Lichtenberg

Surprisingly, neither Doc nor I had outside business commitments
that evening. For her it meant no one sought emergency marriage
or drug counselling, no one was on death's doorstep and the
church's utility bills were assured of being paid the rest of the year.
For me it meant no angry bankers, disgruntled homeowners or
ankle-biting attorneys were at my heels.

'A movie, Claudia?' I asked sarcastically as I walked into the
kitchen from the garage. She knew I did not like to go to the
movies because, among other reasons, I liked my entertainment
live, in three dimensions, as in theatre, opera or sculpture, or
in nature, meaning golf, the medium that had cemented our
relationship.

'You haven't called me by my name in a while.'

'That's because you look so wonderful, standing there, chopping
onions, your Mediterranean skin glowing.'

'You're either looking for forgiveness or up to mischief.' She
arched an eyebrow. 'Did you bring me flowers also?'

'Ha, ha. Not quite.'

'Mmm. No, J.P.: no movie, no TV, no book for you,' she
answered quickly as she set down her butcher's knife. 'Home
tonight, J.P. Thee and me. This Box has your adrenalin running,
hasn't it? You're pumped up.'

'You've noticed. Good idea . . . staying home.' We kissed a little before she pulled away and she started sneezing from the onion's fumes. 'No Internet either.'

'I like your rules. Can we talk about Scotland and the Valley of Sin . . .'

She brushed me off. 'The Box?'

'Well, maybe,' I answered meekly.

'It includes a trip for me?'

'Of course.'

'You have to promise you'll keep your high-pitched insistence out of the discussion.' She cackled softly, as she often did when our battling heritages – Norway and Italy – became part of a conversation.

'What is this, rule-setting for the Inquisition? What was your caddie's name the first trip . . . Litt . . . ?'

'Little Joe, as you damn well know. All these years later and you're still using Little Joe's "can I get there with a five-iron" line . . . Time you came up with something new. A trip to Fife would help.'

She went back to chopping vegetables, though from her smirk I read her mind was focused on St Andrews and the caddies and perhaps something else deeper in her subconscious. I ignored it, went into the den and put on a CD of Puccini's *Tosca* with Pavarotti and Freni, then uncorked a bottle of Amarone, poured two glasses and tied an apron around my waist in a solid knot.

We toasted as I started slicing a courgette. 'Davey's comment about me when I shanked a shot on the Jubilee Links was a classic also – when I said I was going to go drown myself in the North Sea . . .'

'Remember how he quickly responded: "Think ye can keep yer head down that long?"'

During a drawn-out dinner at the kitchen table we recalled that November 'Bloody Mary' Saturday in Minneapolis, as it had relevance to the idea that had seated itself in my mind – the idea being I could capitalise on ownership of the Starter's Box in my business.

'Golf is an addiction for so many,' I said. 'St Andrews and the Box are a big, passionate and historical part of it. Face it . . . if someone can rationalise playing golf when snow is about to fall in Minnesota, they can certainly rationalise buying a lot or house with an authentic link to St Andrews.'

Doc picked up on her remembrances. 'He was a wonderful man, a good club pro, Jimmy was,' she recollected quietly in a mumbling voice that confirmed what I was trying to get across to her hadn't registered. 'I will never forget him. He spent a lot of time with the juniors – much more than he needed to. He was a character, with his roundish body and wonderfully florid, always smiling face that worked from under his stack of unkempt red hair that always seemed ready to go to seed.'

'He always wore tweeds or corduroy, even in the summer humidity. Remember when we had golf spikes glued to a pair of wellies as a birthday present for him?'

Doc started laughing. 'I do. He played a round wearing them and was one under par.'

'Liked his booze, didn't he? That's what got him in the end, I think – or so his lavender skin seemed to suggest.'

Doc raised her wine glass and studied the deep garnet colour. 'Jimmy's narrow lips were always bloodless, without definition, when he reminisced about Scotland. The sun and wind seemed to seek them out every day. He always managed a cunning little smile.'

'He had the low thick eyebrows of a true Scot as I figured out on one of the trips when he went along; we were in a fisherman's pub somewhere.'

'That was in Anstruther.'

The telephone rang. Neither of us flinched. My elbows were on the table anchoring my wine glass as my eyes marvelled at the beauty of the woman across from me and the unique circumstances that had brought us together. Yet suddenly, there was a hollowness in my vision of her. I had thought this before; now I saw it. The word *vapid* came to mind and my sixth sense said the innuendo I had been reading in her, and I guessed she was reading in me, was correct. We were married, yes, but living by rote process, like robots. Discussing anything of mutual importance was past tense. I swallowed, with the less than subtle realisation that our life together was over. We were being polite, but it was over. The only question was when we would face resolution of the inevitable and formalise it. When would we admit it?

'Back to the Box. I have been thinking, darling, more than you know, about this quest of yours. My mind *has* been in Scotland lately. I remember that Saturday because Jimmy gave

us the depressing news we had already played our last round
of the year. No one was prepared to accept what he said. I also
recall, during a lull in the conversation, that somebody turned
off the television and muttered to no one in particular about
being damned tired of the dummy ads that ran on the sports
shows, which never have anything to do with sportsmanship. It
was all about selling beer, parading big-breasted bikini-clad girls
. . . Remember that? You don't see those ads running when you
watch a golf tournament.'

'You're right, and I do remember because of Morrison and the
expletives that exploded from his mostly vulgar mouth after he
yelled: "So? So what?"'

Doc started laughing. 'Oh, yes, I reminded *your* fellow members
that we were in violation of the by-laws if we discussed body parts
or anything alcohol-related while on the stately grounds of the
club.'

'*Our* fellow members, my dear,' I said in a friendly tone. 'I asked
you to quit pontificating – to loosen the reins a little and give our
wicked minds a holiday . . .'

'I said something directed to you, my heathen friend . . .' Doc sat
up in her chair. As she raised her chin to the ceiling, it accentuated
the curves of her torso. '"I cannot relent when souls as corrupted
as yours are involved . . ." Lord, I can't believe I said those things
in those days.' She looked at me. 'Why are you looking at me like
that?'

'You know why. Sometimes I think you were put on this planet
for only one reason.'

'To torment you with my body?'

'Your mind always does it first. Some days you make my life
pass before my eyes without any fuss.' I slid my foot under the
table until I touched her ankle. I felt it pull away.

'Do you want to finish this conversation?' she asked, barely
raising bushy eyebrows.

'Only if we consider "upstairs" in ten minutes.'

'OK.' She looked around the kitchen enquiringly. 'My knitting
must be upstairs.'

I reached for the wine bottle and refilled our glasses. 'God,
woman. You still have a way of stirring me. Did that come out of
my mouth the way I wanted it to?'

'Well enough, perhaps.'

'Back to the addiction, honey. The world doesn't know, but I do, that you're addicted to golf as others are to other material, shall we say, situations and vices. At the end of the day, the only reason you collected a doctorate of divinity from Cambridge was because it gave you the opportunity to take five years out of your life and play the great golf courses of the UK as often as you wanted. Ah, the joy of being beautiful, smart, a preacher and an Italian. Who could turn you down?'

Doc stopped, playfully shook her hair at me and took a sip of wine. 'Guilty, with no further comment, J.P. We've talked about this before.' She rolled her eyes.

I poured a little more wine in her glass as the telephone rang again. Knowing the unique sound of the ring this time, she went to answer it.

Doc came back to the table and sat down again. 'Another lonely person crafty enough with adjectives to get through my sympathetic answering service,' she sighed.

'I was just recollecting our first trip to Scotland and your sprinting into the eighteenth fairway and kissing the turf. What a photo op that was, but we left the camera at the hotel. I will never forget your kiss and the smell of the air mixed in with the perfume you were wearing . . .'

'Really? Thank you. Another reason for us to go again, my dear. You need more practice driving on the left side of the road.' Her smile was like that of a contented Cheshire cat. 'I've come to the conclusion the vista is really a living museum and that you really do want to let yourself be embraced and swallowed up and absorbed by it all.' She straightened her back again. 'That day, my friend, we became a part of history.'

I sighed and took a final sip of wine and a swallow of water.

'The miracle of life, J.P., is that food, as we may not finish cooking here tonight, is never the main course. It is, like golf, the perpetual appetiser. It's helped keep us together, hasn't it?'

'Let's go upstairs.'

CHAPTER 4

VICTORIAN BATHING BOXES

MID-AUGUST 2001

I am often asked if they play sports in Scotland other than golf and rugby. My answer is yes, I understand they also play a game called shinty. I researched the word and discovered the game was originally called camanachd. In fact, the Scots seem to like the word 'camanachd' so much they use it as the game's principal trophy, much as the Open championship has the Claret Jug.

The author

The pleasant surprise of the next morning, when back on the Internet, was discovering that history is not always boring. I don't say this because I became distracted by reading the words and phrases *witchcraft*, *ruined castles and cathedrals*, *wars and sieges* and *religions at odds*, as well as homilies on the nefarious exploits of the clans. I say it because it quickly became apparent the vista had remained unchanged for as long as 77 years – if the Old Course Starter's Box had been built in 1924, which had been guessed at, the year Puccini died and the Englishman Howard Carter was absorbed in cataloguing King Tut's tomb in Egypt. Youthful, indeed, given golf has been played on the Links for over six centuries.

There was little information on her history, but I guessed, from photographs and what I recalled from our trips, that she was a whimsically quaint five-sided kiosk, about fourteen feet across and fifteen feet high and of stubby proportions. Dressed in light tan stucco with blue trim, she seemed to be topped with a lichen-covered slate roof and a red ball-shaped cap-piece that suggested the stereotypical bulbous nose on a circus clown – or the pompom on a tam-o'-shanter. Windows clearly opened to the south, south-west and west, and a blue door filled out the east facade, which faces the Royal and Ancient Golf Club. The north wall, facing the North Sea, appeared to be solid – for obvious reasons, I was sure, given the unrelenting assaults of ghastly weather that blast in from the north.

'All that is missing to dress her up,' Claudia said, as an afterthought, 'are flower boxes filled with red geraniums, lace curtains and a chimney with wisps of smoke lazily rising to the heavens.'

More research revealed the first Starter's Box was makeshift, at best. In fact, other early photographs seemed to agree with what I had read somewhere – that in the 1890s, on what one assumed was another cold winter morning featuring a hard rain or snow, a starter had probably gone down to the West Sands with a horse, tied a rein to the frame and pulled one of the town's wooden, iron-wheeled Victorian bathing boxes up to the first tee for use as a shelter.

It's so easy to visualise this happening when you remember that St Andrews' winter weather, in which darkness arrives early and lingers long, originates at the North Pole. This gives the elements a 2,500-mile free run across the North Sea until they strike land at the barren, treeless Old Course – their first port of call – and the exposed skin of your face, if you happen to be playing golf on the Links in the wintertime . . . as many do!

(In the summertime the boxes were pulled down to the surf line and used as private changing rooms as the Victorian mores of the period dictated that the sight of people in wet 'costumes' was indecent. Not large enough to house a bed or toilet facilities, they nevertheless afforded some protection when the weather took a sudden turn for the worse.)

I also discovered, not surprisingly given lore surrounding the St Andrews caddies, that the starters were also known for their 'eccentricities', shall we politely say, and often unsociable behaviour.

Andrew Greig, the starter on the Old Course from 1894 until his death in 1915, personified this breed of the chronically dissatisfied. (His duties also included cutting the grass around the first tee, which is what he was doing on an April morning in 1915 when he collapsed and died.) His box was one of the beach's bathing huts, in which an opening had been cut so he could easily communicate with the golfers and collect their fees, if they were tourists (the locals could play for free back then). He also hung a simple hand-painted sign on a nail that posted the day's ballot and the list of available caddies. A tripod holding tin plates numbering the order of play often stood alongside.

One day Andrew was approached by a Frenchman who asked if he could play the Old. He said his name was 'Fouquier'.

'Weel,' Andrew replied after thinking a moment, 'when I cry oot Tamson, jist ye step on tae the tee!'

If you haven't had the good fortune of visiting St Andrews, it may surprise you to know that until quite recently there wasn't a public clubhouse on any of the six Links courses. The clubhouse of the R&A and the other clubs along the eighteenth fairway are all private (as tourists have discovered when they've opened the door or rung the bell, expecting a welcome from a porter). Two excellent clubhouses – the Links, which opened in 1995, and the Eden, opened in 2000 – were built by the Links Trust and are the only non-membership clubhouses in St Andrews where visiting golfers can change, shower, shop and enjoy refreshments and a meal after their game. The traditional process of paying fees and managing tee times, however, is still handled by the starters at each course.

Note the word *clubhouse* as opposed to the more encompassing *country club*, with which Americans are more familiar, as country club connotes activities other than golf. St Andrews is golf – pure Links golf. I have never seen a tennis court in St Andrews (not that I have looked for one) and only one swimming pool, aside from the university's, and it happens to be indoors, on a friend's Easter Kincaple Farm.

CHAPTER 5

··

THE LINKS AND THE
ST ANDREWS LINKS TRUST

FROM OVER 600 YEARS AGO TO THE PRESENT

The Scottish Parliament, adjourned on the 25th day of
March in the year 1707, is hereby reconvened.

*Winnie Ewing, when, as the oldest member of the Scottish
Parliament, she presided over its reconvening in 1999*

When people discuss the Old Course and linksland golf, the
conversation always seems to reach a higher emotional level
than other sports-focused conversations, aside from the currently
popular subject of measuring the greatness of Jack Nicklaus against
Tiger Woods. As the word *links* is essential to understanding
the Old Course, it helps to know the difference between a true
links course and those that are often referred to as links courses
but are really throwbacks to the way golf is played along the
coastline of Great Britain and Ireland: Pebble Beach and Bandon
Dunes in the United States, and Muirfield, near Edinburgh in
Scotland, come to mind. Among the probably fewer than two
hundred courses worldwide that do qualify as real linksland
are the six St Andrews courses; Carnoustie, across St Andrews
Bay in the town of the same name (which is perhaps the flattest
stretch of linksland anywhere in Britain); Machrihanish, on the
Mull of Kintyre; and Royal Troon, Turnberry and Prestwick on
Scotland's west coast.

The eminent golf writer Malcolm Campbell has explained it
best in *The Scottish Golf Book*:

The game of golf developed on the east coast of Scotland for the very simple reason that the ground was perfectly suited to it. From the far north beyond Wick in Caithness to well south of Edinburgh, the east coast of Scotland has mile upon mile of land known as 'links'. This ground was unsuitable for arable farming because the sand was never very far from the surface, but its gently undulating contours, covered in beautiful springy turf, were made for the game of golf . . .

The land, then valued only for the grazing of animals and for leisure purposes, became known as 'links' most likely because it formed the 'link' between the sea and the more fertile agricultural land behind the dunes.

It was, in fact, land just waiting for golf courses to be built upon it.

When it was first used for this purpose is a matter for pure conjecture, but it is possible that some form of the game of golf was being played on the links of St Andrews from as early as the twelfth or thirteenth centuries.

Golf on the links, bagpipes, oatcakes, whisky, tartans, burns and moors are as indigenous to Scotland as champagne, haute couture and bouillabaisse are to France, and as baseball, hamburgers and sweetcorn are to the United States.

The land on which the Links at St Andrews evolved was first granted to the town by King David in 1123. It was to be 'common land', meaning its use was under full control of the citizens. With a few detours along the way, which have been well chronicled, it still is. Over the centuries, citizen or contracted use has included sheep grazing, rabbit farming, clothes washing in the Swilcan Burn, archery practice, football, cloth bleaching, various forms of carnal pleasure, rifle shooting, casual strolling – and *golff*.

Most historians would have us believe golf was first played in St Andrews around 1400, after, the quipsters say, 'its invention in Ireland and gifting to the Scots as a joke'. What is known is that King James II banned *golff* in 1457 because it was distracting young men from archery practice and he needed accurate bowmen for his army. The ban continued through succeeding monarchs until James IV finally relented – and allowed the same golfer's aggravation that everyone else experiences to become a part of his life – and commissioned *golff* clubs, made by . . . one of his bow-makers.

Two other noteworthy dates in the evolution of the Links, which I oversimplify, are 1552, when the town granted Archbishop Hamilton the right to farm rabbits on the Links (rabbit farming was vital to the medieval economy), with the understanding that the citizens retained the rights to play golf, and 1821, when James Cheape of Strathtyrum, a local landowner and golfer, bought the Links for the citizens of St Andrews. It is well documented that he said at a special dinner: 'Gentlemen, I have saved the Links for golf!'

The Cheape family influenced the affairs of the Links for over 200 years and, it is safe to say, the Links as they are known today would never have existed without the economic involvement and wisdom of various members of the Cheape family. Fitting reminders, instead of the ubiquitous 'bronze plaque anchored on a random boulder' or 'fountain in a town square that always seems to be in disrepair', include the Strathtyrum Course, which is partly built on land the family sold to the Links Trust in the 1980s, and Cheape's bunker, which is on the combined second and seventeenth fairway of the Old Course.

The Old Course wasn't set in the biggest dunes of the peninsula but a few yards back from them where the ground was more fertile and organic and less likely to be buried under sand drifts. (The low-lying farm fields near the Links are characterised as having 'heavy soil', meaning it is dense and clayey and not conducive to certain cash crops.) The original course consisted of 22 holes: 11 out, 11 back. On finishing a hole, the player made a new tee with a little sand formed to a point, within two club lengths of the previous hole. (How wonderful to have a short distance between a green and the next tee.) In 1764, the Society of St Andrews Golfers, which later became the Royal and Ancient Golf Club, decided some holes were too short and combined them. This reduced the Old Course to 18 holes, now the standard round of golf, and established the routing plan, which is shaped as if encased in a shepherd's crook because that is the form the land resembles when viewed on a map or from the air.

Nature shrank the 'landing areas' on which the Links naturally matured over time to the point when they became so narrow golfers ended up playing to the same hole going out and coming in. As the game became more popular, golfers often found themselves unsafely and awkwardly playing to the same hole from opposite directions. Wisdom again came to the rescue when someone decided to cut two holes on some of the greens. To avoid confusion, the first nine played to white flags, the second nine to red. Why those colours? A variation on the nautical use of red and green to determine right of way? Or perhaps because they are easy to see against the green or light tan of the turf? No one that I have spoken with has a valid answer.

Old Tom Morris, a legend beyond all others when the Old Course is discussed and winner of four Opens, was born and raised in St Andrews. When he accepted the position of custodian of the Links in 1864, he set about widening the course to respect increased play, part of which was driven by the invention of the gutta-percha golf ball in St Andrews in 1848 (it quickly became popular because it was less expensive than the feathery ball). He also built the first and eighteenth greens, which have never been altered, and made minor adjustments to other parts of the natural, slowly evolving over centuries course-routing plan and layout. In reality, little has changed on the Old Course, as a map dated 1821 suggests, except for the relatively recent construction of some new teeing areas that lengthen the course and are used for the Open Championship only. That it still provides an often severe challenge for professional golfers and has kept its position as one of the greatest golf courses in the world without having to be drastically modified to compensate for the technological changes that began to compromise the game of golf about twenty years ago is a tribute to the wisdom of the Scots, Mother Nature, the weather, the Cheape family and a number of political miracles.

When Tom created the separate green for the first hole, it became more acceptable to play the course in an anticlockwise direction, rather than the clockwise route that had been usual. For many years, the course was played clockwise and anticlockwise on alternate weeks, but now the anticlockwise, or right-to-left, routing has become the accepted direction. (Many of the bunkers, however, clearly catch poor shots from either direction, as I well know.) In recent years the Links Trust, in its refreshing wisdom, re-established a playing of the Old Course in the clockwise direction for a few days each year. This generally occurs in early April. (Trivia question:

who won the British Amateur, and in what year, when the course was, by mistake, played in the clockwise direction? The answer is, of course, Horace Hutchinson, and the year was 1886.)

Given its 600 years of lore and history, it is logical that the Old Course exudes half-truths and legends amidst the many dramatic moments that have occurred on the Links. One well-documented example occurred in 1860, when the local lifeboat captain, W.H. Maitland-Dougall, was playing in a competition and word came of a shipwreck out in St Andrews Bay. Commanding the town's lifeboat, he heroically saved the ship's crew . . . before returning to the Links to complete his round. (A logical question might be: as shipwrecks tend to occur in foul weather and St Andrews Bay is quite small and totally unprotected, how could one possibly be playing golf when there was enough of a storm raging to cause a shipwreck?)

The town of St Andrews is unique if for no other reason than that it owns the six world-famous public golf courses, including the Old Course Links, as well as a seventh course now, the Castle Course, which opened for play on 28 June 2008 and has already received high acclaim. In addition to the Old Course, there is the New, the Jubilee (acknowledged to be the most difficult), the Eden, the Strathtyrum and the Balgove. What many do not know is that the St Andrews Links Trust, under an Act of Parliament, manages the courses and the facilities on behalf of the town, not the R&A. A team of professionals is employed to implement policy through a staff of over 70 people including starters, rangers, green-keepers, those handling course bookings and the clubhouse personnel. Simplified, the entity is independent, with charitable status. The management structure was put in place in 1894, when an Act of Parliament decreed the Links should be managed by a Green Committee consisting of five members of the R&A and two individuals appointed by the St Andrews Town Council. Other Acts and 'Agreements' through to 2005 modified this structure and impacted how the Links and Castle Course were managed. Today, members of the Trust are nominated by the local authority, the R&A and the Secretary of State for Scotland.

The Trust also maintains a St Andrews Links tartan, which is registered with the Scottish Tartans Society. Traditionally designed, with dominant colours of blue and green, it is the only Links tartan.

Having concluded my research into the eventful history of the Links, I meditated over a coffee one evening on the Box and my finding a way to save her from destruction. I realised the Duke of York, the King of Morocco, presidents Eisenhower and Clinton, Scotland's Sean Connery and Jackie Stewart, Hollywood's Michael Douglas and Catherine Zeta-Jones, and every other golfer who's played the Old, have all checked in at the Box. The list grew even longer considering the professionals and amateurs in the fourteen Opens played on the Old while she's been in service, including winners Sam Snead, Bobby Jones, Seve Ballesteros, Jack Nicklaus (twice), Peter Thomson, John Daly and Tiger Woods (twice).

There really is a solid story plus a big-idea marketing opportunity here, I finally and honestly admitted to myself. It was time for me to isolate and quantify my perceptions and begin building a viable business plan for rescuing and exploiting golf's greatest icon as a global marketing tool for real estate and apparel – and, perhaps, sporting goods. Why not? There are certain unique objects in the world with such historic, impeccable pedigrees that they represent the essence of human ideals. In the case of the Starter's Box, these ideals are 'sportsmanship', 'fair play', 'equality' and 'public ownership'. If an image of the Eiffel Tower could sell perfume, a holder of a Royal Warrant of the British Royal Family almost anything, the Rock of Gibraltar insurance, and the shadow of a polo player astride a pony with his mallet poised clothing and a lifestyle, why couldn't the Box fill a golfing niche just as easily?

The upside was that whatever money and time I spent, at whatever level of success I achieved – or did not achieve – I would be content to know I had tried to save this icon. It was the least I could do as my payback to golf for all the joy the game had given me over the years. To me, that would be enough.

I stripped the word *fantasy* from my vocabulary and focused on how I could buy her, even if I did not yet know what that entailed or what the business and financial implications were. I smiled as a bagpipe's music danced through my head and a cliché oozed from my mind: *if only her walls could talk.*

CHAPTER 6

··

THREE COLUMNS

MID-AUGUST 2001

Freedom all solace to man gives:
He lives at ease that freely lives.

John Barbour, The Bruce

I began my crusade to set fires and burn bridges astride a thoroughbred named Obsession – my figurative for: *buy, preserve, exploit.*

It was near midnight. A fresh summer breeze carrying the scent of night-blooming jasmine was drifting in through the open windows to the accompaniment of Kiri Te Kanawa singing Strauss's *Four Last Songs* in a voice of honey and humility. I was sitting at the kitchen table, my laptop screen glowing in front of me. I was contented.

'You're behaving as if she's your mistress,' Doc said corrosively as she walked in and set down a half-empty bowl of popcorn. She passed me, uttering a rather spectacular yawn and, in a 'ding-dong' voice of no emotion, said, 'Good night.' The spell was broken.

'Guilty.' My fingers continued typing into the website of the Links Trust. '"Mistress"? Now I know why so many men are tantalised.'

A quick chop of her hand found the back of my head as she picked up her knitting and went upstairs.

'I love you,' I called out.

No answer.

An hour later, I had another conversation with Alan McGregor of the Trust. I casually asked if the Trust had determined the weight of the Box.

'Why do you ask?' he questioned nonchalantly.

'I have been looking into shipping costs. They add up given that, if I win the bid, she will have to be shipped by a container and lorry to the Leuchars railhead, where a train will transport her down to Suffolk and the Port of Felixstowe. Then she will have to be put aboard a ship and sailed through the Panama Canal to California.'

'I can't imagine you would be a bidder. That all seems quite expensive.'

I let his remark dissipate without comment as it was an indication to me that he did not grasp the worth of the Box as a marketing tool. 'Perhaps,' I said, 'but not as expensive as you might think. I have some Norwegian friends in the shipping business looking into it.'

'You are serious, aren't you, John?' His voice deepened.

'Very.'

'Jolly good,' he replied quickly, his voice light again. 'Well, we'll see what happens on 10 September.'

After I hung up I realised Alan had not answered my question about the Box's weight. I wondered if that silence might imply what materials might have been used in her construction – as in brick, or some other form of masonry, or wood. I shrugged it off. A building roughly fourteen feet square and about fifteen feet high? Certainly a light wood frame, I assumed from my building experience.

I was now spending so much time evaluating her marketing worth and historical significance my business was suffering. I spent a long day at the office following that early-morning conversation with Alan, and alas, when I went home at night, Doc resumed her own level of subtle nudging, as some women know how to do, with their much-too-rational point of view.

'My first question tonight,' she said, barely in jest, as I walked in and she pointed to my filled martini glass on the kitchen counter, 'as I have asked before, where is the money for you to enjoy your *mistress*, er, *folly* coming from? Have you solved that riddle?' She raised her water glass in a semi-welcoming toast. 'Sorry about the Freudian slip.'

I gave her a quick kiss and took a sip of my drink. 'Before I answer that question,' I said, 'answer one question.'

'It is?' she asked, only mildly inquisitive.

'What is the DNA in women that makes your gender so incisive?'

'I don't know, and it doesn't matter. Answer the question.' The coarse sound of her cleaver cutting down through a handful of carrots served as an exclamation point.

'Well, my dear, I have good news.' I smiled. 'The bank offered to finance half the cost today.'

Claudia looked at me. 'How or why would they do that without a budget? You don't have a budget.'

'My friend, Dave, the head loan officer, is a golfaholic. He's figured out how to play golf with customers three or four days a week.'

'Lucky him. I'm in the wrong business.'

'He said he would go along with me on the deal for 50 per cent of whatever the cost turned out to be and set up a contingency account for the balance – once I had some solid numbers. He's beginning to understand her value in selling lots.'

'Honey, you haven't the money to build the houses yet and he's paying half the cost of my trip. Is that what you're telling me?'

'Something like that.' I gulped my drink. 'A detail. An administrative issue. I have the partners and finance for the land buy. The build finance is coming.'

The ringing of Doc's private phone saved me from more oral combat. She set down her cleaver and hurried to the library. I refilled my glass with Hendrick's gin and sat down. She was right, of course, in her inferences – I was being a little too cavalier in my crusade, but I didn't let it bother me as it is a part of me to live by entrepreneurship and liken business to the red-stacked tugboat that chugs from a harbour to meet a ship in uncertain waters, its welcoming whistle blaring, instead of waiting safely in the harbour for something to materialise. (Alas, doesn't modern business demand we be aggressive in order to maximise opportunities? Thanks to the computer and instant communication, there is no tomorrow.)

Still, when I combined what the Box's financial worth might potentially represent as a logo in the apparel and sporting goods industries, and her use as an icon to sell lots and memberships in a golf-course development, there didn't seem to be any reason *not* to continue.

THREE COLUMNS

There was little risk in test bidding, I guessed, as the Trust believed the sale would only actually happen in the last half-hour of live-time bidding. I couldn't fathom that a bid placed in late August would hold until 10 September.

Doc came back into the kitchen, her upper teeth biting her lower lip. 'That was Dr Weinstein. I have a parishioner in grave condition. The family would like me at the hospital.'

'Go, honey, of course. I'll finish with the dinner. Meatloaf is always better the second day anyway.'

She put her arms over my shoulders and faintly kissed me. 'Part of the reason you just said what you did is because my questioning of you is over.'

'If briefly, my seer,' I sighed.

'How right you are.'

When I heard the muffled squeaking of the garage door closing, I took a pad of paper that happened to have 'wonderful ideas' printed in red ink along a border. I wrote in block letters across the top, 'Box – Due Diligence', and drew three vertical columns. At the top of the left column, I wrote *positive*; on the middle column, *negative*; on the right column, *partners, sell, escape*. The left column filled quickly: marketing of dirt, sale of real estate, sale of memberships, enhanced monthly dues, apparel, equipment, 'golf stuff', my give-back to golf. The middle column filled even more quickly, which started to disturb me: unknown administrative costs, unknown costs of time and manpower, cost to buy, cost to disassemble, cost to ship (rail, ship, container), St Andrews to La Quinta, cost of permits, cost to reconstruct, cost for press and promotion, J.P. travel and admin, other. After scribbling a couple of connecting arrows and ending them in the second column, it slowly dawned on me that the third column was the only important column because everything to do with my passion and crusade was an unknown. The third column was still blank.

Coupling this fact with Doc's nudging – and I remembered every word: 'You have no basis on which to judge the value of your little obsession; you've told me no one else probably does either. What will you do if your bid is the final bid? I'll bet you've already bid once or twice and haven't told me. As in being stuck with a win, J.P. Consider the moral issues and hard-cash issues, J.P. We have been to charity auctions, haven't we, where someone opens with an outrageous alcohol-fuelled bid for a week on some exotic island, or some city no one wants to visit in January, and everyone else sits on their hands. Then what? Remember when that *someone* was you, and *you* won the long February weekend in Chicago? The weekend of the big blizzard that kept us hostage in our hotel for four days?'

Claudia's hammer hit home. What the hell was I doing?

Something else became daunting. It was the sudden swing of mood I felt between us – the constant focus on drinks, religion and the mundane and minutiae every time the Box crept into the conversation. Nothing I had considered in business before had consumed as much of our private time as the Box. Sure, I understood: it was because it confirmed our mutual passion for golf . . . or was the Box just the catalyst for our festering . . . ?

CHAPTER 7

....

TIMING AND LUCK

MID-AUGUST 2001

Scotsmen take all they can get, and a little more if they can.

Lord Advocate Maitland

The adage is: 'Mathematics and money can rationalise anything. Sometimes we need more for the right answer.'

With the thought firmly embedded in my mind, I ignored my personal issues with Claudia and continued supporting my original premise of doing anything necessary to preserve the icon. This included calling Alan McGregor and others at the Trust more frequently with one question or another, mostly to gauge the strength of genuine interest. One day Alan dropped a bomb when he said the Trust had no idea how the Box had been constructed and the staff had decided not to break into any of the walls, or the roof, to find out. 'As is, with the important sign and our logo,' he said firmly. 'That's how it is being offered. We don't want to be interrupting the check-in process or unduly inconvenience the golfers.'

'Oh?' I questioned.

'We are firm. Now is the proper time for you to submit your credentials for evaluation. We are advising others of the same. May we have your package by 1 September?'

'Of course,' I replied. 'I have been working on it.'

In mid-August, Alan told me interest had taken a strong upturn, as is routine in the case of auctions when bid day approaches and the truly committed players join the bidding. 'Interest is now being shown by groups representing many European countries, as well as Australia, Japan and others in the US. I still think, as we have discussed, the successful bidder will be UK- or Continent-based, don't you, because of the shipping cost?'

'No,' I answered slowly. Clearly, he still didn't envision use of the Box beyond serving as a shelter for a golf starter. Unknowingly, however, he touched on an interesting subject. In most fine-art auctions, the auctioneers, potential buyers and sellers have a very strong idea of the economic climate (the willingness to buy) and market depth and prepare themselves accordingly. The Box and its unknowns, which my three-columned sheet so clearly illustrated, shattered all these givens.

I began to compile a list of who other bidders might be. The Koreans came to mind since interest in their country for golf was intensifying; so did some of the US's obvious equity-rich golf resorts, including Pinehurst, Pebble Beach, and a few properties in Florida and Arizona. I was also sure the Japanese would be more than interested because they are such golf fanatics – especially at the corporate level. Even with the recent changes in the world's economy, they were still roaming the world with open chequebooks buying almost anything that interested them – five-star golf resorts included. (This I knew as I had recently closed out a joint venture with the Mitsubishi Corporation. In the heyday of the strong yen it was rumoured that a Mitsubishi-chartered 747 filled with executives and customers flew from Tokyo to Scotland every Thursday night for long weekends of golf and its rumoured associated delights . . .)

After more calls to Alan, I began to feel an affinity for him, and I think he did for me as he allowed the conversation to border on the personal. We often chitchatted about family and whom we might know in common. I assumed this was because he wanted to get a professional 'read' on me and my intentions with regard to the Box. This proved true – no unprepared executive he – but it also became clear the Trust was seeking assurance the successful bidder would give some form of guarantee, if only a moral, unenforceable guarantee, that the Box would be reinstalled in an appropriate setting and used either as a starter's box or a museum artefact available to the public, including, with great hope, junior golfers.

As 10 September approached, the question-and-answer game I played on my 'wonderful ideas' sheet of paper took another twist when I wrote, 'Where are the preservationists? Why doesn't the vista – including the Box – with its intertwined historic, archaeological, architectural and even horticultural significance, have landmark or "Listed" status, as they refer to the preservation system that often dominates life and development in the UK?'

Though my mind accepted Alan's answers regarding the R&A renovation and the Box's weight, it still seemed too simple. If she had outlived her usefulness, why not move her out on the Old Course to an area near the ninth green and use her as a refreshment stand? (It was only recently that snacks or beverages had been made available on the Links.) It seemed an obvious solution. Convinced something was wrong, I revived every due-diligence trick in my arsenal that I had ever used in evaluating opportunity. Nothing connected; instead, I collected more unknowns.

I gave myself a bit of comfort when I remembered a real-estate opportunity in Carmel, California, I had read about in the *Wall Street Journal*'s want ads, no less, in the early 1970s. 'Fully permitted, approved property, with water,' it advertised. Huh? I had asked myself. Developable property in Carmel and not sold to an insider? What was wrong? It turned out nothing was wrong and I made a very handsome profit.

A year after that triumph, I remembered receiving a tip from a fellow San Francisco developer. She told me of an apartment complex in Silicon Valley that was for sale. Every developer in San Francisco – including the Canadians, who were investing heavily in the US, and particularly California, at the time – had taken a look at it and passed. 'Why?' I had asked her.

'Because the zoning only allows current use or conversion to condominiums. Condo conversion is too innovative, it seems. Do a drive-by on your next trip to Pebble Beach.'

I did, liked what I saw, spent two weeks in intensive due diligence, bought it, converted it to condominiums – and sold out all ninety-one units of housing in ten months, close of loan to close of last escrow.

One evening, over dinner with friends, Claudia managed to control the conversation and answer all the questions directed to me and my 'affair' – as she seemed to be doing more and more often. Injecting her own brand of Mediterranean causticity when describing my adventure, she regularly used the words *fantasy*, *crusade* and *obsessive* – and sometimes even less sophisticated adjectives such as *obstinate* and, once, an eight-letter, hyphenated word one would associate with a Manhattan trash-hauler, not someone of the cloth. 'He's treating her like the daughter he never had!'

Our friends filled the room with mirth and asked genuine, intelligent questions including: 'Why and how will it change your life?' (Stay tuned – film at eleven, plus it's my give-back to golf); 'Brilliant marketing potential' (Thanks for the confirmation); 'Sounds like an excuse to go back to St Andrews?' (Of course, thank you again!) The last question was the only one that drew an appreciative laugh from Claudia.

I felt the temperature of her smouldering Italian personality rise as I went through the interrogations. Still I answered dutifully, if with meekness and embarrassment. More often than not I took the occasion, later, when we were alone, to remind her that her business, the business of religion, only existed because of the potent adjectives she had chosen to describe my 'adventure'.

A little more than two weeks before the auction, my crusade imploded. The bridge over my moat was burned – and not by any of my listed unknowns. Instead it was by an adversary I had never had cause to consider. The land-development housing project I had earmarked as the Box's home had been identified as a potentially important archaeological site.

At a hastily called press conference that included the mayor and the county supervisor, City Hall announced: 'As of today all permitting on this controversial project are suspended pending full university and Federal review of the preliminary findings . . .'

I was devastated. It was as if I had heard the dull sound of the ropes fall on my coffin after I had been lowered to my grave.

CHAPTER 8

JACK FRANKS

SATURDAY, 1 SEPTEMBER 2001

It is never difficult to distinguish between a Scotsman with
a grievance and a ray of sunshine.

P.G. Wodehouse

Resort environments are real-estate-fraud country. Some
transcend and become murder country. The Coachella Valley of
Southern California, which includes Palm Springs, Palm Desert,
Rancho Mirage, Cathedral City, Indian Wells, La Quinta and
Indio, is no exception – except that there have been few homicides
of consequence in the Valley. (Those involved in such nefarious
activities have historically seemed to prefer the glamour of
Beverly Hills and Hollywood to the west, and Las Vegas to the
north, for showcasing that brand of thunder.)

Pained by the overnight evaporation of my real-estate dream
and the increasingly unpleasant innuendo that snaked though my
conversations with Claudia, I needed a diversion and relaxant
– mentally as well as physically. 'Stay off the booze,' I told myself,
'and forget about diazepam – I still have my passion for the Box
and she is unaware of my travails. Continue with your crusade,
J.P., ensure her preservation and consider it a victory. We will
survive together.' I inked the words across my now battered sheet
of 'wonderful ideas' paper.

My due diligence had included listening in on conversations at
selected watering holes in the Valley – where, as is the case in most
resort towns, every night is New Year's Eve – to ascertain if any
local development was a candidate to house the Box should my
project, for whatever reason, not find fruition or be compatible.

Number of employees at R. Forgan & Son at the height of their
golf club- and ball-manufacturing business

37

Rumour suggested the Country Club of the Desert, a new, very ambitious private golf-club community in La Quinta that had the potential as their marketing staff was publicly touting the quality of their golf courses, along with the words *heritage* and *sportsmanship* being bandied about.

I was warned by local lenders, developers and friends in the development business that the Country Club's developer, Jack Franks, had a chequered past – chequered, that is, if alleged jail time and nasty lawsuits that included the *f* word, as in *fraud*, were of concern. (This was pre-Google, mind you.) One friendly wag put it quite succinctly when he said, 'Some people believe filing for bankruptcy is a legitimate extension of a business plan. Others say the same about jail time – as in, if you haven't had a vacation at the expense of the government, you haven't been crafty and seized opportunity.'

It was easy for me to shrug off the comments as they were only hearsay and usually spoken with a vodka on ice or wine glass in hand and when the lips had become a little rubbery.

Indeed, I was completing a partnership land acquisition across Avenue 54 from the Country Club for a project in which the Box offered no marketing value – even when I stretched my imagination. As I wanted to buy additional land, to buffer and protect my environment, I methodically called all the landowners whose lands abutted mine, asking if they wanted to sell. Most were speculators and did, but on a cash-only basis, of which I had very little. (Hard money was very difficult to come by in the late 1990s and early 2000s.) I offered substantial down payments with the balance on participating terms once our project was generating profits. Darned if Jack Franks didn't have the same idea, but he was offering cash. Guess who won out – in all instances. A quick and sincere respect for him prevailed, no matter his reputation.

Pete Dye and Clive Clark – the latter a former European Tour and Ryder Cup player who had recently moved to La Quinta – were each designing a golf course for the Country Club. I had met Pete some years before when he was designing and building the Mountain and Dunes courses at the La Quinta Resort for Ernie Vossler and Joe Walser and their Landmark Land Company, and I had come to know Clive through an introduction from the writer Malcolm Campbell. When I told him of my quest, Clive introduced me to the project's manager, Nancy Aaronson. Nancy, I quickly discovered, was a fine golfer who respected St Andrews and all it stood for. Logically, she liked the idea of the Box showcasing her project. Over lunch, I emphasised the auction was less than two weeks away.

'How many other developers are you talking to about this opportunity?' she asked firmly. 'Are you playing us against someone else in the interest of self-serving?' Her bold brown eyes were vacant.

'Very few,' I answered with a fib. (In reality, her project was my last chance saloon.) 'The rumours around town suggest it would be a fine fit for you.'

She smiled weakly. 'Two weeks? We have a staff meeting this afternoon. I'll mention the idea. Tight schedule, isn't it?'

She called me the next morning and excitedly said she had scheduled a lunch with Jack Franks, lead developer of Country Club of the Desert, at the La Quinta Resort. 'Could you make yourself available at 12.30 today?'

'Tell me about this Box and this idea you have,' Jack Franks called out somewhat rudely. He arrived at the table where Nancy and I were seated, squinting, without sunglasses in the brilliant sunlight. 'I don't play much golf.' He offered a handshake without eye contact, sat down and pulled his chair to the table, the sound of the iron legs screeching on the tiled floor like fingernails on a blackboard. Unceremoniously he reached for a menu. It was all accomplished in one smooth motion. Rather short in stature and portly, he wore well-wrinkled Bermuda-style cargo shorts, simple sandals and a garish gold Rolex wristwatch.

He ignored my attempt to answer his question and started talking project issues with Nancy, most of which I couldn't hear as their voices were drowned out by the resort's ever-present pre-recorded mariachi music. Then he scanned the menu and waved off an approaching waiter. His condescending persona made me nervous.

Nancy had prepped me to begin the conversation with small talk, including a comment or two on the very hot weather the desert had been having, with near daily temperatures above 110 degrees; his ranch in Mexico; and his participation in a new project I was contemplating in the Pebble Beach area. 'Go slow,' she had said. 'Try to get him to relax and focus. It will be tough, but try.'

Instead – to this 'big-hurry' man with a mind swarming with issues and ideas – I said, as gruffly as he had spoken, with the same Gatling-gun delivery he had used on Nancy: 'The deal is to lend my credibility and horsepower as your agent, for a fee, and buy golf's greatest icon, the Old Course Starter's Box. I will oversee its disassembly, packing and shipping to California and the Country Club of the Desert. It will give your project instant credibility through its tie to St Andrews, the Home of Golf. Every prospective lot purchaser, whether they have dreamed of playing or actually played the Old Course, will relate to the Box. *Perceptions* sell lots, houses, memberships and lifestyles – especially when a golfer and his passions are involved. I believe you agree.'

'Through osmosis?' he asked, as he looked at me for the first time and cracked a wry smile.

'Osmosis? I haven't heard that word since college biology. It's a terrific word. Plenty of people are caught up in celebrity and think osmosis works – as if they can acquire a celebrity's lifestyle if they eat in the same restaurant or think they can become better golfers if they rub elbows in a pro-am. Yes, it's about wanting to absorb a celebrity icon's aura. Passion makes the sale. To put it a little more crudely, people want to emulate their favourite stars. We live in a copycat culture.'

A quick grin betrayed hidden warmth. The ice was broken. He studied me again, his eyes becoming small slits that went vacant as he spoke slowly. 'I do this . . . you get a couple of trips to Scotland, have some fun, you make a little money . . . and you garner notoriety as the saviour of an icon that, for some reason, you have a hard-on for . . . and you save face because you can say you rescued a piece of history. Correct?'

'Precisely.'

He looked at Nancy as he spoke to me. 'How much money do you need for yourself and the buy?'

I gave him the price range as I pulled a draft budget from my briefcase.

'Forget it. You know what you're doing.' He waved off the paper with a flip of his wrist and pushed his chair back, the legs screeching again. Then he stood up, pulled a thick wad of bills from a pocket, slid off a thick rubber band and dropped two one-hundred-dollar bills on the table. 'Enjoy your lunch.' He smiled approvingly at Nancy, then glared at me with open, iron eyes as he started to leave. 'Get it!'

Year in the twentieth century Provost John Reid unveiled the plaque presented by Polish soldiers to the citizens of St Andrews

41

CHAPTER 9

THE AUCTION

MONDAY, 10 SEPTEMBER 2001

Beautiful, glorious Scotland, has spoilt me for every other
country!

Mary Todd Lincoln

The live final-bid portion of the Internet auction was set to begin
at 11.30 a.m. GMT (3.30 PST), with the hammer down half an
hour later, at noon GMT on Monday, 10 September 2001. There
wasn't much for me to prepare for other than to make sure my
alarm clock was set for 2.30 a.m.

(It turned out to have been an easy decision for Jack Franks,
Nancy told me after he left us to enjoy a $200 lunch, because
the evening before that he had already approved the project's
marketing slogan – 'Continuing the Great Traditions of Golf'.)

The Trust had approved the Country Club's financial statements
and marketing package, and Nancy had orchestrated calls of
recommendation to the Trust by those charter members of the
Country Club who were also members of St Andrews golf clubs,
including the R&A.

The alarm clock proved unnecessary. I woke nervously at 2 a.m.
I went to the kitchen, made a pot of coffee and tried to calm myself
by doing a crossword puzzle and reading the morning paper – as
if anything else in the world was as important to me that day as
the auction.

Five big stories greeted me. Sven-Göran Eriksson and England's
football fortunes were a lead, as was Barry Bonds finally breaking
Roger Maris's home-run record the day before by hitting three
against the Colorado Rockies. In golf, Scott Verplank won the

Canadian Open by holding off John Daly and Sergio García, among others, for a three-stroke victory. The win vindicated Curtis Strange, who made Scott the first-ever rookie Captain's Pick for next month's Ryder Cup at the Belfry, Warwickshire, England. In tennis, the banner headline of 'Hewitt Sprints Through Generation Gap' celebrated Lleyton Hewitt's one-hour-and-fifty-four-minute triumph over Pete Sampras for the US Open title. It was the first year Sampras had not won at least one of the four major titles since 1992. A secondary headline rehashed Venus Williams's Saturday win over her sister Serena for the women's title.

The arts section was quiet, which allowed a writer to devote too much attention to Michael Jackson's Saturday concert in a sold-out Madison Square Garden. The article said the tickets had gone for as high as $2,500.

The front page was Monday boring. Most stories were summaries of the political positions offered by the talking heads of both political parties on the Sunday-morning news shows. If any story dominated, it was the proverbial fear of a recession intertwined with possible tax cuts. There didn't appear to be anything happening in the world that couldn't be solved over time if a heavy dose of rational thinking were applied.

I read the horoscopes, finished the crossword puzzle (Monday's crossword is always the easiest) and at 3 a.m. (11 a.m. GMT) did an online dial-up and logged on to the Links Trust's website. After a couple of dropped lines, I finally got a good connection at 3.15.

As I did, I recounted the antics – and that is what they were – of the bidding the previous week. Some days the bidding was flat; some days, for whatever reason, the bids rose by a few thousand pounds. Early on there was a five-pound bid from a St Andrean who sent a cheque to the Trust with a note saying that if his bid was successful he was going to relocate the Box to his back garden for use as a potting shed! One day I deliberately upped my own bid by £500 to see what action it would draw. It drew a raise an hour later. Weird. By 8 September, the bidding had climbed to £12,000. I went to £13,000 to test the waters again. The next morning, the price was £17,000. My passion for the Box suddenly ratcheted itself up to another level.

Today was different. Real players, all qualified, but with profiles and nationalities unidentified. Real money. The bidding was to continue, as before, by Internet, only now the Links Trust was to confirm each raise in 'real time' with only the qualified bidders participating – though because the Links Trust represents the residents of St Andrews, anyone, theoretically, could still bid. (I was never told how many of us there were actually bidding.)

Silently, almost secretly and mysteriously, as in a black-and-white Second World War espionage movie, a ribbon of time-dated text announced the Trust was starting the bidding at £25,000, which was £2,500 above the posted bid. I made the first raise. In 30 seconds or so, my bid was countered; in another 30 seconds or so, it was countered again.

My stress level exploded when a thought hit me like a blow between the eyeballs from the fist of Muhammad Ali – I wouldn't be able to see the faces of the other bidders. This was a pure gamble, and with someone else's money – Jack Franks's money. This wasn't a conventional auction – far from it. The *auction* word, which implies almost always knowing the strength of the bidders beforehand, had been on my mind and had lulled me into a false sense of security. No! This wasn't like high-stakes poker, where success was measured by your ability to interpret the personal expressions and nervous tics, the thresholds of pain, of the other players in real time – as does a golfer when participating in a friendly Nassau on the golf course. The problem was I was going into the auction blind. I couldn't *read* the other bidders because I couldn't see them.

I took a swallow of coffee and then chuckled for a moment or two because I realised the playing field was level. They didn't know any more about me than I did about them – which was nothing. Nada! What fools we mortals be when passion and the word *she* is involved . . .

The bidding continued at a reasonable pace, though it seemed an eternity between the times a bid was made and confirmed. Once, my adrenalin caused me to tap the wrong key and send a bid below what was posted. Later, another bidder did the same thing. Then a raise was made in French francs instead of pounds sterling. Alan caught the errors and kept things moving along smoothly.

When the bidding reached £45,000, or about $90,000, the pace of bid and raise changed. The time between a raise confirmed

44 Number of rounds in the Open Championship Tom Watson has played under par (through 2009)

and a new bid offered slowed dramatically. I realised I was now dealing with serious money on what many, including members of the press, and Claudia, called a 15-square-metre (150-square-foot) folly.

In an attempt to keep the momentum going, Alan, who had auction-company experience, lowered the minimum raise to £1,000 from £2,500. I became very edgy. As it was nearing noon GMT, I took a chance and called the Trust on the telephone to ask if the bidding could continue by telephone because the time lapse between typing and sending my bid over a dial-up connection – if the connection didn't drop – and the Trust's receipt and confirmation varied, depending on the speed, at the moment, of the Internet. 'I don't want to be in the middle of a bid and have the 12.00 GMT hour cancel me out,' I said.

One of the other bidders, speaking in heavily accented English, had made the same request. Alan agreed and put us on a speakerphone.

I upped the ante to £48,000 and tried to listen to the languages of the others, sensing now that there were probably only two or three people still bidding. Alan acknowledged my bid and asked for £49,000. Another eternity seemed to pass before £49,000 was confirmed.

When Alan asked for a raise to £50,000, his voice tone changed from business formal and matter of fact to one that carried a generous amount of surprise, astonishment and joy.

I quickly bid £50,000. There was acknowledgement. Alan asked for £51,000. It came. In rapid-fire succession he asked for, and received, £52,000 ... £53,000 ... £54,000 ... £55,000 ... £56,000 and £57,000, from me. He had to ask twice for £58,000 but got it. Then, from me again, and quickly, £59,000. It stayed quiet: too quiet. I looked at the clock. It was 3.39 a.m. (11.59 GMT).

Alan asked for £60,000. Again. And a third time. Finally, in words that sputtered from his mouth, he said: 'The time is 12.00 GMT, 10 September 2001. The Starter's Box is sold to the gentleman from California for £59,000!'

I heard applause and a few typical Scots 'spot-ons' and 'hip-hips' shouted out in the background by what I assumed was Links Trust staff and board members.

Instantly, the shock of what I had done exploded in my brain. I felt euphoric and wonderful, yet disbelieving. I belly-laughed at the absurdness of it all . . . my being entrusted with and spending over $120,000 of someone else's money – so far.

'Congratulations,' Alan said, almost shouting into the telephone. 'If you were here, we would toast you with a spot of whisky.'

'Don't worry,' I said eagerly. 'I have a bottle next to me here in the kitchen of my home and I'm pouring myself a wee dram of a 15-year-old Glenlivet as we speak.'

He laughed. 'Ah! Fine, fine whisky. Confident, were you?'

'Not at all, though you have to believe in yourself and your ideas, don't you? Off the record, I will admit I had a good feeling about this. I so love Scotland. In another life I must have been a Scot, not a Norwegian. Either way, win or lose, I knew I would want or, rather, need . . . may I say it now . . . a wee nip?'

Alan laughed again as we began discussing business matters such as when I could wire payment (ah, the Scots and their national disease of principal-and-interest on the brain), when I could fly over to make arrangements for the take-down and shipping, and what needed to be done immediately with press releases.

'I want to meet you and inspect the Box before any money is sent.'

'Jolly good, John,' he said, finally ending the conversation. 'Jolly good.'

I ended my part of the conversation by saying I needed two days to tend to some other business but my wife and I would fly to Scotland on Wednesday, 12 September, arriving in St Andrews late on Thursday afternoon for a meeting on Friday.

'We have a concessions rate at a new hotel that is about to open: St Andrews Bay. We will make the arrangements for you. The carpets may not be down, but you will be comfortable.'

I called Nancy Aaronson and woke her. She was shocked. 'Really? God, what do we do now? I'm . . . I've got to call Jack in Mexico.'

'I leave for Scotland in two days. Remember the schedule you approved if we won?'

'Oh my God.' The phone went dead.

I left the kitchen table and went up to our bedroom. It was 4.30 a.m.

'Doc,' I whispered, 'I won the auction. I got the Box!'

'Huh,' she said, waking. 'You're *kidding*?' Her eyes squinted as she zeroed in on the tumbler of whisky in my hand – like an archer's arrow finding the bull's eye. 'You're keeping your promise? We're going back to Fife?'

'Yup. And it's not root beer in my glass either. In case you were going to ask.'

'How much?'

'£59,000.'

She slid up a little, rearranged a pillow, then studied me through half-opened eyes, her mind elsewhere, calculating. '$120,000? That's over $800 a square foot . . . £400 a square metre.'

'So what? It's a marketing-icon buy. Square feet and square metres don't count.'

'It's over $800 a square foot. You're *nuts*!' After a weak smile, a lazy air kiss of congratulation floated up to me before her head slid back under the pillows and she turned away from me.

'Mission impossible. Mission accomplished,' I said softly as I leaned down and kissed her shoulder.

I went back downstairs, poured another whisky, a full gill this time, and made a toasted peanut-butter-and-marmalade sandwich. *Loose change*, I said to myself, *small potatoes*. In the world of marketing, this is loose change compared to what Madison Avenue pays a Hollywood idol, or supermodel, or one-dimensional athlete to be a marketing icon. And those icons bring baggage. The Box brings *no* baggage. The Box is a known icon of history, of sports . . .

I called one of my closest friends, Angus Locards, in Scotland. His wife reminded me that he was on a ship in the Antarctic on an Explorers Club expedition. He was to return in a fortnight. She said she would try to relay my message. (It was unlike her to be so kind and courteous as I was sure, subconsciously, she blamed me, probably the only American she knew, for causing the American Civil War, which disgraced Lord Palmerston when he was the prime minister.)

The intercom buzzed from our bedroom. 'You *really* won the auction?'

'I really bought her for Country Club of the Desert.'

'God save your soul. Come upstairs.'

'With a wine or whisky for you?'

'At this hour? Mmm. OK, a wine, but a coffee also, thank you. Bring the newspapers.'

'So she's coming to America, J.P.?' Doc said later as she came out of her dressing room in a swimsuit, her white latex Esther Williams-style bathing cap covering her head. 'This *is* exciting. Well, with the Country Club's slogan being something about "continuing great golfing traditions", it sounds like a match made in heaven, or at least it should be.'

'Bad pun.' I sat up in bed and dropped the papers on the floor.

'I am so happy for you.' Claudia's voice became more focused and serious as she sat down on the edge of the bed and forced a quiet half-smile. 'Not to take the wind from your sails ... but I have been thinking about the dynamics of this quest – this obsession of yours – and its parallels for me in religion as a leveraging of your investment.' She winked almost playfully.

Despite the wink and almost arched eyebrows, I sensed hollowness in her voice. She did not sound sincere. 'Really now; you're waking to reality?' I fluffed my pillows and forced a smile.

She shrugged me off. 'I'm being serious. This new book I'm writing on the mixing of work with personal life and community service is giving me fits. I need a hook for the parables and reasoning of our *new* – if you can call it that – contemporary living of life. Perhaps, just perhaps, I may let our beloved game of golf and your odyssey with the Box become my fulcrum. Your rules, and tools, are really the same as mine. We both know that.'

'Interesting idea.' I paused, thinking. 'But isn't the triangle of life enough of a hook for you, where the legs of the triangle are *sleep*, *work* and *shop* – the shorter the legs of the triangle, the happier the human should be because it allows more time for healthy conversation? The parable of the smaller the refrigerator, the happier the soul. You have always said that there are really only 15 or 20 rules for achieving success in anything – including hitting a golf ball. Thousands of professional golfers are only needed because there are so many ways of communicating the same mantra.'

'The hard part is finding the right tool for communicating the lessons. Particularly in this age, with our obsession with technology and instant gratification.'

'Ah, yes, the Archimedes principle: "Give me a lever long enough and a fulcrum on which to place it, and I shall move the world."'

'In this day and age, freedom of choice may be the most important element to achieving a better life.'

'It may sound trite to you, and I can't explain why – but I feel the Box is going to give me a fresh direction.'

'A spiritual transformation? You, J.P.? My, my. That is a *big* statement.' She locked her hand in mine, leaned over and pecked me with a soft kiss.

'I wouldn't go so far as to say that,' I whispered.

'Get ready to deal with envy. A lot of people are going to envy you – and loathe you – for what you've done. When are we leaving for Scotland?'

Less than 24 hours later, the al-Qaeda attacks were launched on the World Trade Center towers in New York and the Pentagon in Washington DC.

I had read. I had discovered. I had learned. I had laughed along with many others at the margin of daily existence we all experience when we dream and strive towards a better life and renewal and the cause and effect of living. Now this. Suddenly my life and the lives of everyone in the free world were marinating in tension because of moral slippage on the other side of the planet. Immediately I remembered Doc and the patented question she used on herself when she was working to resolve a moral quandary: '*What hath God wrought?*' I sat down, shocked and bewildered.

CHAPTER 10

THE FIRST VISIT AFTER
THE AUCTION

WEDNESDAY, 10 OCTOBER 2001

I had occasion, not for the first time, to thank heaven for
that state of mind which cartographers seek to define as
Scotland.

Claud Cockburn

I was finally able to book a flight to London and Edinburgh on
10 October, almost a full month after 9/11. Even to fly that early
after the attack took a near act of God. A letter to the president of
United Airlines pleaded my case on behalf of golfers everywhere
and what was rapidly becoming a cause célèbre – the tale of the
sale of the Old Course Starter's Box. I was able to buy one of
the early tickets released after the US's National Security measures
were modified and those stranded outside the country had returned
home safely. (Requesting one ticket instead of two also helped.
Doc decided to forego the trip because, she said, her parish needed
her for emotional support and counselling in the aftermath of 9/11
and running off to Scotland, under the circumstances, would not
be looked upon favourably. She was right, of course: it was a solid
answer, but we also finally agreed we needed time apart from each
other, as our personalities, when we were together, had become
wooden and laconic.)

I felt elated yet anxious and nervous as I drove up to the Kingdom
of Fife and St Andrews from Edinburgh Airport. Though I knew it
was futile, I ignored the beautiful dry-stone, often tessellated walls
along the A91 and attempted to catch a glimpse of the Old Course

as I circled around the Guardbridge roundabout, which leads north to Leuchars Royal Air Force base, Perth and the Highlands.

On the east coast of Scotland, between the firths of Forth and Tay, in a shape – if you use your imagination a little – resembling a Scottish Terrier with raised, alert ears pointing towards the North Sea and Norway, lies Fife. Adding the dog's glistening eye to the form identifies the first tee of the Old Course Links.

On the left lay the Eden Estuary, its bramble bushes thick with berries; on the right the Cuthill family's Easter Kincaple Farm; then a roundabout that led to the university's science buildings and the Links' golf-practice facilities.

At once, I was in St Andrews again. I turned off North Street onto Grannie Clark's Wynd. Fife's classic autumn weather of periodic sea mist mixed with light rain greeted me. A grey sky hung low to the sea, except at the vista, where, gloriously, in a freshening light, the Old Course Starter's Box loomed bright in its soft colours.

I stopped the car halfway to Bruce Embankment, the street that runs along the sea wall and looked towards the fanciful, almost stately Box. I smiled as I reflected on what she has always been to golfers all over the world, so much a symbol of expectation and people enjoying life.

When Alan McGregor had told me the R&A was in the middle of a three-year renovation, the extent of the work really hadn't registered. The R&A Clubhouse protected the Box, as it always appears in advertising copy and television images, but the clumsy hulk of the building was in terrible disrepair. The large, ornate clock on the west-facing facade, with its gold numerals and hands, was damaged, and many of the large windows facing the Old Course were broken. The chandeliers were missing and the spotlights in the grassy berm behind the first tee that lit the building at night had been crudely ripped from their anchors. Most of the roof had been stripped away, with the opening covered by a false roof that seemed bolted to the scaffolding and a dark-blue tarpaulin that flapped and snapped recklessly in the wind, shroud-like. Complementing the downright ugliness of it all was the R&A's debris-filled car park mixed with the drab green construction trailers of the club's undertaker. (*Undertaker* is an often-used Fife word for general contractor.) I contrasted this with the building's normal condition: an always accurate, sparkling clock, polished

Year in the twentieth century the Greenside Works won a medal at the Fife Agricultural Show for its production of turnip seeders

51

windows and brightly lit chandeliers in the parlour rooms facing the first tee.

The sandbags at the base of the R&A's scaffolding caught my attention. Each bag, a giant heavy-canvas pillow two feet or more across by four feet high, was filled with sand – about two tons, I was told later. It was obvious the bags were stabilising the scaffolding and the false roof, acting as anchors, because I didn't see any bolts tying the scaffolding to the building. Ah, I thought, the preservationists may have exerted their influence. The scaffolding was free-standing! (The engineering proved brilliant as winds were to be clocked at 99 miles an hour that winter on the nearby Tay Bridge, which connects Fife to Dundee and Carnoustie.) The lack of a roof also meant, however, that the club's anemometer, which is normally anchored on the roof, to warn golfers of the conditions as they go out to play, would not be operating.

Gulls were feeding in the fairway as a flock of birds pealed overhead, while the mist thickened and became annoying. Patches of sea fog, or haar, as the Scots call it, began to settle in. My elation on arriving changed to depression.

Walking up the fairway towards the tee, I remembered Sandy Tatum, who had been president of the United States Golf Association (or USGA) from 1978 to 1980, and his invitation (which I'd had to decline) to attend the 'driving-in' of the new R&A captain in the late 1970s. Historic, silly and yet serious, it was another ceremony the Box had probably been a part of for over three-quarters of a century. The phrase 'driving-in' refers to the newly elected captain ceremonially confirming his election to office by driving off the first tee at eight o'clock in the morning. Of course a huge contingent of the membership is there to applaud as the event is held during the R&A's Autumn Medal competition. For emphasis – as if any is needed – a single cannon is fired at the moment the new captain's driver strikes the ball. Lining the fairway are the caddies, for the one who retrieves the captain's ball is presented with a gold sovereign (worth about £400 or $775 in 2009). As the caddies know the skill level of the captain-to-be, they can pretty well guess where the ball will likely land and, therefore, where they should position themselves. More often than not it's on the right side of the fairway or even out of bounds. (Most right-handed golfers, when under stress, slice the ball or hit it to the right. When the Prince of Wales, who later became the Duke of Windsor, drove himself into the captaincy in 1922, it was reported that 'the caddies stood disloyally close'.) There is no respect for protocol, at any level, I assure you, when a caddie and a gold sovereign are involved.

I took pictures, then looked at the Box critically from her design and construction perspectives. The blinds were drawn so I wasn't able to see inside, but the window- and doorframes, covered with several generations of paint, looked solid. The roof didn't have any discoloured or lichen-free slate tiles, which led me to believe it was likely no replacements had been made. Other than the addition of an incongruous cheap, tasteless plastic eave around the roof, she seemed to have good bones.

Back at my car, I stopped before opening the door as I felt the absence of Claudia. Maybe it was the melancholy of the moment. If so, it pained me and served to remind me of my flaws and issues and her increasing need to openly fault my success – and use it as an excuse for ignoring and failing to confront her own emotional problems. Reluctantly, I admitted our marriage was in a shambles. Still, I wanted her with me. I wanted to share this event, this achievement. But I knew we would never see Scotland together again. I felt hollow and as lonely as the flag I saw fluttering atop a building behind the seventeenth green. It was the Saltire, the flag of Scotland – thought to be one of the oldest national flags of any country, dating at least to King Angus's victorious battle against the Saxons in AD 832 – which shows a white cross on a blue background, representing the cross of St Andrew, the patron saint of Scotland, who was crucified in Greece by the Romans.

I looked west to the mounds of gorse defining the seventeenth fairway, then north to the rest of the Links where the Old Course goes out and back and hardly respects the long, broad beach where the actors portraying the Olympic hopefuls were filmed to Vangelis's mesmerising anthem. It was more welcoming and invigorating, and yet somehow validated what I had always believed about dusk in Scotland: that late in the day, these most civilised, placid lands of St Andrews are one of the loneliest places on Earth.

It also reminded me of what an old Scot had told Claudia and me in a heavy brogue some years before as he removed his snap-brimmed tartan cap, held it to his heart and lowered his head reverently: 'Time here is not measured in days or weeks but in seasons, each one blending with the other, yet every one so different.

Aye, time not only tends to stand still in St Andrews, but the town's a symbol of eternal peace.'

At once the haar was pushed back to sea by an icy west wind. Bands of black clouds started to sail ominously across the sky as rain suddenly bucketed down in torrents and a freshening wind pummelled and churned the ocean.

Year in the eighteenth centur y the Society of St Andre ws Golfers was created by 22 noblemen and gentlemen of Fif e

CHAPTER 11

∙∙

LUNCH WITH THE LINKS TRUST

FRIDAY, 12 OCTOBER 2001

Oats: a grain which in England is generally given to horses,
but in Scotland supports the people.

Samuel Johnson

Alan McGregor hosted a welcoming lunch at the Links Clubhouse
that included Peter Mason, external-relations manager, and the
Trust's communications manager, Carolyne Nurse.

'John,' Alan began solemnly, after we had toasted the Box, 'we
want to offer our sympathies for the terrible tragedy of a few weeks
ago. It is difficult for us to fathom what actually happened and how
Americans must feel. And we certainly understand the absence of
Claudia. We look forward to meeting her another time.'

Peter and Carolyne added their own comments. I must say
the three of them spoke with as much eloquence and sincerity as
anyone I had heard, including heads of state and more than a few
peers of Claudia.

Alan briefed us on the effect 9/11 had on the burgh's business.
Given that more than half the golfing visitors to Scotland each
year are American, the effect on the hospitality industry had been
devastating. Eventually he focused on the Starter's Box, the issues
of dealing with the press and a few noteworthy local citizens
who were making more-than-vague political threats to have the
auction overturned in the courts.

Eternal peace, hell, I thought to myself. I'd like to be talking to
that old Scot with the heavy brogue now!

I passed out copies of the auction's US press clippings while
stressing that most people, including the media, tended to listen,

smile, ask questions and laugh with a real sense of caring when the Box was discussed.

'Because of 9/11, I would think?' Alan asked.

'Probably,' I answered. 'People also think she's charming, compared to the insensitive brick-and-stone piles that surround her. It's also wanderlust and it reminds them of how much they love being in Scotland. This is not a case of the grass seeming greener – they really do have more fun when they're here and around her than they do when they're home at their own golf clubs. The reality is they come here for the Old Course, and then a few others, as long as they've made the trek. As for the media, well, they have been searching for lighter but newsworthy human-interest stories as a counterpoint to 9/11 – especially the sports media now that next month's Belfry Ryder Cup has been pushed to next year. But they've also discovered the reality of her international appeal and her ability to resurrect pleasant memories and make people feel good about themselves again – as women who are romantic legends often do.'

Polite laughter lightened the mood, the conversation became less formal and I sensed Alan's staff was beginning to understand the Box really was a welcome tonic from the new grim realities we were facing in our lives, whether we were ready to admit it or not.

I went on to tell them where we were in the scheduling process and said we were treating the Box as the icon she was – emphasising *icon* and *Old Course* to convey how seriously we were treating the project, as the words implied a certain level of credibility.

Alan took a sip of his wine and said, 'You are being properly formal – British formal – about this.'

'Yes, we are. The Country Club's marketing slogan doesn't harm our cause either.' I paused to sip some water. 'More often than not it helps when someone suggests I am a nutcase, or worse, for attempting to take the Box apart and ship her through the Panama Canal to California. One wag even suggested, "You're undressing her . . . you're raping a supine maiden . . . !"'

There was more laughter as we focused on the waiters serving our meals and Alan's ordering of another bottle of wine.

'On the subject of museums,' I said, as we settled in to eating, 'I've contacted the National Museum of Scotland for guidance. I thought it a good idea as packing and insurance are important issues. To me, maybe because of my background in architecture and art history, I believe, buildings don't die. They get bulldozed, dismantled, restored and rehabilitated and reconditioned – or transformed into something else as a reincarnation.

'I also contacted the Museum for political reasons because, when my mind began wrestling with the "why the sale of a national icon" question, I knew if push came to shove, it wouldn't hurt our cause if we had a prestigious national institution as an ally. It might imply veiled endorsement. In the email I sent to the National's director, I explained our task in as simple and professional terms as possible – without, I hoped, causing him to wonder who these nutcases from California actually were.'

Peter laughed. 'Interesting.'

'Believe it or not, I received an answer a day later. He wished us well and told us who to contact for assistance. The note was parenthetically signed off with, "He's a *Fife man*, though he works in Airdrie. We'll miss her, we will. Take good care of her."'

There was more laughter around the table.

'Ah, again,' I interjected, 'the emotional, passionate power of this Box, this global icon.' (And the Fife man proved to be a perfect advisor for us in our dealings with our shipping company in England.)

Peter Mason entered the conversation as his responsibilities included marketing, merchandising and licensing. 'As an American,' he asked wryly in his melodious baritone, 'I am sure you have considered the Box as a logo?'

'Yes, of course,' I said softly, not wanting to push the proprietary-icon-and-merchandising button just yet. 'There are some obvious cross-marketing opportunities for us to discuss,' I said, shifting my enthusiasm down a gear or two, while trying to be humorous. 'For instance, we'll let the Trust continue to use the Box's image on its merchandise – as you seem to feature it on everything from shirts to bag tags to single-malt-whisky bottles – if you let the Country Club use the Links Trust tartan on a special line of merchandise.'

There might as well have been an earthquake. The silence was deafening. Peter and Alan looked at each other; it was clear neither sensed my humour. Alan's jolly voice and rubicund cheeks, which usually serve him well, don't mask the workings of his incisive mind when his mood is more precisely focused and businesslike.

'My God,' I could hear him saying to himself as he looked at Peter and a reality check set in. 'It is an icon on the Old Course's stage; now the bloody Yanks own her.'

'She and the sign are marketing icons, yes,' I said softly, perceiving the thoughts racing through their minds, knowing this was as good, or bad, a time as any to open the icon-marketing conversation. 'I think that's what I read from your expression. Obviously it is an important reason we wanted to buy her. But there is more to it than that. We understand she is golf's greatest icon and, therefore, a de facto brand with global reach. In our opinion she may be unparalleled in the world of marketing, or at least in the world of sports when pure sportsmanship for both the professional and amateur dominates. It's a part of my "Fruit and Vegetable" rule.'

'Eh?' Peter said. 'I've heard about you and your marketing ditties. Some quite funny, actually. Have you considered a chapbook?'

'Really?' I said, surprised. 'From whom?' The look on his face said ask no more questions because there will be no answers. His due diligence on me and the Country Club had been thorough. 'It goes something like this. What you own, or control, is not always what you think you own, or control. What you see is not necessarily what you . . . The illusion that life is almost always better somewhere else is very real. The Box has been in your stable, as they say, for so many years you've never taken the time to assign her asset value – what she can mean economically if marketed properly. She is unique and can't be duplicated, like Big Ben. You have only been concerned with the new, not the historical. You have become,' I added as I softened my voice, 'a wee bit complacent, perhaps?'

'Well, I never . . .' Peter said, before he dropped the thought.

'As someone said, a fruit is a vegetable with looks and money. If the fruit rots it turns into wine, which is something Brussels sprouts never do. The Starter's Box is our fruit.'

Alan laughed politely as he studied me again, and his face and words sought a pained assurance we were not going to exploit the Box in a non-golfing environment.

'Hats and logo merchandise, including apparel,' I answered before he could ask. 'I have been thinking about an equipment line, but that is probably unrealistic. No, nothing that is not tasteful, golf-related or doesn't have to do with the Country Club of the Desert. Remember, it is a private club.' I took a sip of wine and suggested we discuss junior golf and the possibility of an annual, one-school-term exchange between the juniors of La Quinta and St Andrews. 'The climates certainly lend themselves to the idea of the La Quinta juniors spending their summers in St Andrews when the desert weather is hostile – and the St Andrews juniors schooling in La Quinta in the winter when the conditions in Fife, shall we say, reciprocate.'

'That *is* a good idea,' Alan said, emphasising the word *is* as only a British subject with a proper brogue can do. 'Yes, let's explore it. We can base it first on academic achievement, then athletic skills. We are committed, after all, through our junior-golf programme, if you didn't know, by one means or another, to see to it that a Scot and, we hope, a St Andrean wins the Open again.'

'How long has it been since a Scot has won?' I asked.

'1985, down in Sandwich at Royal St George's, with Sandy Lyle. Though born an Englishman, we claim him. For a native St Andrean, well over a hundred years,' he answered drily.

'I suppose you want the win here on the Old Course?'

Peter raised his eyebrows. 'Lord, we're not that picky. A win anywhere.'

Alan dropped a bomb as we ordered dessert. 'I received a fax from the R&A's undertaker this morning. It says the Box has to be off the Old by the end of the day on Saturday, 10 November, because utility trenching is to begin the Monday following.'

'Why, that's impossible,' I said, choking on a forkful of trifle. 'We haven't hired an undertaker yet. Are you serious?'

'Very.'

He handed me the fax. I read it. 'The way things are going, maybe I'll need the other undertaker,' I quipped in a whisper as I handed back the sheet of paper.

Alan flinched. 'Well, we'll see what we can do to help. Little can be accomplished next week, with the Dunhill Links Championship using the Old Course. Oh, by the way, we're going to put you in contact with Fraser Smart, our architect for the new box. He will help you hire a local joiner and undertaker, and in the cataloguing of her "body parts" – as I think you referred to them – on a computer drawing. Why don't you stay the week in St Andrews and enjoy yourself?' He smiled, barely baring his teeth, then chuckled.

I casually opened my agenda and fibbed that I had a business meeting in Los Angeles the coming Monday. I did, but with

Year in the sixteenth century John Knox incited the Protestants to drive out Catholicism by ransacking St Andrews Cathedral

59

Claudia, and the business was our marriage – our differing goals in life, our growing apart.

I also knew there probably wasn't a hotel room to be had in Fife because of the tournament. I shook my head. 'Well, it looks like I'll fly to California tomorrow and fly back next weekend.'

Peter laughed. 'If you embarrass the Trust when you return, on the golf course or elsewhere, including the pubs, we'll politely blame your actions on the sixteen hours of jet lag you'll be incurring from two trips between California and Scotland in the same week!'

CHAPTER 12

....

EUROPEAN TOUR PRODUCTIONS

FRIDAY, 12 OCTOBER 2001: AFTERNOON

Don't play too much golf. Two rounds a day are plenty.

Harry Vardon

After lunch I went over to the Box, as Carolyne had arranged for me to meet with Tim Lacey, a London-based television producer for European Tour Productions. He was in St Andrews covering the Trust's efforts to provide beach nourishment and other protection work to the dune areas severely eroded in the harsh winter storms of 1999. He was also producing a television story on the auction and, I quickly found out, looking for an invitation to play the Old Course.

We stood on the first tee under billowing white clouds and in a blustery, whistling wind as the last of the morning's rainy weather dissipated in the expanse of St Andrews Bay. Tim introduced me to his camera- and soundman and then reviewed the script of questions he was going to ask.

'I'll want video of you coming down the steps. You've been interviewed so many times we should be able to do the audio in one take.' His hand traced the lazy pattern he wanted me to follow from the R&A's front door to the steps leading down to the Old Course, the Box and the first tee. 'It's a fine afternoon for golf,' he added. 'Do you want to play when we finish?' He nodded to his golf bag leaning against the fence post.

I begged off, telling him I had a photo session with Alan and the junior golfers later, then a meeting with a photographer.

'Where are you playing?' I asked casually.

'I would hope here?' he said sheepishly as he scraped his chin. He was wearing spiked golf shoes.

'The Old is closed, obviously. Last tee time is twelve thirty this time of year, but let me see what I can do.' I called Alan on my mobile.

Alan put me on hold as he called a course ranger. When he came back on the line, he said, 'Yes, he is free to play, but he should begin play on the second hole. Actually, as the ranger reminded me, it is a good idea he plays and shoots his video on the Old today, given the favourable weather this afternoon. It will be less of a disruption than later in the week as the last group of today's golfers will be well ahead of him. The rangers will assist; tell him he will play as a guest of the Trust because he can't finish the round before dark with the late start. Oh, I'll be at the Box for a faux Passing of the Keys ceremony with the the juniors at 3 p.m. Remember you haven't paid for it yet.'

I caught Alan's innuendo and smiled, as if I had come all the way out to Fife to tell him we were reneging on our commitment. I gave Tim a thumbs up. 'You're good to go on the second tee, plus you're playing for free. They rarely do a concession for anyone. He mentioned you won't finish the round before dark.'

'Ah,' Tim said, his face brightening, 'the power of the Hut. She's a very handy tool for you socially and politically, isn't she?' As his right hand found his right hip, he raised his left hand, curved it above his head and danced a short jig. 'You must have gained a lot of new friends in the past month.'

'Even my enemies remind me we're friends when the Old Course is involved.'

He laughed. 'With plenty of envy added in, I'm sure.'

'True. No one believes I still have to queue for a starting time and pay green fees like everyone else (and I do, by the way). I'm now getting a couple of calls a day asking for me to assist with starting times – false loyalties are too often sacrificed on the altar of greed. Golfers crave identity with celebrity even if the celebrity is the Box.'

'Welcome to Marketing 101,' Tim quipped.

'Ah, yes, the claustrophobic, competitive world of fans and the lengths they will go to in their quest to get close to their heroes.'

'As if the trap of life they think they're caught up in can be remedied by hero identification and communication.'

'By one-dimensional, terribly insecure people.'

'Which is why their heroes socialise with each other – for the ego boost.'

'You've been around sports and show business too long.'

'How true.' Tim looked up to the clearing sky. His rather obese cameraman took the hint and tested different lens filters around the tee area.

'If I may say so, your monarch is the quintessential marketing icon.'

'She has been good for commerce and she's a symbol of family,' Tim said quite seriously, 'in spite of the shenanigans of her children.' His eyes warmed as he signalled to his cameraman again.

'Shenanigans are in a royal's blood, it seems – they enjoy tattling more than we mortals do.'

'I understand that. What I don't understand is the level of energy Americans exert on celebrity worship. Having no Queen or true family dynasty or anything else as strong as many seem to need is part of it, I suppose.'

I raised a questioning eyelid. 'But you do have to be careful because of the scar tissue. Celebrities are human; they have their own agendas – arrest records and controversial political leanings, at the extreme. The joy of unforeseen frontiers.'

'How well I know.' He rubbed an eyelid. 'Read *The Sun* or *OK!* or *Tatler* lately? What you're suggesting is that your icon over there is bulletproof.' His eyes focused on the Box.

I beamed. 'Exactly. She's a known commodity. We know her pedigree and what she stands for. Inanimate objects and dead celebrities are foolproof icons. The companies or governments who use the inanimate such as the London Eye, Rock of Gibraltar, Great Wall of China and phallus-shaped lighthouses in Cornwall have it right. As do those who use Marilyn Monroe.'

'Now the Starter's Box,' Tim added with emphasis. 'I know my friends in the advertising business are forever worried about the consequences when they sign a celebrity for an endorsement contract.'

'As well they should. Marketing is truly global and the sensitivity of national politics carries so much weight. It is a significant variable; the potential for negative impact is huge. Sometimes I think the celebrity is hired more for the personal vanity reasons of someone in the ivory tower than for sound marketing reasons.'

'Rational decision-making does not transcend the tabloid.'

I laughed at the joke. 'You are so right.'

Tim rushed the interview. 'Now to the hallowed, barren links.' He shook my hand, picked up his golf clubs and sprinted towards the second tee.

CHAPTER 13

··

FISHER WIVES AND MOZART

Victory anywhere is always sweet, but to win at St Andrews is so special it rises above everything else.

Seve Ballesteros, winner of five major championships:
the Masters, in 1980 and 1983; and the Open Championship
in 1979, 1984 (on the Old Course) and 1988

Wandering the quaint commercial streets of St Andrews is a joy. The burgh, which became 'royal' in 1620 but had been a market town for centuries, is often called a three-street town – North Street, South Street and Market Street. (It is still laid out as it was when the streets were full of market stalls and traders' stalls.) Tourist shops cater to golfers, of course, but unlike what has unfortunately occurred in many other towns of tourism, they are, for the most part, tastefully integrated into the commercial fabric every community requires to support daily life. I passed a shop on South Street with kitchen aprons displayed in the window. One had printed on the front, amid a smattering of musical notes, 'The Frying Dutchman'. Another said 'Too Hot to Handel'. I bought one of each as gifts for friends along with the eleven different Box-emblazoned postcards I found on the racks outside the shop door.

With a population of around 14,000, the town did not until recently have parking meters. The town had instead 'scratch-off' parking cards and what seemed a London-sized contingent of constables. A good place to buy the cards was the Visit Scotland store on Market Street because it also had a great selection of local-interest books and maps – and, yes, also some of the similar dumbed-down curios one also finds along the Champs-Elysées in

---

Paris or in New York's Times Square, the profit from which pays the rent. Each 60-pence card had a block of squares for day of the week, date, month, hour of arrival at the parking place and minute of the hour. You simply scratched off a grey gluey substance covering the appropriate squares with a fingernail or coin and placed the placard on your dashboard. (If you needed more time than you had scratched, with two hours the so-called maximum in any stall, you returned to your car, as you would a parking meter, and scratched another card.) The constables always seemed to be out in force – even when the rain was pounding and you engaged your brain in the game of 'thee or me'.

A look into Visit Scotland offers a bonus, which is the friendliness of the staff and their knowledge on all matters Scotland, particularly Fife, and their ability to assist with last-minute accommodation.

'Why, welcome,' someone said pleasantly from the counter at the rear of the store.

I walked around a bookcase to be greeted by a middle-aged lady and her soft-spoken brogue. 'What is the music I hear?' I asked. Wonderful crescendos from a cello and trumpet being practised filtered throughout the shop.

'Lovely, isn't it? Quite lovely, yes.' The lady rested her elbows on the till and beamed a partly open smile. One corner of her mouth was lower than the other, but it was natural and really quite becoming, though I didn't know why. 'Students from the university, upstairs; practising their Mozart, they are. Missed a run-through of the *Serenade No. 9*, the "Posthorn". They have concerts booked throughout Fife during Reading Week. Lovely to hear the music, really. All that's missing is the fancy tastes of Vienna's tortes.'

I smiled at the innocence of her words as I eyed the racked postcards and my ears listened in on the sounds of the rehearsal. 'You have a good selection.' Many of the cards featured images of the Box.

The clerk's motherly face flushed with a glow of happiness. 'A nanny in me youth, in Vienna, I was. Forced their music on me, the family did. Wise they were. Forever grateful.' She straightened her spine, stretched instinctively and wiped her hands across her apron in a matronly manner, then folded them in front of her boiled-wool tunic. 'Oh, very well, I suppose you are in need of parking cards?'

'Yes, I should think,' I said, aware I was beginning to incorporate the syntax of the Scots into my conversation. 'Thank you.'

'Aye.' She reached under the counter for the parking cards before counting out the postcards I had chosen with a moistened finger. 'You've only seven. More would do.'

I added more to the pile. 'Sometimes I think postcards were created for grandfathers. Before I came over for this trip, my granddaughter informed me that I needed business somewhere other than the UK because my cards were getting repetitious.'

'Aye.' She started ringing up the sale, her natural brogue lyrical and soothing. 'A few Princess Di and Prince of Wales cards are 'nuf for anyone. Prince William was in yesterday, he was.' Her voice brightened, with a musical, expectant quality. 'Had a wee nosy with a few friends and a pretty girl. Kate, I think her name was . . . Handsome, he is.' She sighed and seemed to dream for a moment before reality set in. 'Five pounds eighty, please.'

I paid the bill.

'Mind you, it would be a good day to trek to the restored fisher house, it would. Few visitors today.'

'You're right,' I agreed. 'The trek.'

(*Trek* is an often-used word in Fife. If you cannot park directly in front of the shop you want to visit and have to park a few shops away, you trek. If you walk a couple of miles to town, as many do every day when the weather is fair, and often when the weather is quite miserable, you trek. If you walk the 78-mile Fife Coastal Path, from the Forth Bridge to the Tay Bridge, you trek.)

With time still available before meeting Alan and the kids at the Box, and then Iain Macfarlane Lowe, a respected photographer whom the Links Trust had introduced me to, I decided to make the fisher wives' trek – all of two small city blocks from Visit Scotland. Distances are measured in tight, finite terms in Fife.

I started to leave the shop, but the clerk interrupted me. 'A ceilidh is being celebrated in Lower Largo this afternoon an' tomorrow. Rather a trek, but worth the effort.' Her twinkling eyes added emphasis. (*Ceilidh* is the Celtic name for what an American cowboy would call a hoedown. Ceilidhs feature singing and dancing, with fiddles and accordions and plenty of whisky, though nowadays beer and wine, in copious quantities, rival whisky as a vein-clogger.)

I waved politely and started my trek.

The address of an old 'fisher' house is 12 North Street. It has been restored to house the museum of the St Andrews Preservation Trust.

Near the ruins of the cathedral and castle (which was a palace built for comfort as well as a fortress and a dungeon), this part of town dates to the twelfth century. In its medieval heyday, the town had a sizable fleet and it was not unusual to see 300 boats tied up in the harbour, or split haddocks hanging on lines to dry along with the laundry, or to experience nautical disasters with many men dying throughout the years, often on their return from the Low Countries of Europe, their principal trading partners. Mending nets, baiting lines and tearing mussels from the Eden Estuary mussel scalps were everyday tasks for the fisher families (or jobs at very low wages for other women and children) up to 1882, when the council appointed a keeper to control the beds and charge people for the privilege of gathering. Suddenly, selling bait to the fisher families became a source of the burgh's revenue. Well known in those days was a recipe for mussel brose, which combined oatmeal and mussels. (Whisky with oatmeal and mussels, anyone?)

The sight of the stocky fisher women with their creels and wheelbarrows – which were large, often three feet high, with wooden spokes and a metal strap nailed to the wheel – and baskets, which they used to haul the bait mussels home on their backs, must have been impressive, if oppressive. (They walked across the Links to the Eden Estuary, where they took their harvest bare-legged and bare-footed in the freezing waters of St Andrews Bay. It was a four-mile walk out to the end of the Eden Estuary and back to North Street. West Sands Road, now partially paved, replaced the mussel path in the early part of the twentieth century.)

It was common for the small houses – many with only two rooms – to be given names. One, often referenced, was named the Royal George in honour of a naval vessel of the same name that capsized in port with her one hundred guns in 1782. Most of the crew was on board, as were many visitors. The loss approached 900 lives. It wasn't until 1848 that she was finally raised.

When some of the older fisher houses were demolished in the early 1900s, in the name of urban development, recognisable stones and mouldings from the ruins of the 1318 St Andrews Cathedral (consecrated by Robert the Bruce) and the castle were found incorporated in the walls. How convenient to have a centre-of-town stone quarry for many centuries, including the early 1900s, for houses being lived in today.

CHAPTER 14

··

LADIES LAKE AND TONTINE

FRIDAY, 12 OCTOBER 2001: AFTERNOON

May the road rise up to meet you,
May the wind be always at your back,
May the sun shine warm upon your face,
May the rain fall soft upon your field,
And until we meet again,
May God hold you in the palm of his hand.

A Celtic Blessing

With time still available, I crossed over to The Scores, where I came upon three signs crudely but lovingly painted by an unsteady hand. One hung askew from a simple wire tied to a nail that had been wedged into a high wall's masonry crack. It said [*sic*], in black-and-white letters:

Polite notice. This road lead only to a private house. Please do not trespass.

The wall was scattered with climbing tea roses held in place by a geometrically contrasting thin grid of wire. The road was no more than a very narrow, well-kept gravelled lane, wide enough for only a small car. A partially hidden home seemed to perch on the sea cliff around the lane's bend, its canted roof an uninviting dark slab of asphalt. The second sign, tied to the open gate, was a simple board that had a combination of written and printed block letters scrawled across it in nail-polish-thick red-and-white letters. It said [*sic*]:

ST ANDREW MOST SPECTACULAR GARDEN?
YOU BE THE JUDGE!
GARDEN OPEN. £2.00 ADMISSION £2.00.
ACCOMPANIED CHILDREN FREE. SORRY NO
DOGS.

Next to it, another, smaller, nondescript sign announced:

Proceed divided between maintenance and charity. Wow!
4000 bedding plants now in full bloom. Fantastic!
Lawn like a green!

I smiled at the typos and walked down the lane, noticing again that not one weed protruded from the length of the lane. The sterility reminded me of a barren moonscape. When I came to the lane's bend, another simple sign stood out, this one a shredded piece of cardboard with pencilled lettering. Lying on top of a stone wall, it said: 'Honour Box'. A little tattered wooden box sat alongside looking like a historic church's candle-altar coin box. To the left, a small greenhouse was packed with a profusion of potted plants, which casually hung from the ceiling structure, sat on the floor or leaned against the glass walls.

As my two pounds fell through the box's slot with a hollow *thunk*, I looked at the now visible house. A woman was watching me with a wary eye. I followed the words of another simple sign – 'This Way' – and then another stating: 'Some Steps'.

I walked down to a blizzard of flowering begonias, and other flowers I didn't know the name of, all symmetrically and too perfectly arranged in dome-shaped beds. The signs had not lied – there were thousands of flowers!

Given the signs I had passed, I found it curious there were no 'Keep Off the Grass' or 'Do Not Enter' signs or pointing arrows, so I walked across the lawn, as perfectly manicured as any green on the Links, to the stone wall that grew out the cliff that barricaded the sea. A medieval stone staircase with a rusted gate locked with a heavy metal chain sat along the sea wall, foreboding and dungeon-like.

The sky was a quite clear sparkling blue and the view to the north and east spectacular, as was the thin golden ribbon of sand-dunes across St Andrews Bay at Carnoustie, and even land's end at Arbroath. I guessed the next point of land to the east was probably the Skagerrak fjord on Norway's craggy southern coast. It was fitting as the word *scores* is a Norse word for 'clifftop'. It reminded me of standing on the deck of Frank Lloyd Wright's 'Walker' house in Carmel, California, the house featured in the film *A Summer Place,* starring Sandra Dee, Troy Donahue and pregnancy tests.

The setting – too perfect, surreal and unsettling, with no till marks or weeds, and utter silence – caused me to question whether the flowers were plastic or silk fakes. As I turned to leave, I glanced up at the moderne house, and in its view-of-the-world I saw the top half of a man's head. He appeared to be sitting down and reading a newspaper. A telescope was bolted to a nearby tripod. The woman I had seen earlier was standing in the porch's open doorway.

'Good afternoon,' I said. 'This garden of yours, and this setting, are spellbinding.'

'Oh, I know,' she answered quickly. 'Thank you. We love it here.' She greeted me with a studious half-smile. Her attractiveness replaced her wary eye. I guessed her to be of retirement age.

'I have been coming to St Andrews for years. I never knew this house existed.'

She smiled again. This time her eyes were warm and kind. 'In some form or another since 1811.' She ran her hands down her hips and the sides of a flowered smock that covered a simple cotton day-dress that ended well below her knees. Her feet loomed in front of me. Her shoes were sensible. 'Would you like to come in?'

I was shocked. In all my years of being in Scotland, I don't think that I have been in but a dozen private homes. 'I'm in town now because of the Links Trust,' I said quickly, attempting to legitimise myself.

'Oh, well then, my husband would like to meet you. I'm sure of it.'

I tentatively started up the steps. She looked the satisfied Scot, without any pretensions. 'How long have you lived here?' I asked.

'Oh, me? Five years. That's how long we've been married. He's been here for many years. We were childhood sweethearts.'

'Congratulations,' I said, smiling to myself.

'Come in, won't you. Please come in.' She showed me to a large room overlooking St Andrews Bay. I recognised the telescope. A large flat-screen television was turned on, the sound muted. Given the view, it seemed a sacrilege. A waist-tall, long bookcase ran along one wall. The tan-and-green chairs and sofa were arranged to focus on the view.

'I have tea on the boil. May I get you a cup with a biscuit? He'll be in straightaway.'

'No, thank you. I've just come from a lunch with the Links Trust.'

'Ah, yes, the Links Trust.' Her nod was approving, if questioning.

Her husband appeared and stepped down into the room. 'I am Gordon Senior and this is my wife, Joyce. Do sit down.' He went to a chair near the window, took a look at the cricket match being broadcast and sized me up at the same time. 'Links Trust?'

'Yes,' I said. I went on to mention the Starter's Box.

'Ah, yes. The man who bought the Hut.' The simple sentence was followed by an uncomfortable silence. He knew exactly who I was. When he spoke again he used the 'bull's eye' phrase in referring to the auction as his eyes went back to the cricket. 'This property was a tontine.'

Embarrassed, I told him I didn't know the word.

He turned to look at me, disbelievingly. 'Hmm. Let me tell you about tontine.' He was smiling now and getting comfortable as he moved his medium frame around in his chair and sought his favourite position. 'The word was coined after a Signore Tonti, an Italian banker who started a scheme – *scheme* not being the controversial word in the UK as it is in the US, as you know, meaning it does not suggest secrecy and collusion but simply implies a forthright method, plan or strategy instead. Mr Tonti's scheme was to have investors pay monies into a fund. In return, the investor received a dividend on his investment. What made Tonti's plan unique was that, as each investor died, his share was divided among the other investors until only one investor remained, who collected all the benefits or assets.' He turned away from me to focus on the cricket again. 'Tontines were eventually banned because there was too much incentive for the investors to kill each other off to increase their share of the fund – or to become the final survivor. Ah, the cunning Italians.' His smile appeared again, this time with a bit of comedy attached. 'For that reason, it's a wonderful plot device for detective-story writers, who use it as a motive for serial murder. Remember Robert Louis

Stevenson's *The Wrong Box*, which was made into a film in the 1960s?'

I had to admit I did not know the story or the film. 'Sounds similar to timeshare and fractional housing, which are a part of my business.'

'Without the opportunity for evil deeds,' he said. 'When I bought the property, a very old woman was alive who had worked here. I met her. Her job was to heat the salt water that was hauled up from the sea. This was a tontine bathhouse for women. Hot and cold seawater baths and secluded bathing were available up here and down on the rocks. The girls were taught to swim down there.' He raised an eyebrow. 'Can you imagine nude bathing in St Andrews?'

'Hardly.' I was becoming fascinated. 'St Andrews' first swimming pool.'

'In a way, yes. When I saw you look over the wall, you may have noticed man-carved depressions in the rocky shelves – little reservoirs, they are. When the tide was out, and if there was sun, the water became heated. Slightly heated, that is.' He laughed.

'I just noticed the beautiful rock formations and the nesting fulmars. It reminded me of parts of California.'

'Would you like your tea now?' his wife chimed in dutifully.

'I'll wait, thank you, my dear,' her husband answered. The action on the television screen seemed to change his mood from hospitable to reserved to out of sorts. 'There were six baths up here where the house stands. It was hard work working here and hauling the water up from the bay, the old woman told me. We have an 18-foot tide here, so when the women couldn't bathe down there, the water had to be hauled up here. It was quite a chore.'

'I assume they used the stone steps I saw at the end of the garden?'

'That's correct. I forget just how many steps there are, but I can tell you they're almost always slippery and dangerous.' He stood up, stretched and looked out to the small sailboat that was navigating along the shoreline. 'That lad had best mind himself. The currents and undertow along here are treacherous.' He sat down again, turned off the television with his remote and refocused on me. 'It all went to hell in the middle of the last century, Mr Hagen. This property was derelict. St Leonards School owned it for a while but did nothing with it. They still own Castle Cliffe house next door and the grounds between my land and The Scores, where students often come over with footballs and golf clubs to practise.'

I had noticed the walled square, about half the size of a football pitch, through a slit in the wall when I was walking down the gravel path – and the painted signs posted on each side that said 'No Ball Games'. 'How wonderful an open space, and it gives you a fine view of the university.'

'Of course.' He nodded to his wife. 'Do we have an extra copy of the Ladies Lake tontine information?'

'I'll see.' She scurried away.

'"Ladies Lake"?' I asked.

'The name of this property,' he answered proudly, as his wife returned and handed him a sheet of paper, which he glanced at then passed to me. 'You can keep it. In 1968, Robert Howe, an antique dealer on North Street, bought the site and built a house around the baths. I bought the property from him in 1985 and about doubled the size of the house. I also had the engineering done for the terraces and gardens. We are about forty feet above the water here, and the foreshore is about thirty feet.'

I quickly scanned the sheet of paper. It appeared to be copied from a book. Questions started spinning though my mind. How did the bathhouse really work and how much had he paid for the property were the two obvious questions – as was how had he and his childhood girlfriend reunited . . .

'How long have you been in St Andrews?' I asked innocuously.

'I come from Glasgow.' He stood up.

Sensing it was a signal to leave, I asked one more question: 'How much time do you spend on your fantastic garden?'

'Play golf three days and spend an equal time in the garden.'

'I was at a friend's house, in Lower Largo, on Sunday after a christening. I must say parts of your garden resemble theirs.'

'Oh,' he said, interested. 'Who do you know in Lower Largo?'

'Malcolm and Jane Campbell,' I answered.

'We had drinks and dinner with them on Friday night,' he said, shocked that I knew Malcolm and Jane.

'Malcolm said he was going to be in town Friday for a reception and dinner with friends when I called him from London.'

'Hmm.'

I wondered if he was a member of the R&A or any other local

golf club. I decided not to ask. 'I want to thank you for your hospitality. This has been very kind of you.'

He looked me over again. 'You're a good balm to bad cricket.' He offered his hand and laughed as we paused at the top of the stairs.

'Perhaps when I return next month you will have tea with me?'

'That would be lovely,' Joyce said for both of them, 'quite lovely. Bye for now.'

An elderly couple using canes were peeking around the corner as I approached the honour box. I assured them the visit was well worth the two-pound donation and continued back to The Scores, smiling. I was sure Gordon Senior was surely placing a call to Malcolm to discuss his pay-as-you-go interloper.

I turned left, towards the castle ruins, pausing at Castle Cliffe, the name of the set-back house next door, to admire the facade and proportions of the Romanesque architecture. An ugly sign was posted at the drive. It said:

University of St Andrews
School of Economics and Finance

CDMA
Centre for Dynamic Macroeconomic Analysis

CRIEFF
Centre for Research into Industry, Enterprise, Finance and the Firm

'Huh?' I said to myself. I kept walking.

A few minutes later I was at the castle ruins, which date from the 1300s. A well-designed sign said that the relics of St Andrew had been brought here by a Greek monk around AD 700, and over time, and intervening religious atrocities throughout the Reformation, the name of the town became St Andrews and he was adopted as Scotland's patron saint. An adjacent sign commemorated the death of George Wishart, who had been condemned for heresy and burnt at the stake in March of 1546, while his captor, a cardinal, was caught two months later, killed and his body hung in public view from the battlements.

Enough. I drove to the Jigger, ordered a wine, and carefully read the sheet of paper Mr Senior had given me. Ladies Lake and Castle Cliffe? Appropriate names for a gothic novel.

CHAPTER 15

THE PASSING OF THE KEYS CEREMONY AND THE DUTCH JOURNALIST

FRIDAY, 12 OCTOBER 2001: AFTERNOON

I'll guarantee you'll seldom enjoy a more stunning ride than that going from Dundee over the rolling, sometimes craggy mountains, passing Balmoral Castle on the road to Inverness. While some of us may have been in Scotland afore ye, if you can go anywhere, include truly Bonny Scotland.

Malcolm S. Forbes

While we were waiting for our photographer, Mike Joy, to re-anchor his tripod, the weather changed again. The sky remained clear, without clouds, but the wind stiffened, making it difficult to stand in place. 'I have heard a lot of lame-brain excuses for skipping classes – including a few I concocted when I was your age – but this is ridiculous,' I said as I buttoned my blazer. The cherubic-looking junior golfers from Madras College who were standing around the Starter's Box with Alan McGregor and me began to laugh bashfully, and one of the lasses turned her tan Country Club of the Desert cap askew and faked a pout. The kids had been excused from school to be part of the photo shoot and press conference announcing the junior-golf programme.

I had already passed out baseball hats and golf shirts emblazoned with the Country Club's logo, an artistic representation of a nautilus. As with golfers everywhere, it received most of the attention. When I told them the hats and shirts were the only ones in the UK, they shyly giggled as only teenagers can do.

Alan took the time to tell them what they could expect from the junior-golf programme. 'If you keep your grades up,' he said, 'you're all candidates to travel to California for the Box's unveiling this coming February.' More giggles and applause followed.

Reporters and photographers from local and national newspapers arrived, including *The Courier*, the *St Andrews Citizen* and *The Scotsman*.

'None of the photographers seems to be using a digital camera,' I said to Alan when we finished and the kids started to tee off on the first hole. 'How are we going to get photos to the foreign press and efficiently catalogue the take-down and shipping process?'

'No need to worry,' he answered. 'This vista, as you call it, is certainly the most photographed block of land on the earth. We have a tremendous archive. Digital cameras are too new an invention for us, I suppose,' he answered politely. 'Few of us even use mobile phones.'

I looked at him. 'You don't have a digital camera?'

'Not me, certainly. I don't know about staff. Interesting question.' He went into the Box and called Andy Eccles, the Trust's IT manager. After a short conversation, he said, 'We do have a digital camera. Andy will be available to you for photo-taking.'

Digital photography was a quite new medium, yes, but it had never crossed my mind to question whether the Trust would have access to digital equipment given they were constantly badgered for images of the courses.

As Alan and the photographers were leaving, a casually dressed man who had been standing with a local reporter walked over and introduced himself. He had a full head of unkempt candy-coloured hair and smoked a cheroot. He was a Dutch journalist on a Scottish holiday with his wife. His editor in Amsterdam had called him in his Edinburgh hotel the day before and told him to cover the story of the Starter's Box. We chatted as he scribbled rather copious notes in a well-worn brown Moleskine and I made a few notations in my journal. At the end of what turned out to be a quite formal, fact-focused interview, he asked if I had anything else to add about my experience with the Box.

I sensed the real interview was just beginning. 'Yes,' I said, '9/11 seems to have given my fairy-tale inanimate object a living, breathing life. In a few weeks she's become a symbol of something totally unrelated to the playing of golf. People relate to her now in the same way they relate to a good book of fiction – where the lives and problems of others help them escape their own lives and problems. She is beyond the tabloid, as I told a television reporter earlier. She's a symbol of the morally robust, which is something we all need given the slaughter of 9/11.'

He looked at me, puzzled, turned a page in his journal and started sketching the R&A and the Box. 'One of the reporters said words to that effect as we watched you having your picture taken with the juniors.' He fingered the stub of his cigar, decided it was dead, and put it in his jacket pocket. 'Those are quite strong statements. A stretch there, surely,' he snickered, 'but philosophically you may be right. Why do people care so much about animals, particularly horses, or buildings in general, with which they have no personal connection? I'm not a golfer, but I can tell you I've travelled the world on assignments and I've never been told to interrupt my holiday to cover a story before. Never. What is it with this Box, or this Hut, as I also heard it called? My editor said the press has been covering the story as if she were a head of state.'

I looked down at his drawing, noting he was an accomplished artist. 'How well I know. But people are grasping at any conduit of hope and humour these days, aren't they? I think that within a twenty-four-hour period, my giving interviews to Spanish, Japanese and Australian newspapers in the morning, then an interview with a reporter for one of Scotland's nationals in the afternoon and telephone interviews scheduled later with Swedish and American newspapers is a pretty solid demonstration of that. Other than the events of 9/11,' I added, without being coy or cute, 'is there anything else happening on this planet today that's commanding the same level of attention, in its own way, as the Box? It's golf's greatest icon, certainly, which means it represents a game that is based on humility, honesty and sportsmanship, without any dilution from the scandals of drugs and cheating that badger other sports. There's more than a little local politics thrown in, naturally – but she's also about having fun and living the adventure of being in Scotland. The whole process of buying her, taking her apart and shipping her through the Canal really is quite funny.'

He looked out to the North Sea, closed his journal and secured it with its elastic band. 'Travel is a reality tour for all of us.'

I waved and called out to the parent of a junior golfer I had met earlier. 'I would think they're on the third hole by now.'

'May I follow?' the mother asked.

'Of course. The course is now closed to golfers; you can follow the kids. It is *your* course, you know. You have the rights.'

She smiled, waved back at me and walked on towards the second hole.

The journalist's face brightened. 'I suppose almost everyone can relate to the Box as an icon in one way or another – whether they play golf or not, which must be the case if you're getting all these calls from the press. Yes, it is quite funny.' He cracked a smile, then made a comical face. 'An icon without a foreign language or a Roman numeral attached.'

I studied him again, with more interest this time. His sculptured, ruddy face suggested he was in his mid-50s. 'What do you mean?'

'Marketing people are enamoured with using foreign languages and other gimmicks for emphasis, I've noticed.'

'I like marketing rules that are easy to remember.'

He thought for a moment. 'I am talking about the principle of Latin. Think about it. Latin may be dead as a language, but a Latin inscription or a series of Roman numerals, like nothing else I know, indicates strength, culture, even sophistication.'

'Interesting.' I reflected on what he had said. 'You're right. The logo of our professional-football championship game is a Roman-numeral logo. Our national public-television network uses *carpe diem*.'

'As do the names of the popes and your Apollo lunar missions. The corollary is . . . ?'

'Keep talking,' I teased. 'The dais is yours.'

'"Aye", as the Scots say . . . On the use of language: a well-turned phrase in a Scots brogue is worth millions. Just ask Sean Connery. On the use of words: *Paris*, *Hollywood* and *St Andrews* perk people's ears.'

I clapped my hands.

'Thank you. Thank you.' He laughed in appreciation. 'After I got the call in Edinburgh, I went on the Internet and did some research to put the founding of golf in St Andrews over 600 years ago into perspective. I wanted to know what else was going on six centuries ago. It was interesting.' He shielded himself from the freshening wind, lit a fresh cigar and then turned back to face me.

Scored by Allan Robertson, the golf-ball maker, born in 1815, on the Old Course, the first to do so

'In the fifteenth century, the Florentine sculptor Donatello carved his *David*, and Jeanne d'Arc became the heroine of France and changed history. Leonardo da Vinci had only just been born in 1452.'

'Very good.' I reached into my briefcase for my scarf.

He methodically checked to make sure the cigar was properly lit. 'To think in the grand scheme of things, opera is only 400 years old.'

'If it *was* opera,' I said, 'this would be an aria opportunity. Golf on these hallowed grounds is pre-Shakespeare, pre-printing press. The Ming dynasty was just beginning to expand the Great Wall of China when the *golff* began.'

The corners of his mouth turned upward playfully. 'Ah,' he said, taking a long contemplative draw on the cigar. 'Perhaps I should have concentrated on 1924, when the Box was supposedly built. That's actually what's important, isn't it?'

'The two are intertwined. I looked into it.'

His eyes warmed. 'I'm sure you did.'

'Lenin died in 1924, bringing Rykov into power. Gershwin's *Rhapsody in Blue* was first performed that year; Puccini was finishing *Turandot*. It was also the year of the first Winter Olympics.'

'In Chamonix.' He emphasised his answer with a puff of his cigar.

'Very good. In golf, 1924 was the year Cyril Walker won the US Open at Oakland Hills, beating Bobby Jones. The Open was down at Hoylake that year; Walter Hagen won. (No relation.) In boxing, Jack "Manassa Mauler" Dempsey was heavyweight boxing champion of the world.'

He interrupted me. 'I think Proust died in 1924, or maybe it was 1922.' Unsure, he shook his head and wrote a note in his journal, which he turned to show me. Underlined, it read, 'The Box is about life. To some, the Box represents life.'

There was a certain portentousness to his statement, which I took as his own reaction to 9/11. 'My friend,' I said, 'to many who have walked these blessed grounds, golf is a matter of life and death. But to others, it is much more than that.'

'Perhaps this legend will become a cause célèbre?' He raised an eyebrow.

'She may already have. Yes. The required passion is certainly there.'

A self-satisfied smirk crossed his face as he closed his journal again, this time with a sense of finality. As we turned to walk away, he saw his wife coming out of the Trust's golf shop behind the eighteenth green. She was carrying four well-filled shopping bags. He introduced me as the man responsible for disrupting their holiday.

A youngish, vivacious, athletic woman, she spoke with the soft lisp you often hear in the south-east of the Netherlands, around Maastricht. She pulled out a tea towel and waved the printing at us. It said, 'Golf is an endless series of tragedies obscured by the occasional miracle.'

'I could have spent a fortune,' she said. 'There are the most wonderful things to buy in the shops.'

'The Trust will be happy to hear that,' her husband replied as he raised his hands in exasperation. 'My lovely wife personifies the fact that women do the buying.' He tapped his journal a few times with his knuckles. 'It looks as if you have outdone yourself again.'

I cracked a smile. Better his wife than mine.

'John, you have met the golfer who believes it is her divine right to have a cap and shirt from every course on the planet – whether a journalist's salary can support it or not.'

'Actually,' I said, pointing to the Box, 'she's responsible. Do you play golf?'

'Oh, yes,' she answered quickly, as if there was any question. 'But only three to four days a week.'

I reached down and repacked a tissue-paper-wrapped cable-knit cashmere jumper that was falling from one of the bags. 'Tell me, impulsively, what you think of the Box as a marketing icon.'

'I don't have any ideas; I just know you will make a fortune,' she said seriously, without hesitation. 'A fortune. Every golfer in America will want a shirt or a cap with the "SB" logo and every golf widow will be happy to buy it. It's better than a designer's name tag hidden in a dress's collar.' She looked at the Box again, only this time studying it a little more closely. 'Why, with a . . .' She stopped, realising she was caught up in her own enthusiasm. 'She is homely, though, isn't she?' A laugh followed. 'But that is what's so *right* about her. She's as common as we are, yet she is inspirational and represents so much, doesn't she?'

'That pretty well sums it all up,' her husband said, as he reached to shake my hand. 'We should go now, before she finds another shop.'

'May I ask your wife one question?'

'Yes?' she said expectantly, before he could answer.

'You're a sportswoman. Tell me about celebrity, logo merchandise and icons . . .'

She didn't let me finish. 'It's simple. Fire my passions – I'll buy anything you want to sell me.'

'If Catherine Deneuve or Tiger Woods endorses it . . . ?'

'More so.'

'Oh, oh,' her husband chimed in. 'A rule of marketing is about to be announced?'

'Ah,' I answered, as I explained the prompting of her husband's comment. 'The Paris Principle, because, as you said, women are the buyers. Which means that to succeed, a retailer must cater to the needs of women and infuse magic into the mundane. If he can find an icon that is compatible with the product that also symbolises the dream of glamour and romance, all the better.'

She planted her feet in a posture of strength. 'Even the modern "can-do-it-myself-thank-you" woman wants passion. Retailers are lucky that men seldom think . . . at least when it comes to buying something. No offence dear.'

He mumbled something in a playful snarl and picked up two of the bags by their handles as Danny Campbell, who heads the Links Trust's retail operations, walked over from behind the eighteenth green.

I introduced him as the journalist's wife said the words that would make any merchandising manager's day – or month: 'See an image of the Old Course Starter's Box and the Swilcan Bridge and think a trip to Scotland – and a shirt and cashmere jumper!'

Danny's expression deepened into a knowing smile. 'Is this conversation a set-up?' he asked.

I was still laughing after I described the spectacularly beautiful misty moors that lay waiting for them along the road to Inverness and the Highlands – all interspersed with dreamy deep-blue lochs and often craggy mountains. They waved a farewell from their car as they headed west, towards Perth. I nicknamed their car the 'Brand Wagon'.

CHAPTER 16

··

IAIN MACFARLANE LOWE

FRIDAY, 12 OCTOBER 2001: AFTERNOON

Lord Aberdeen was quite touched when I told him I was
so attached to the dear, dear Highlands and missed the
fine hills so much. There is a great peculiarity about the
Highlands and Highlanders; and they are such a chivalrous,
fine, active people.

Queen Victoria

It is safe to say all golfers' mindsets reach a heightened level of
excitement when a game of golf on a storied course is in the offing
– be it the Old Course, Royal St George's, Winged Foot or Pebble
Beach. Many also become excited when an invitation is offered to
visit any of the private, tradition-infested clubhouses in St Andrews.
I am one of those people and I was happy to be invited for drinks
at the St Andrews Golf Club by the renowned photographer Iain
Macfarlane Lowe.

As I made my way towards the clubhouse, down the simple
lane called The Links, there was a strong spring in my step as
I passed the Playfair ship's mast, its lanyards snapping in the
wind. (The mast, and its accompanying plaque, honour Sir Hugh
Lyon Playfair, a provost of the university, who had been a strong
political force in the construction of the R&A's clubhouse, and in
the 1850s, it was reported, in reversing the town's slide towards
near decrepitude.) The club is one of the local golf clubs that line
the southern boundary of the eighteenth fairway and are separated
from the Old Course by The Links. (Until the mid-1800s, The
Links was 'in play', meaning that if your ball landed on the road,
you played it as it lay.)

Founded in 1843, the St Andrews Golf Club has Jack Nicklaus as an honorary member. The other men's clubs along The Links are the New Golf Club, founded in 1902, with Arnold Palmer as an honorary member; and the St Andrews Thistle Golf Club, founded in 1817. It shares the facilities of the St Andrews Golf Club.

The women-only clubs lining The Links are the St Rule Club; the St Regulus Ladies Golf Club; and the Ladies' Putting Club of St Andrews, established by wives of R&A members in 1867. (It is not uncommon for ladies to have their own golf clubhouses in the UK and, in a few cases, their own courses.)

The Ladies' Putting Club leases a wedge of land for a many-holed putting green near the Links Clubhouse under a contract that expires in 2016. It is the only part of the Links courses that is not under technical control of the Trust, though they assist in maintenance. Most know the property as the Himalayas because of the green's enormous size and severe undulations. (If you are ever in St Andrews with an hour to spare, pay the Himalayas a visit. You'll find the putting green great fun and you are sure to be in the company of a hundred or more other happy souls.)

Iain is one of a handful of international photographers who have managed to build an envied, rewarding life photographing golf courses. I wanted to buy a few large-format images of his for display in the Country Club of the Desert's clubhouse, including the image used on the dust jacket of the book *St Andrews & the Open Championship*, along with his classic photo of John Daly with Costantino Rocca, pounding the ground, from the 1995 Open, and Arnold Palmer's final wave from the Swilcan Bridge during the 1995 Open.

We met at the steps of the club as David Joy, the historian who had written *St Andrews & the Open Championship* and the historical narrative for *Scottish Golf Links*, happened by. Iain introduced us. David confirmed a meeting we had scheduled by email as he proudly showed us the first copy of his new book, *The Scrapbook of Old Tom Morris*, which he had just picked up at the post office. As he hurried off, we went inside.

Iain ordered a gin and tonic for me and a whisky for himself from the ground-floor bar, which is just inside the front door. (No wasted footsteps between holing out on the eighteenth green and the club bar here!) We took them up to the first-floor dining room, where a series of his three-feet-by-six-feet photographs were hanging, as was a collection of historic photos by others dating back into the nineteenth century. Looking out through the expansive windows, he reflected on the professional pre-planning, patience and luck involved in shooting panoramic photographs, like those in the vista spread before us, from an angle I hadn't seen before.

The sky was quite clear and the day's last rays of sunlight splashed a low light across the fairways – so low the Valley of Sin had nestled into the soilscape as an uninviting shadow. The few clouds with any definition were a mixture of soft grey, bright blue and tints of pink, as if painted by Gainsborough. The dunes of Carnoustie across St Andrews Bay were visible as a reed-thin sand-coloured line. The R&A, the Box and the Caddie Pavilion were all bathed in soft yellow light. A squall, well out at sea, was being tracked by a rainbow.

'We're witnessing a quality of light I've never quite seen before,' Iain said, almost apologetically. 'Aye, another sapphire sky on a St Andrews afternoon in late autumn.' His statement shocked us both from our lethargy. We grabbed our cameras and took photographs until we ran out of film.

''Tis a shame,' he muttered later, with a tinge of sadness in his voice, when it became too dark to take photographs, 'that she's leaving us. 'Tis a shame, really. Really 'tis.'

I didn't know him well enough to pry or challenge his comments, but decided to subtly test him anyway. 'I hear some of the locals are angry she was sold.'

'More than that,' he said with a lowered head, as he packed his cameras. 'I heard in Edinburgh this morning that David Christie is trying to get the local MP involved to stop the sale.' He looked at me. 'Do you know either?'

'Your Member of Parliament? No,' I said softly, 'I don't know him. Nor David Christie.' I wasn't about to divulge that the Trust had asked me to stay clear of David Christie – the controversial Old Course starter before the formation of the Trust who had been rumoured to accept a ten- or twenty-pound note, on occasion, from someone who turned up without a tee time. Working on the 'hand-in-the-cookie-jar' principle after the Trust made its comment, I had, of course, booked a meeting with Mr Christie at my hotel to discuss the Box because he was the only pre-Trust starter still living. (Dave gave me the names of the other Old Course starters who had collectively served in twenty major championships, including seven Opens, six Walker Cups and many other professional events. It was about the only interesting comment of note elicited during our meeting. They were Bob Black, Donald McKenzie and Jimmy Alexander, the last of whom Dave thought dated from 1924 to around 1958, when he died.)

'Dave was the Old Course Starter from 1975 to 1988,' Iain said. 'The Box is owned by the town, along with the courses, you know. I've heard others are threatening to sue. So there may be some bloody hell to pay yet.' His voice trailed without much interest attached. Not being a golfer, he was probably suggesting he didn't understand what all the hoopla was about.

I cringed. 'Just what I need,' I said, looking out of the window and down on the foursome that was putting out on the green in almost total darkness. 'I'm not in the mood for a legal action, and I don't think the Box's new owner, Jack Franks, is either, from what I know of him and his reputation in business.'

'I wouldn't be too worried. I have a feeling you'll be all right. You seem to speak the language you need to speak. Even to a Scot.' He looked at me with a blank expression for effect, then stifled a laugh. 'You're not a Scot, are you?'

I shook my head. 'No.'

He changed the subject by beginning to tell me about some of his experiences in photographing golf courses, including the boredom associated with travel and the frustration inherent in waiting for nature to deliver perfect weather.

'You can't possibly be bored, or frustrated, as you call it, waiting for the weather in Scotland?'

'Oh yes, you can,' he replied seriously. 'When the weather wants to change every ten minutes for days on end and you want it to hold – and often for only a few minutes' time, or even half an hour, at dawn and dusk – it becomes challenging.'

I brought up the landmark question. 'There's been very good press but little editorial comment in the papers.'

His weathered brow creased. 'In spite of what I said, be careful. People here are always looking for causes. A large percentage of the population of St Andrews is elderly, which means they have plenty of time on their hands. Causes give them something to complain about and a level of power they may not have had in their business lives. I'm as surprised as you are that the landmark-heritage bomb hasn't been dropped with your icon, as you call our Shack. I would stay away from using the words *landmark* and *heritage*. Substantial words, with passion involved, they are.' He put a lens cap on one of his cameras and imparted a small smile. 'We are very proud people, as the history of the clans attests. Some say we've been betrayed. Anything that gives cause to fault the Links Trust most often creates an increased level of interest – even though, all things considered, the Trust does a very fine job. You can easily become the rock from which sparks fly in a verbal dust-up.'

'I have spent some time in *The Courier*'s archives. There seems to be an editorial condemning the Trust every other month – with an occasional accolade, of course. Between attacks on the cost of the green fees for the locals to course maintenance and the food-and-beverage pricing in the Links Clubhouse, nothing seems to be sacred. Even the potshots taken at the university.'

'"Sacred"? We're very secular here. How do I remember it from when I did go, in my youth? "Everything has its time. For everything there is a season . . ."'

'Close enough. I still legally share my life with a preacher,' I answered ominously.

'Brave man,' he said in quick response, without emotion or any questioning. 'More simply put, you may want to store the fact that, to some, you are a marked man.'

I squinted and looked out of the window, then back at Iain again. 'I've heard that from others but not as succinctly. Thank you. Hasn't the fact the proceeds from the sale are being used to launch junior golf diffused some of the flak?'

He took a small sip and looked at me ruefully. 'The Trust and the citizens are always at loggerheads over one thing or another. It may well have been a clause in the Parliament Charter that gave the Links Trust its birth.' He sipped again. 'I suppose you think the Shack is as important to golf as the lone cypress along Pebble Beach's 17-Mile Drive is in your country?'

'More so, and not only because the Box is the physical focus for collecting green fees. Every golfer can identify with it. They can't with your club or the R&A, for example, because they're private. No, the Box is every man's – amateur and professional alike – iconic symbol of St Andrews, golf and sportsmanship.' Without being overly impolite, I looked at my watch as an embarrassing loud, uncontrolled jet-lag yawn fell from my mouth. 'Excuse me.'

He smiled wisely. 'I must leave also. As the farmer's forecast says, the weather will hold two days out. I'm driving off in the night to Sutherland, Royal Dornoch and then Brora to shoot a whisky advert.'

'To think of you going to all these wonderful destinations and you don't play golf.' I marvelled that he was going to one of the most special golf destinations anywhere, after St Andrews, and would not be taking advantage as I had done.

'Golf is less a test of skill than human spirit,' Iain said. 'I catch the human spirit with my camera.'

'Indeed you do.'

CHAPTER 17

···

PITTENWEEM, BUGATTI
AND FERRARI

SATURDAY, 13 OCTOBER 2001

The Scot will not fight until he sees his own blood.

Walter Scott

The farmer's weather forecast was spot-on again. I pulled up the blinds and opened my bedroom windows wide to a refreshing, almost warm Saturday morning and the autumn odour of rustling, sooty leaves of decaying colours.

I decided to call Doc. As it was approaching midnight California time, I guessed she would be in the tub for her before-sleep bath, knitting – a private guilty pleasure of hers. I was right. We conversed wearily, reviewing our respective days' adventures. She covered the gossip of Los Angeles and I made idle comments about the ceremony at the first tee and the Dutch journalist – and his wife, who must have had a separate income, given the strength of her shopping habits. An hour into our call, Doc signed off by splashing the water with her feet with enough force that I could hear the noise, above the sound of her knitting needles thrashing one another . . . It was a conversation loaded with deception, sarcasm and innuendo. I wondered if I was going to enter that abyss, as so many others have, in which my love of the game of golf was going to last longer than any other relationship in my life (or at least those made of my own choosing).

I went into town and made my ritual rounds. The first stop was at J&G Innes Ltd, the newsagent's on South Street, for the day's papers. The second was nearby, at the Sweet Shoppe, for a non-

Year in the twentieth century Nick Faldo won the Open Championship on the Old Course

alcoholic, 'naked' Highlands coffee (three shots of espresso and filtered coffee, without a dram or two of whisky added) and the local gossip.

'Good morning, lassies,' I said in a sing-song fashion that complemented the tinkling of the bell crudely nailed to the top of the door frame.

Sophie squinted at me as I started separating the news sections from the ads and inserts of my newspapers. Her eyes were more than a little bloodshot. 'Aye. Mornin'.' That was it. She started a coffee for me on the espresso machine. 'Noisy, the steam is this mornin'. Bloody noisy.'

Her partner, Lucy, flashed a rolling, cheery smile as she flipped a nod towards Sophie's affliction and set a plate, dwarfed by a large soda roll and a dollop of marmalade, on the counter. 'Sobriety is terrible at times, 'tis,' she said, 'an' when ye have a cold and a tussle with the boyfriend involved all together, 'tis all the worse.'

'Tell me about it,' I mumbled, thinking of my own personal problems.

'Huh? Problems with a lass?'

'You might say that. Sophie should drink a couple of Irn-Brus,' I said, referring to the soft drink that has been marketed as a hangover cure under the slogan 'Scotland's Other National Drink'.

'Might work but tastes like melted plastic. Yuk.' Lucy made a face.

'So?'

'Maybe right. Becoming a Scot, ye are, if ye know aboot oor other national drink.'

I had quickly come to understand that the agenda and demeanour of these two mid-20s lassies could – no, *would* – be driven by whatever abuse they had inflicted on their bodies the night before, particularly Sophie, who truly believed her body was a vessel for transporting pleasure. Generally, it was refreshing because you never knew what the subject of conversation was going to be. As I looked out the window, one of the junior golfers from the previous day's photo shoot was crossing the street near the ruin of Blackfriars Chapel on her way to Madras College for what I assumed were Saturday-morning classes. Her uniform of box-pleated skirt, navy blazer, school tie and white shirt was topped off with the logo baseball cap.

'Thank you, Sophie,' I whined as she set down my coffee. 'Maybe you should have one of these quad bullets yourself, with a wee dram of *correction*.'

Sophie ignored my suggestion to partake of the four shots of espresso, but sneered at the mention of whisky.

Lucy laughed. 'Whisky may not be a cure for the common cold, Sophie – or the boyfriend problem – but it fails more agreeably than most other things.' She made the sign of the cross across her torso and went to wait on another customer.

I folded the papers, grabbed my takeaway coffee and went off to meet Malcolm and Jane Campbell.

After an enjoyable catch-up, I took Malcolm's advice, and advantage of the unusually dry, warm weather, and drove off to Edinburgh the long way – meaning along the A917, which more or less follows Fife's eastern shore, except when it turns south and bypasses Fife Ness. I passed Boarhills and pastures dotted with stone walls, grazing sheep, cows, manicured fields filled with stubble – and, nestled in among it all, the Balcomie Links at Crail – and a windmill. The mixed smells of the soil and the sea were overwhelming.

Scotland's ubiquitous speed cameras braced me to drive slowly through the sleepy villages of Kilrenny, Anstruther and the small picturesque harbour of Pittenweem, where I stopped to stretch in front of the fishmonger's stand. A red-hulled short-masted fishing boat lay on its side, stuck in the mud and silt, awaiting the tide.

A while later I passed Earlsferry, the childhood home of James Braid, the golf-course designer who won five Opens in the early 1900s. I stopped at the Elie Links to seek out the fourteenth hole, set tight under the escarpment of Kincraig Point, because Braid said it was the best hole in golf. While taking the short walk to Chapel Ness, the sound of shotguns echoed in a grove of trees to the right. Two solid pops, returned echoes, and then more pops and echoes. Finally silence. Double-barrel or over-and-under 12-gauge shotguns, I was sure, recounting my youth and hunting in the corn-stubbled fields of the US's Upper Midwest states. I wanted to believe that someone's dogs had flushed a brood of pheasants from a thicket.

A few minutes later, as I drove through Lower Largo up to the Lundin Links and the Links of Leven, I rolled down the car windows. There were smells again, but this time from the oily, odorous exhausts of a deep-blue 1939 Bugatti Type 57C and what looked to be a partially restored red-orange Ferrari Dino 246 GT as they flashed past me, racing each other. They were a blur, their sounds a welcome, refreshing intrusion on the peace of the countryside.

I turned onto the A955. Over another leg-stretch and a ha' pint of ale in a Wemyss pub, where I was the only patron, the pleasant-looking brown-eyed bar girl started a conversation.

'Visitin'? From where?' she asked, as the boredom that mapped her face faded to a soft, inquiring smile.

'California,' I answered, noticing she had an exciting frontage.

'Castle Wemyss dates from the twelfth century,' she offered. 'Still inhabited by family members.'

'I have an acquaintance who lives in Napa, California,' I said. 'She is a well-respected wine historian. She is from the family.'

'Aye?' she answered, somewhat disappointedly. 'Heard that story afore. Can do better than that, can't ye?'

CHAPTER 18

··

PRINCES STREET

SATURDAY, 13 OCTOBER 2001: AFTERNOON

So long as we love we serve; so long as we are loved by
others, I would almost say that we are indispensable; and
no man is useless while he has a friend.

Robert Louis Stevenson

By mid-afternoon, that fine, still-warm October afternoon, I was
in central Edinburgh. Princes Street, like most high streets in the
UK on a Saturday afternoon, was a swarming mass of people – not
unlike New York's Fifth Avenue or Paris's Madeleine during the
Christmas season. There were no signs of 9/11 remorse here as far
as I could see. I tried to be positive. Perhaps the Scots were going
to teach me something about the living of life. I was ready to learn.
I left the car at my hotel and took the long walk up to the Castle
grounds, where I sat down on the pedestal of the bronze statues
of Robert the Bruce and William Wallace and dialled in to the San
Antonio Saturday-morning radio golf show that was to interview
me. (The joy of a mobile phone, differing time zones and no one
really knowing – or caring – where you actually are at any given
moment.)

The host of the show, Andy Everett, introduced me as being in
the clubhouse of the R&A, or so he thought. 'Now that you've
owned her for a month or so,' he said, 'I have a question – by
that folks, for those of you who haven't been following the story,
I don't mean to suggest that Mr Hagen has bought a woman.'
He paused for emphasis and humour. 'What he *did* buy on 9/10,
the day before 9/11, is the St Andrews Old Course Starter's Box,
which in gender has always been considered a female.' He paused

again. 'John, has the significance of what you've accomplished sunk in?'

I laughed at the introduction. 'Andy, before I answer your question, I do have to comment on your use of the phrase "bought a woman" because my wife, and not necessarily in a joking manner, sometimes references the Box as my *mistress*.' I paused to change my voice tone. 'To be serious and answer your question: no, Andy,' I said, 'no; it hasn't sunk in. I am still shocked and it has been – what, over three weeks now since the auction?'

He went on to inquire about the Old Course, Scotland's weather and single-malt whisky – the usual common questions his audience was interested in – before he asked a very intelligent wrap-up question: 'What do the natives think of all this? I'm sure 9/11 has impacted them to some degree?'

'9/11 has been devastating for business here, though it is nearing the end of the season. People are in shock, of course. They respect the enormity of the holocaust and perhaps are better able to deal with it because terrorist attacks are more common in Europe. What has been interesting is the intense passion people have for the Box: not only the UK, but all over the world, too. The press has been enormous. It is as if she's become an antidote to 9/11.

'I've also discovered that for a lot of people, sports fans and otherwise, that as an icon, she clearly represents the good in the world, with friendship, sportsmanship and adventure at the top of the list. Think the Box, or see an image of her, you plot a trip to Scotland.'

Andy quickly interjected a spirited: 'I do! That's for sure!'

I laughed. 'I'm happy to say, no drugs and middle-of-the-night sensationalism here, no police-blotter reporting in the morning papers, as is too common with celebrity athletes and Hollywood celebrities. There's probably a book of parables that can be tied to the Box; parables for living life.'

'Well, I asked the question; I got an answer,' Andy said, pleasantly surprised, as he went to a commercial.

During the commercial break he told me how happy he was to interview someone who wasn't repetitive, used non-figurative sentence fragments laced with cliché and 'you-know-what-I-means', or believed the word 'like' was a conjunction.

The next morning I counted only 31 people in the pews for the Sunday service at St John's, the beautiful little church in the West Princes Street Gardens. It was a little strange to me, given the carnage. The rector's sermon did focus on 9/11, America and how 'all our hearts are in a pilgrimage . . .'

CHAPTER 19

DUNHILL LINKS CHAMPIONSHIP

SUNDAY, 21 OCTOBER 2001: AFTERNOON

For, as long as but a hundred of us remain alive, never will we on any condition be brought under English rule. It is in truth not for glory, nor riches, nor honours that we are fighting, but for freedom – for that alone, which no honest man gives up but with life itself.

Declaration of Arbroath, 1320

My return to St Andrews the following Sunday afternoon came at the end of what BBC Radio reported was 'a week of the worst autumn weather many remembered'. I had to agree, as I had taped the Golf Channel's Thursday and Friday coverage of the Dunhill Links Championship – the last tournament the Box would host.

Most amazing, the sportscaster said while summarising the tournament, which ended an hour before, that Paul Lawrie – despite the conditions – had set a record in distancing himself from the rest of the field over the final 36 holes of the weather-delayed tournament. He scored birdies on seven of the first ten holes of the final round on the Old Course and capped it off by holing a forty-foot birdie putt on the eighteenth hole from the Valley of Sin to edge Ernie Els by a single shot and win almost $1,000,000.

I listened to this while sitting in the Hertz car park at Edinburgh Airport. Thirteen hours of fly time, plus a change of planes, terminals and waiting out a four-hour weather delay at Heathrow, were wreaking havoc with my senses. I needed a few minutes to adjust my brain for driving on the 'other side' and navigating the always clogged Barnton roundabout at the airport's entrance.

Year in the eighteenth century the St Andrean John Baine cast, in his type foundry, the first dollar sign ($) ever used in America

97

Important as weather issues were, I was unable to keep my mind off Claudia and the gut of our meeting – and the realisation that our relationship had run its course and neither of us was any longer the person with whom we had fallen in love, or, more crushingly, the person with whom we wanted to spend the rest of our lives. We admitted a mutual love and respect for each other was not enough, as we agreed – with slightly teary smiles – that the Box, bless her, was the catalyst that had allowed us to discover the unseen fissures in our relationship. I accepted the fact that the stress of my losing a deal to archaeology and my Boxaholic obsession had cracked our relationship wide open. Claudia said similar words, as she admitted she had been using religion as a crutch and an excuse to avoid facing and resolving her own emotional problems, and announced she was taking a sabbatical to write a book. Nothing quite so esoteric with me; I still had my 'mistress' to contend with, even if I didn't have to worry about the bed being big enough for three of us any longer.

Half an hour later, I crossed the Forth Road Bridge and drove very slowly up to Fife, as almost everyone did. It was foolish to challenge the M90 at over 30 miles an hour in a torrential downpour with high, gusty winds.

If this was the end of the storm, what misery had the golfers played in earlier in the day, and yesterday? And Paul Lawrie – seven birdies in ten holes on the Old Course? In this slop? *Impossible!*

CHAPTER 20

∙ ∙

JIM BROWN: STARTER

MONDAY, 22 OCTOBER 2001: MORNING

Scots, wha hae wi' Wallace bled,
Scots, wham Bruce has aften led,
Welcome to your gory bed,
Or to Victorie!

Now's the day, and now's the hour,
See the front o' battle lour;
See approach proud Edward's power –
Chains and Slaverie!

Robert Burns

Normal drive-time from Edinburgh Airport to St Andrews –
without any bridge-related delays, or being stuck behind a farmer
on his tractor or combine (farmers have the right of way) – is
around 90 minutes. The drive took four hours.

Twice, all traffic was stopped on the M90 because of flooding.
Twice more I had to pull over because of vision-obscuring white-
outs caused by the patchy fog.

Once back in my room at the St Andrews Bay, after the obligatory
welcome glass of claret from the hotel's general manager and then
a hot shower, I unpacked the equipment I had shipped ahead from
Los Angeles as United Airlines had told me to expect problems with
airport security at both LAX and Heathrow. How right they were!
My leather belt, with a simple, undistinguished buckle, didn't clear
security at LAX. I left the US without it. Then, when going through
customs in London, a detector took exception to the screws in my
right ankle, the remnants of a skiing accident in the 1960s. (I didn't

mind, for obvious reasons, and felt very sorry for the detained man standing next to me in Heathrow who was in danger of having his false teeth confiscated. 'The only set I have,' he said, dumbfounded by the confusion.)

My equipment included an old rain suit, two pairs of heavy corduroy trousers, a down coat, long-sleeved turtleneck shirts, cases of film in X-ray-proof containers, a camera and a tape recorder, marking pens, spray paint (in various colours), a geologist's axe, a compass, grid-lined paper, a journal, a laptop computer, a tape measure, canvas gloves, waterproof boots, trainers, a stocking cap, two umbrellas and a tam.

As corporate gifts, I had shipped a case of Nike golf balls, four bottles of Hendrick's gin, six bottles of Jack Daniel's and two bottles of Oban whisky, all of which cost twice as much, or more, in the UK than in the US.

Looking at it all spread out on the floor, I thought that if long underwear, a tent and a Coleman stove were added, I'd be ready for the Antarctic or ice-fishing in Wisconsin.

During the drive into town the next morning, a radio newsreader informed her listeners that the worst of the weather had moved south to the north of England. A simple all-day rain was forecast. I bought the papers and went to the Sweet Shoppe. 'Good morning, Sophie,' I said, happy to be out of the steady heavy drizzle.

Her cheery mood and my gazing at the ripeness of her robust Scottish frame were a fine start to the week. 'Lucy's off to Edinburgh an' an auction where there's another espresso machine on the block. Aye, you're the celebrity who knows the biddin' business. You should be biddin' on our behalf.' She flashed her usual warm smile, stifled a morning yawn and started making me a double espresso. 'Story on you in the *Scotland on Sunday*, there was. With your photo. Need one taken here for publicity's sake.'

'I'll see what I can do. We call that "value-added", the capitalising on celebrity icons. A lot of restaurant and even car-wash walls are plastered with celebrity photos in the US. It is an association issue, as it is with the Box.'

'Pubs in Edinburgh have pictures of the celebrities an' football players. They seem to be the most popular with the tourists. Here, the Dunvegan's walls are covered by golf photos.'

'People like to be associated with what they perceive as success, whether real or imaginary. We can talk about that some other time.' I changed the subject. 'What's the news? What's happened in Fife this week?'

'Terrible car accidents again. Fast drivers. The drink. Tourists forget what country they're in an' start drivin' on the other side of the road. Others don't mind the right of way in the roundabouts an' overtaking of the farmer an' his tractor on the narrow roads. Usual. Business is bad, ne'r mind the time of year. 9/11 has seen to that.'

When I arrived at the Old Course a few minutes later, the drizzle had matured into one of those famous drenching cold winter rains in which the gods of Fife rejoice. Unmoved, the usual contingent of golfers were standing around or sitting on their bags at the Box, umbrellas open, waiting to tee off or hoping for a no-show or cancellation. (Weather conditions have almost nothing to do with playing golf in Scotland.)

The day's starter, Jim Brown, invited me inside the Box. Mike Horkan, property manager of the Trust and the person responsible for overseeing the Box project, stopped by. It was a tight squeeze for the three of us as the Box's clear inside dimension is only about six feet by eight feet. But who cared? The electric heater was working and we were dry.

We chatted a bit about Paul Lawrie's feat and the wholesale cancellation of tee times after 9/11.

'It must be tough in the US,' Mike said, 'because it's bad here.'

'You're right about that,' I answered. 'Surprisingly this Box has found a role in the horrors of that day. She's become an antidote, a placebo. Mention her name and people smile or laugh. Even the sceptical press.'

'Hmm,' Jim said noncommittally as he handed Mike the telephone.

'On my way,' Mike said, as he turned to me. 'Off to meet our head starter, Steve Jones, at the Jubilee Box. A golfer wants to share his bag of clubs with a second player, which is not allowed.'

Jim became engrossed in a conversation with a golfer, which gave me the opportunity to look around from a 'taking-it-apart' point of view. I'd obviously never been inside the Box and in all the times – over 20-odd years – that I had checked in to play the Old, I had never had reason to take the time to study her. Instead, the pre-golfing process had always been the same for me and what

'Play Away Please'

Peter Mason guessed had been at least a million other golfers. That is, check in 30 minutes before your tee time, pay the green fee, have the almost always mandatory pictures taken, avoid antagonising the starter, maybe stretch a little and take a few practice swings.

Listening to Jim, I began to understand how all-consuming the starter's job actually is. It requires the insight of a psychiatrist, the constitution of a judge and the patience of a parish priest – not unlike a telephone operator or a concierge working at a resort hotel. One eye is focused on the clock as the starters keep to a very exacting schedule. Tee times are set at ten-minute intervals on the Old Course and seven minutes on the other Links courses. Lateness is not tolerated. The other eye is on the computer screen: monitoring the check-in and green-fee-payment process (most fees are prepaid these days), answering the occasional telephone call from a ranger and confirming handicaps. The maximum allowable handicap on the Old Course is 24 for men, 36 for women. Finally the starter announces a tee time over the tannoy after the group who last teed off has started down the first fairway. Then the process begins again.

Jim turned to me. 'Some people think they can turn up late as they do for a restaurant reservation or their hairdresser's.' He answered the telephone, said a few words and then picked up where he left off. 'Once they admit they're late, they think that a ten- or twenty-pound note, or something more substantial, can solve their problem. Not true.' His voice was firm and resolute.

Jim is correct. The reservation process is squeaky-clean, though anecdotes about the business practices of the starters before the Trust became involved are numerous – with many probably apocryphal. In the old days, at the end of the nineteenth century, feeding a 'padded palm' was quite normal, as one of the old starters is supposed to have attested when he told a golfer, 'Aye, the whisky has a price on it, ye know.'

Similarly, A.W. Tillinghast – or 'Tillie the Terror', the great American-born course designer (San Francisco Golf Club and both Baltusrol courses among them) – wrote: 'After the nightly inspection of the starting times for the morrow ... if our hour was not to our liking the passing of a half crown to Greig probably would slip us in somewhere. Probably? Absolutely!'

Indeed, one of the first questions the press asked the undertaking crew when we began the demolition process was: 'How many twenty-pound notes did you find stuffed in the walls?' The too quick answer was: 'Nane.'

Jim had a short chat with a passing local he knew and checked the wall clock. As he seemed to have a free moment, I asked, 'You are prepared for everything, aren't you?'

'More than you think,' he replied. 'The Links courses are public, so many of the citizens believe they own the Links – as does the woman who just happened by – and that we work directly for them, or that we are their own personal concierge. 'Tis an added twist that often turns unpleasant.'

'There must be a new tactic tried every day as far as playing the course without a reservation is concerned.'

'Oh, yes. A fresh idea almost every day, with many from the journeyman professional.' He turned to check the connection of a cable coming out of the side of his computer. 'Many believe they're entitled to special treatment – as if their various logos connote golfing skills. After a practice swing or two, you almost always know who will, or will not, find their form.'

'At least they go through a focused preparation not unlike most superstar athletes,' I said, slipping in an aside, 'as they prepare to compete and strive to improve themselves. Everyone can always get better. The baseball player tapping his bat on home plate, the tennis player bouncing the ball with precision before serving, the sprinter testing the track's surface before anchoring his feet in the blocks: they all come to mind.'

'The business leaders I see do something similar, even if it is only a waggle or continual re-grip of the club – to calm nerves and relax muscles. You can tell they're focused, very focused indeed. But most times, too tense to play a proper game of golf.'

'I understand. When you think about it, the demands on an executive exceed those on an athlete, don't they? Athletes train their body to perform for very small periods of time: say, two seconds for the batsman, nine seconds for the sprinter, four hours for the golfer.'

'Haven't looked at it that way, I have to say.'

'In business, everyone is expected to perform 100 per cent all of the time, no matter the circumstances and amount of preparation. The Japanese have a principle, I believe, that dictates continual improvement, regardless of achievement.'

Jim thought about what I said as he fingered his microphone, then announced a tee time. 'What did I hear on the telly, when I was watching a poker tournament? "It's not the cards dealt; it's how they're played"? The fun part is the struggle to get better?'

'So true, Jim. So true.'

He looked at me, smiling over the top of his half-glasses. 'Being the businessman you are, I trust *you* are prepared for our weather at this time of the year.'

'There is no bad weather, only bad planning.'

'Nae, dinnae count on that statement offering truth in Scotland.'

An omen? I nodded anxiously and glanced out at the caddies, quietly evaluating the swings of their players before wishing them the round of their lives. 'A perfect example of a caddie-businessman in preparation.'

'For a larger than normal tip,' Jim answered.

'We call it revenue enhancement.'

A woman started tapping on the window with the head of a golf club. Her actions were annoying and terribly impolite. Jim opened one of the Box's little windows. 'I'll be with you in a moment, ma'am. Let's not break the glass, please. Thank you.' He closed the window. He had obviously spoken the same words countless times as he carried it off with such a pleasant, kindly voice it most likely led the lady to believe that Jim considered it an honour to bear her abuse.

He had told me earlier that when he had arrived at the Box before dawn, she was already standing there, in the rain, along with others who hadn't won a tee time on the previous afternoon's ballot. As he prepared himself for the day's business – before he had raised the blinds – she had begun her tapping on the window. She had threatened discrimination, for some bizarre reason, because he wasn't paying attention to her, the only woman in the queue.

'She's a classic, she is.' He grimaced at me as he opened the window again. 'Your handicap ma'am?'

'Forty,' she shouted arrogantly, in a loud voice.

He slowly closed the window and turned around, his eyes rolling over the top of his glasses again. He was chortling. 'Do handicaps go that high in the States?' he asked, trying to contain himself.

'I have no idea,' I said with a chuckle.

This time he opened the window more slowly. 'Ma'am, I am terribly sorry but the maximum handicap for ladies on the Old

Course Links is 36. Please visit the Links Clubhouse just down the way and make a booking for one of the other Links. You will find them most enjoyable.' He went back to his work, made easier now, as the daily block of tee times reserved for the local clubs and residents was approaching. They knew the procedure.

'I think one of the reasons I love this game so much, Jim, is because it's such a wonderful forum for observing the human condition. As a preacher I know says: "It's best to keep your composure, as every hockey player knows, because you can't score from the penalty box or when God is mad at you."'

'Ye get a fresh set o' conditions here ev'ry day, ye do,' he said, using his brogue for emphasis. 'Human and natural.'

Having a 40 handicap means a person will probably shoot a score of 40 over par, on their very best day – or in the case of the Old, 112 strokes altogether, as ladies' par is 76. (As all golfers are aware, a 'best day' is a rarity.)

USGA data suggests that only about 9 per cent of the thirty-two million people who play golf in the US – fewer than three million – have the skills to shoot under 100 for 18 holes. Only about 1 per cent of the 9 per cent – or 30,000, to be generous – score under 80 on a regular basis. Other than the fact that it takes more time to hit 112 shots than it does, say, 80 shots – and forgetting the fact that many of the 112 shots are being hit into unplayable locations instead of where intended – a handicap of 40 correctly suggests the golfer possesses only the most rudimentary golf skills. (This data has changed little since the technological revolution in golf equipment and instruction began over 20 years ago. As Michael Lamanna, one of America's finest golf teachers, suggests, 'If you want to improve your game, forget the $400 driver and $200 putter; take a block of lessons instead.')

A more important point is that slow play impacts enjoyment of the game for everyone as poor golfers, generally, play slower than those who are more skilled. My friend Jack Nicklaus once said something to the effect that you can have friends if you're a slow golfer, and you can have friends if you're a bad golfer – but you don't have any friends if you're both.

On the St Andrews Links, they strive to have rounds completed in fewer than four hours, which is certainly possible as the courses are flattish, conducive to walking, caddies are available and tees are close to greens just played. (Electric carts, or 'buggies' as they're called in Scotland, are not allowed on the Old Course, nor will the caddies carry tour-professional-size vanity golf bags. When you go to Scotland, pack your 'Sunday' bag as if you were to carry it yourself.) A perfect example for demonstrating that fast play and low scoring can go hand in hand is what occurred during the last round of the 1970 US Open at Hazeltine. The first twosome off on Sunday morning, which I followed as an observer, as Leon Crump was one of the competitors, played their rounds in one hour and fifty-seven minutes. Both, without any real motivation to focus, except to get an early plane out of town, broke 80.

At the height of the summer season, about 250 golfers will play the Old Course each day – except Sunday, when it is closed. (It is also closed during the month of November for maintenance.) The other Links courses are open every day. The Old Course generates about 40,000 rounds of golf a year. The seven courses generated over 220,000 rounds of golf in 2008, including the rounds played on the Castle Course after it opened for play on 28 June that year, which is remarkable when the relatively short tourist season, chancy weather and short periods of daylight from autumn to spring are factored in. In support, however, the longitude of St Andrews, roughly the same as Moscow and Juneau, aids in the summer when the sun rises around four in the morning and you can play past ten in the evening.

Another incident that morning demonstrated the difficult situations the starters often face. An R&A member and a relative who had made the trek from Australia for the purpose of playing his once-in-a-lifetime round on the Old arrived late. Being late, their tee time had been given to a couple who had been standing in the rain since early morning, just waiting for such a no-show situation to present itself. There was a heated, unpleasant exchange when the R&A member and his guest were told they could not be accommodated. (I think Jim will agree with me that there is a reason many starter and club-secretary positions in the UK are famously populated by retired military personnel, who are accustomed to remaining unflappable in sometimes difficult situations.)

Street number on South Street where, in the early 1900s, a perfumier sold antiseptics as a cure for head lice

CHAPTER 21

....

FRASER SMART, MIKE HORKAN
AND ROB DONALDSON

MONDAY, 22 OCTOBER 2001: LATE MORNING

Why Golf is Art and Art is Golf,
We have not far to seek –
So much depends upon the lie,
So much upon the cleek.

Rudyard Kipling

The fantasy was over. The real business was at hand. It was time to scrub with the surgeons.

This was my thought as I arrived back at the Box after lunch. That, plus understanding some things in life never improve, one of the more prominent being the general quality of the pub food in the UK. Walking back to the Old Course after a typically overcooked, fatty – no, *gristly* – pub lunch, it occurred to me that sometimes when you're too close to a situation, you lose perspective. I sensed that that might have happened with the Trust from the way I'd read the facial reactions the week before. I detected their selling the Box probably wasn't a unanimous decision. They really didn't understand they were selling an icon with important history and human emotions attached. I remembered my last trip and what Iain had said – or not said – about the Links Trust and politics. I put it out of my mind because Mike Horkan was waving as I approached the Box.

We shook hands again before he introduced me to the other 'surgeons': Fraser Smart, the Links Trust's architect for the new box; and Rob Donaldson, a joiner and undertaker from a hamlet near

Lower Largo, whom Fraser had recommended we hire during our last telephone conversation. The local rumour was that it wasn't a good idea to interview a St Andrews or Glasgow company for the work because they sometimes practised 'ring-fencing', meaning they often inflated their bids to outsiders. (The phrase is taken from the literal 'ring-fences' used to contain animals on a farm.) Ever the realist, Fraser had said that Rob's firm, based a 'goodly' distance away by St Andrews standards – almost 15 miles – was qualified for the challenge.

'Living 15 miles from St Andrews means you are an outsider?'

'Oh, yes; 15 miles is a goodly distance in Scotland,' Fraser replied seriously.

Rob thanked me for bringing California's *Baywatch* weather to Fife.

'Thanks,' I said, derisively. 'We can do better. This is not a pleasant day in Southern California.' The rain had softened to a nasty thick drizzle, but in parts of the sky the cloud cover had broken and allowed a hint of sunshine. The temperature was in the high 30s and I flippantly wondered if the blustery, cutting wind was not a harbinger of things to come.

'Near a Fife tannin' day, 'tis,' Rob said. His short-sleeved shirt was completely drenched.

I smiled. '*Baywatch*? Well, at least you watch sophisticated American television.' As we laughed I took the time to study Rob. I guessed he was in his early 40s.

He became serious. 'Aye, nuthin' like it on the BBC,' he said. 'All lassies look like that o'er there?' he questioned with a genuine curiosity.

'Well, you'll find out if you come over and put the Hut back together for us in California.'

Rob's face lit up as he smiled broadly and jammed his hands into his trouser pockets. 'Aye, ne'er been oot o' Scotland.'

Fraser asked, 'You must have thought about the possibility of going to California?'

'No till now,' he answered quickly, his face beaming. 'Only bird I often see here is a seagull.'

Fraser was a scene unto himself. He wore what was to become his daily uniform of a knee-length, unzipped, flame-orange down-filled seaman's parka, blue dress shirt and exotic patterned tie. A roll of drawings was tucked under his arm and a video camera hung from his rather brawny neck. He took a minute to light his pipe, a routine I soon discovered was an all-consuming, all-the-time activity – one that seemed to give him the time to let another project's worries run through his mind. He had a thatch of wild grey hair, struggling to become white, and a face that rippled with humour and irony. I took him to be in his early 50s. He was the classic image of Gary Cooper portraying the architect Howard Roark, Ayn Rand's protagonist in the film adaptation of her novel *The Fountainhead*.

After the telephone conversations I had had with Fraser and Rob, it was fascinating to finally match the burrs and brogues of voices to faces and personalities. Rob's brogue varied from slight to thick depending on his mood and level of seriousness. Fraser's never varied. It was always studied, calculating – so much so it was sometimes difficult to tell whether he was serious or just spicing his conversation with a dash of wry Scots humour. Mike's, on the other hand, was blended with the light lilt of the Lowlands, which complemented his easy-going demeanour.

Because the combined area of the first tee, putting green, Caddie Pavilion and Starter's Box is barely 500 square metres (about 5,000 square feet), or around an eighth of an acre, Mike took the time to thoroughly brief us on the issues associated with the marshalling of our equipment and the staging of the shipping container. It was important that Rob's men stay out of the way of the Old Course crew. As if on cue, Eddie Adams, head green-keeper of the Old Course, came by, introduced himself and reiterated Mike's statement. The pecking order was obvious. Work on the Old Course took precedence over everything else, including the R&A's restoration. Anything to do with the Starter's Box was in a very distant third place. I didn't argue.

Mike apologised for the change of construction schedule but said we could work over the weekend of 10 November if we needed to.

I looked at Rob. I was about to sign his contract. He knew what I was thinking.

'Nae problem,' Rob said. 'An' I'll nae charge ye o'ertime if we're inta the weekend, but ah think it's only 'bout a four-and-a-half-day job anyway.'

'Thanks,' I said. 'Does your time calculation have a weather allowance included?'

'Nae. 'Tis only late autumn or early winter as yer soul may judge.'

Mike brought up the potential for petty theft. 'We will increase security because the university will be in Reading Week.' The souvenir value of the slate roof tiles was a concern as was the Old Course's putting-green sod, which Eddie's crew had already started to remove and stack in the first fairway. 'They can swipe your trim and sill bricks also.' As Eddie knows, they even often try to put their divots in their golf bags instead of replacing them in the turf. The caddies are always on watch.

The implication was that with no classes in session, the students had more time available for the inevitable college pranks. As can be imagined, the Old Course is besieged by 'collectors' looking for souvenirs at all hours of the day and night. As a deterrent, the flagsticks are collected at the end of the day and almost everything else of souvenir value is removed from the course. Even so, the grounds crew occasionally find rakes, hunks of turf, bunker sand, tee signs and the crushed sea shells that still define a few of the on-course pathways missing when they prepare the course for play in the morning.

I noticed that about a hundred feet or so of the classic white Old Course fencing running down the right-hand side of the first fairway was missing. 'Where is it?' I asked casually as I didn't see it stockpiled anywhere.

'Probably at the dump by now,' Mike said.

I was speechless. 'You mean you've trashed the fencing that's been a part of this wonderful natural stage for so many years – that's framed this most glorious historic vista and been the ribbon that's held it all together?' The intensity in my voice must have emphasised my frustration and bewilderment.

'"Vista"?' Mike shook his head, clearly not understanding or concerned.

I looked at Rob for consolation. His face was blank.

'What about the *history* . . .' I stopped suddenly as the 'everything has its time' comment of the Dutch journalist started rapping in my head.

Fraser's eyes went warm and had a calming effect. 'Meet us at the pub at half five. To discuss the fencing.' He nodded towards the Dunvegan over on North Street. His eyebrows rose above his steel-rimmed glasses as his lips worked his pipe.

'Yes, sir!'

CHAPTER 22

IAN JOY'S PHOTOGRAPHY SHOP

MONDAY, 22 OCTOBER 2001: AFTERNOON

> Golf appeals to the idiot and the child in us. Just how childlike golfers become is proven by their frequent inability to count past five.
>
> *John Updike*

With time to spare, I decided to walk the town's core again – as in immersing oneself, wherever you may be, into the fabric of day-to-day local life. It is more important, to me, than being the 'in-and-quickly-out-of-town' golfing tourist.

The Ian Joy photography shop, now closed, was on Bell Street, one of the cross streets that runs from South Street to North Street. I stopped in because Mike Joy – Ian's son, who ran the family shop – had been hired to take our daily construction photographs and I had not been able to talk to him the week before at the photo shoot. A little brass bell rang out when I opened the window-paned red door, its tone a little lower than the Sweet Shoppe's. A one-hour photo-development service was prominent, as were a wide variety of film cameras – but no digital cameras. Part of one wall displayed for-sale photographs of the Links for varying amounts, depending on the size. I made a quick calculation and decided they were probably being sold by the square centimetre.

Mike came through a doorway, curtained like an arch in a mysterious Moroccan cafe. We chatted. I asked if he would also take digital shots of our construction activity on a daily basis for my emailing back to California. 'No digital,' he said. 'Film-selling and developing is what I do here. It's my business.' His tone was firm.

'I understand,' I said, not prepared for a discussion on emerging technology.

He caught me eyeing the Old Course photos. 'I have some images I took of the Box last winter during a snowstorm. Are you interested?'

'Yes,' I said.

'Let me get them.'

(I was later told that David Joy, the historian, and Mike Joy are cousins, if somewhat distant. Or as a San Andrean said in abbreviated Scots fashion when I asked if Mike and David were related: 'Cousins, I think, but not often seen together in public.')

He returned with a panoramic photograph of the vista. The Swilcan Bridge, Swilcan Burn and first and eighteenth fairways were covered with a few inches of snow, as was the Box's roof with the red pompom cap piece sticking up through it all. Passion sold me. I ordered personal Christmas cards with the image.

All the evocative photographs of the Old Course stirred memories in me of all the facts I had discovered during the course of my research. Prior to the first Open Championship at St Andrews in 1873, and the filling-in of Halket's bunker, the Swilcan Burn was a natural water hazard that ran close to the centre of the first fairway and not the evil-looking, moderately deep, narrow channel it is today. The burn was also used by local women for the washing and bleaching of laundry before laying it out on the fairway, over the whin, to dry. The R&A made changes to the local rules in 1851, and again in 1888, to account for 'domestic chores'. Finally, a few years later, a finite rule was arrived at which read: 'When a ball lies on clothes, the ball may be lifted and dropped behind, without penalty.'

The hole was more interesting and a more formidable test of golf back then, as the fairway was less than a third of today's width and the rest of the fairway was a natural sandy hazard. The burn was reachable most days with the tee shot, even with the balls and clubs of the day.

I went back to Market Street and walked the cobblestoned pavement until I came to the fountain in the small square at the street's eastern end. Until I'd heard the rehearsal when I was in the Visit Scotland shop the previous week, I had completely forgotten I had arranged an apartment for a friend's daughter, who had spent a summer in St Andrews five or six years before. She was a violinist who was graduating from the Juilliard School of Music in New York and wanted to spend the summer in St Andrews to practise her violin and prepare her recital material for a coming concert tour.

'In St Andrews?' I had asked, a bit shocked by the question. 'People don't go to St Andrews to play the violin. They go there to play golf, drink and trek.'

'Well,' my friend said, 'my daughter told me that, among some musicians, the St Andrews weather is rumoured to behave kindly to the wood of string instruments.'

I had found an apartment for her, on this square, but didn't remember the address even though I had negotiated the lease. I took a panoramic photo of the square to take back to California. In St Andrews for a summer and, as I remember, she didn't play golf or drink?

CHAPTER 23

DUNVEGAN PUB

MONDAY, 22 OCTOBER 2001: 3.30 P.M.

Join a Highland regiment, me boy. The kilt is an unrivalled
garment for fornication and diarrhoea.

John Masters, Bugles and a Tiger

Many of us have faced the unpleasantness of booking two meetings
at the same time. Fortunately, for those I inconvenience, when I am
the guilty party, it most often occurs when I have scheduled the
meetings in the late afternoon, in restaurants. (I do not refer to
those who are habitually late. Long ago, I made the decision to
refuse to deal with the inconsiderate. Life is too short, with time
being the most precious irreplaceable commodity we have.) I have a
tactic for minimising the emotional strain I cause. It is to discreetly
pass my credit card to the waiter as I enter the restaurant, tell
him my dilemma and let him know I will make an unannounced
exit. Then, when I do leave the meeting, after apologising, and
my guests are beginning to wonder about me, at least they are
pleasantly surprised when they find the bill prepaid.

Such was the case with Mike and Fraser and my scheduled dinner
with long-time friend Angus, a member of the House of Lords (and
an early arrival for a conversation with Will, a workman who has
lived and worked on Angus's property for 70 years).

I need not have worried about my meeting in the Dunvegan
with Mike and Fraser. When I walked in, Mike was well into his
first ale and bag of salted crisps. 'Fraser had an emergency, had to
drive to Leven,' he said as I sat down. 'Good news,' he continued,
getting to the point as he ordered me a ha' pint I had no intention
of finishing. 'I found about 50 feet of the fencing. It has been saved

Number of strokes, minus 50, of Greg Norman's final round in
the Open Championship, Royal St George's, 1993

The classic iconic photo of the R&A Clubhouse and the Box, which served golf on the Old Course for 77 years. The photo was taken the week before the disassembly process began on 5 November 2001.

A snowman made by two university students and me on the Swilcan Bridge, 12 February 2009.

My friend Ron Beard, Chairman of Callaway Golf, and me, with caddies Davey and Little Joe (wearing 'two left shoes', though it doesn't show), in 1989.

My son Drew, Ron and me, on the Swilcan Bridge, during the same summer trip to Scotland. Who 'woulda thunk' that 12 years later . . .? The pre-digital photo is one of only three I have of me with the Box.

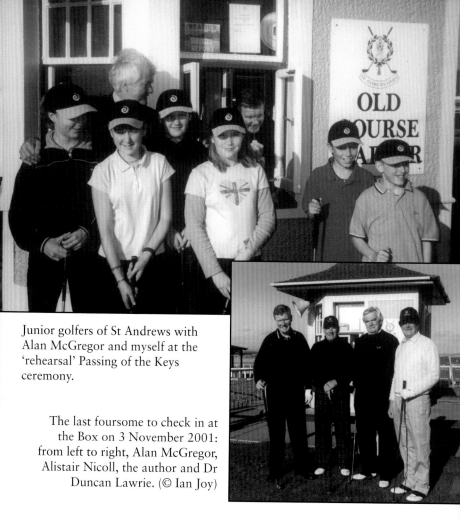

Junior golfers of St Andrews with Alan McGregor and myself at the 'rehearsal' Passing of the Keys ceremony.

The last foursome to check in at the Box on 3 November 2001: from left to right, Alan McGregor, Alistair Nicoll, the author and Dr Duncan Lawrie. (© Ian Joy)

The merry foursome beginning to enjoy what would prove to be the year's last day of good golfing weather.

The rook sections on the ground, the west wall partially down and the R&A's two-ton sand pillows anchoring the scaffolding. The roofing tiles are one-centimetre-thick slate.

Ringo, Shadow and Ox taking a break and, probably, cursing the weather, the Box and the Yankee who bought her.

Mike Horkan, Eddie Adams, Fraser Smart (with his back to the camera) and the author discussing strategy to assure no damage is done to the Old Course.

Fraser, a handsome man, as he endures a gale-force biting wind and tries to shelter his video camera. Another snowstorm is about to pummel the Old Course. Passing behind him, with his back turned, is Rob, the undertaker.

The brick-grab about to remove a section of the unnecessarily thick south wall. Fleet Foot and Ox watch closely, as does Mike Horkan, but from a safer distance.

Nancy Aaronson and a friend, Wells Marvin, surveying the laid-out Box in her barn in December 2001.

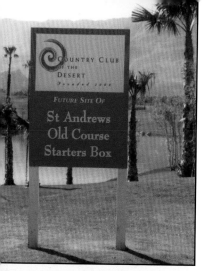

The sign constructed at the Hideaway to 'welcome' the Starter's Box.

A partial view of the 18-hole 'Himalayas' putting course at the Madison Club, in La Quinta, California, the Box's home and shrine.

The iconic view taken after the Box had begun its sea voyage to California from Felixstowe, England. Do not be deceived by the blue skies; it was a bitterly cold November day and if the photo had been taken from the frozen eighteenth green, you would have been able to see the ice pond in the Valley of Sin.

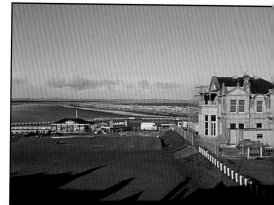

Stockpiled brick pallets with their spray-painted location coding that corresponded to the architect's computer drawing of the Hut.

She's gone. The sandbags of the R&A as fallen teardrops . . . A fitting metaphor, perhaps, for a sad farewell.

for you. The rest had already been carted to the dump or taken by a local.' His sentences ran together with indifference.

I sighed a little in anticipation of chatting with Will and decided to ask the 'no-no' question, betting that Mike, a construction man, probably wouldn't be sensitive to the situation. 'Don't you keep anything for historical purposes?'

'Not old fencing,' he said.

'Maybe the Box and fencing qualify as historic landmarks.' I took my first sip of the Guinness, the sip that's always the best. 'Hasn't a tree-hugger ever raised the issue?'

'Over here we call them brick-sitters, or stone-stealers.'

'"Stone-stealers"?'

'Gravestones – a phrase from the old days. Some are still being used as door steps, or what you would call "stoops".'

I ignored the blasé quality in his voice. 'Think of the potential money that could be raised for junior golf, or another charitable cause, by selling sections of fencing as souvenirs.'

'Huh?'

I had considered it on the flight from Los Angeles in the context of what had been done in San Francisco when the cables of the Golden Gate Bridge were replaced in the 1970s. Someone had the enterprising idea of selling the old cable in small sections as souvenir paperweights. I started to multiply one-foot sections of fencing by several thousand feet by ten pounds per section . . .

Mike finished his pint and apologised for not buying a round as he had a meeting to attend.

'Not a problem,' I answered quickly.

We were stopped by four big, brawny, kilt-wearing Scots in the hallway on our way out of the pub. They greeted Mike automatically and introduced themselves, as those in their mid-30s almost always courteously do in Scotland. The reverent tone in which they related their day working the Links green-mowers disappeared as the conversation turned to football and women. The testosterone level was high.

Mike and I shook hands and parted ways in the car park behind the British Golf Museum. As I drove away, I reflected on the day's activities and how refreshing it was to be involved with professionals who didn't seem to have hidden agendas. I was also looking forward to being with Angus and hearing about his voyage – and what would be my first whisky since the auction.

CHAPTER 24

WILL

MONDAY, 22 OCTOBER 2001: 4.30 P.M.

I could take out of my life everything except my experiences at St Andrews and I would still have had a rich and full life.

Bobby Jones

There is a fine man known only as Will who lives on Angus's large farm spread out over the rolling hills and tangled woods above Strathkinnes. He has life tenancy in a three-roomed sandstone cottage, which has a prime view out to the Eden Estuary and the Links. The first time I visited Angus and his family in Scotland, he introduced me to him with the powerful words: 'Will is the most honourable human being I have ever come to know.'

Will's age is either 93 or 94; he is not sure; neither are the Council record-keepers in Fife nor the sexton of the kirk he has attended since his youth (the only kirk he has ever been in, let alone attended regularly, except for a wedding or funeral). Age is not important to Will; nor is a family name, since he has no family. Nor is golf important, as he has never played the *golff* and never will.

What is important to Will is having a car. It is all he has ever wanted since he saw a photo of King George V riding in a car, in a London procession, in 1915.

Will has never had a bank account. No one ever thought about this until early one Saturday morning in 1975, when Will walked into the kitchen of the manor house in his wellingtons and church clothes. He was holding a plastic grocery bag. It was filled with banknotes. He wanted advice from Angus on the purchase of a new car. (Will's first car was an Austin 7 Box Saloon from the late 1920s.)

Will does not recall having been involved in an accident in any of the three cars he has owned over seventy-nine years – except when he killed a deer some years ago while driving on one of the unpaved, rutted lanes of the farm at dusk. The incident was the fault of the deer, of course, and there was little mention of it as the deer was slaughtered, bled, scalded, scraped, cut up, cured and smoked by a local butcher in exchange for a bottle of Bell's whisky and half the meat.

Though Angus's father retired Will with a full pension some 29 years ago, Will continues to involve himself in the farm's daily life, doing what he believes needs to be done. He often says, 'I like to help out.' Angus still pays him a full wage every Friday, as he did when he was formally employed, and as Angus's father did before him, and his grandfather did, for a brief period of time, before his father.

The 16 full-time workmen on the farm hold Will in high regard and take great pride in working alongside him. It is said that other workers who are brought in to work the harvest in the autumn do so because of Will.

If you want to talk to Will, you go and find Will, because he has never owned a telephone.

The last time I saw Will was about a year before the auction. He had returned from Sunday services, cooked his hot noontime meal and changed into his work clothes, which consist of wellingtons; baggy teal-coloured corduroy trousers; an unironed shirt buttoned to the neck, often with a collar-point splayed upwards; a pullover in a blizzard of muted earth-toned colours; and a snap-brim leather-and-tweed cap. Never having seen Will without his cap on, ever – but then I have never been to church with him – I have no idea if he has a full head of hair, is bald or something in between. He does, however, have wide, thick sideburns. They are the colour of a roan horse. I have also never seen his teeth – how many he has remains a mystery because he always speaks through pursed lips. (I say this because old Scots, and too many young ones, do not frequent the dentist.)

I had found him working in his garden. 'How was the sermon this morning?' I asked as we shook hands.

'Aye, a baptism took time so the sermon be brief,' he responded, smiling, as he rested his gnarled and calloused hands around his mottled hoe handle. 'It was a quite good sermon.' He went back to making rhythmic, fluid motions with his brawny shoulders – motions that made the hoe seem as if it were part of a ballet as it scarified and carved the earth.

'The leeks appear ready.'

'Aye, another week, if the weather holds. I counted a bit ago. Only 201 now. The rabbits were here in the night and took most of 23 for a meal. Bloody rabbits. Need more hawks!' He glanced over to the herbs and rows of perfectly aligned and manicured potatoes. 'Potatoes are ready for wintering under straw in the barn.'

I smiled, quietly watching him work for a moment, before saying reverently, 'I heard Mrs Anderson passed a month ago.'

I referred to his next-door neighbour of many years. Will's wife died in 1971, and Mr Anderson passed away soon after. When an appropriate period of time had lapsed after her husband's passing, Mrs Anderson took the initiative and decided she and Will should do some sharing of life together. They worked out an arrangement where both contributed to the buying of food and other provisions. She did the cooking, laundry and other household tasks, and Will fixed things, tended to the garden and made the five-mile Saturday drive into either St Andrews or Cupar for the groceries. They spent parts of their days together in each other's cottages, but never their nights.

'Aye.' He kept hoeing but turned his head to look out towards the estuary in reflection, his still-clear blue eyes focused and unblinking.

I lowered my head, said a silent prayer for his friend and gave thanks for the sunny day.

'The carrots are ripe,' he said, as I looked up. 'Do best to try one.'

I reached down and pulled on a smallish stem. It emitted a soft, suctioning *womp* as it left the security of the soil. The fresh smell of the earth and dark-green stalk were intoxicating. I wiped off most of the dirt and took a bite. 'Wonderful carrot!'

'Aye. Dinnae hae tae do much to grow 'em, ye know. The difficulty is keeping the bloody rabbits away. Nature works most o' the rest.' He paused briefly. 'Made protection last night, I did.' He pointed to a stack of long oval cages crudely constructed from a fine-mesh chicken wire.

'Will,' I said, feeling there was a lot on his mind, 'can I do anything for you before I leave Fife for California tomorrow?'

'Nae. We hae trouble with the buzzards again.'

'Buzzards?'

'Aye, they're back tae peckin' out the eyes o' the sheep,' he said matter-of-factly, in a cool voice without stress. 'Blind them, they do, then the sheep fall and die and they have a meal. Nature is cruel most days.' He paused and looked at me blankly. 'Nae. Quiet now with her gone, and quite peaceful. Now I can eat the food I like.'

He went back to working his hoe, back and forth, in the same rhythm and tempo as before – scraping and digging at the soil – only pausing to pull an occasional stubborn weed.

CHAPTER 25

....

LORD ANGUS LOCARDS

MONDAY, 22 OCTOBER 2001: EVENING

There is not such a word
Spoke of in Scotland as this word fear.

Shakespeare, The First Part of King Henry IV

Lord Angus had called me the day after the auction, from the Antarctic, to congratulate me for playing the role of a 'buccaneer who had filched one of his country's sacred icons'. He also said he was going to be in St Andrews for golf and a visit to his oldest granddaughter, a graduate student at the university, at the same time I was in the burgh tending to the Box. We arranged dinner at his manor house in Fife.

The Locards family is very old, even when considered in relation to other established families, who can often trace their roots back to the thirteenth century or before. As with all these families, when history and lore are discussed, fact and fiction become intertwined and modified to suit the current patriarch. In the case of the Locards family, references to the practice of witchcraft by certain members of past generations do seem to have some validity.

Having been friends for many years, I was well aware Angus was a successful farmer, an environmentalist, an oil man and a very old-world private financier. (The phrase 'old-world private financier' can be quantified in a single word: *discreet*. Indeed, when windmills were prevalent in the East Neuk [east corner] of Fife, his family prided itself on operating the farm without the intervention of the authorities until well after they had brought power to Scotland. At the same time, his grandfather started buying North Sea oil leases.)

Angus is a classic large and cumbersome Scot with sandy-red hair and mutton-chop sideburns the texture of straw. His appearance often suggests the personality of a bluffer, but he has the heart of a poet and exudes gravitas.

As a butler led me into the east parlour, I saw that his chin was lowered, his cheeks blown out and that he was, as usual, wearing a kilt.

He pushed a dram of malt across the table towards my chair and studied me, obviously aware I was taking note of the large folio of maps that lay untied and open on a long, distress-finished, solid-oak parson's table. A magnifying glass rested atop a page. A crystal ashtray and a 15-year-old Linlithgow-whisky bottle were set to the side.

Exhausted from the drive out from town, which had been made unpleasant by the sudden, intermittent squalls and stiff, sharply shifting winds that blew in off the North Sea, I parked my chilled body in an overstuffed, well-worn leather chair. The view through the massive, north-facing, leaded window was poster-perfect, even in the faint light. The streaks of lightning that raced in the distance to the thunder's muffled applause were a fine accompaniment to the opera playing in the background – the second act of *Tosca* with Callas, certainly, and probably Tucker. 'It only took me an hour to get here, but that felt like the longest drive I've had in my life.'

Angus said nothing as he topped up his glass with the amber whisky. This is how it almost always is when Angus and I meet alone, even after long periods of not being together. We don't have to bother with shaking hands or other courtesies because a look and blink into each other's eyes can convey days of stored information and questions. Friends never cease to marvel at the strength of our deep friendship, which only came after years of sharing joy, sorrow and trauma in business and our private lives (with wives, children, girlfriends and temporary irregulars), as well as the unconditional respect and love we have garnered for each other because of it all. Indeed, we have been known to continue a conversation you would think, on listening to us, that had been interrupted only a few minutes before, when in reality it may have been a few days, or even a month or more. We never worry about such things because, sooner or later, everything will be hashed over, debated, resolved and laid to rest – including, this evening I expected, the dissolution of my marriage and my resolve for finally ridding myself of the volatile internal casino that was controlling too much of my psyche.

'Aye, Will is always happy to see you. A fine nosy with him, I trust.'

'The best, as always. I learn more about life and values from him in ten minutes than . . .'

Angus's laugh interrupted me. 'When you can understand him, that is!'

'He does have a thick burr, almost as thick as one of the officers of the Trust. Thank God he speaks very slowly and deliberately.'

'He, he. I've been thinkin' on the words of Thomas Hardy, I have.' Angus raised his hands and touched the fingertips together as if he were going to pray. Instead he spoke from memory:

> When friendly summer calls again,
> > Calls again
> Her little fifers to these hills,
> We'll go – we two – to that arched fane
> Of leafage where they prime their bills
> Before they start to flood the plain
> With quavers, minims, shakes and trills.
> > 'We'll go,' I sing; but who shall say
> > What may not chance before that day!

'That's warming,' I answered, as I began to relax. 'Is spring scheduled on the Scottish calendar next year?'

He ignored my barb. 'We dinnae spend enough time together,' he answered in his brogue as he raised his glass, and we finally toasted each other, and Hardy and Burns, the Old Course, the Hut, St Andrews and Scotland in general.

I added: 'To tolerance in the world, or at least solidarity.'

'Aye. Would settle for one, would we not?' He put his elbows on the table and moved his massive frame closer to me. 'So ye got the sacred Hut. Good work, lad. Good work.' He picked up the magnifying glass, held down the map and studied a stretch of coastline off a grouping of small islands in the Hebrides. 'Very funny bit of business, 'tis.' He chuckled and coughed. 'Rarely happens that business has humour.'

Earnings position of Ian Woosnam on the European Tour in 1979 (£1,049)

I didn't pry because I knew from his restless body movements that something more important was on his mind. Instead, I asked about his wife. 'How is Lady Locards? Or should I not ask?' I watched his eyes as they feigned contentment. 'When she took my call after I won the auction, she actually sounded humane.'

He squirmed in his chair, took a good draw of whisky and let his bushy eyebrows and melancholy facial expression answer the question.

'Have you considered divorce?' I asked for the umpteenth time.

'Aye, leave Sarah? Never! Murder? Never!' He smiled meekly. 'To paraphrase your Clarence Darrow: "I would read her obituary with great pleasure, however."' A hand wave suggested I catch up with him in the sipping department. 'Dare I ask about Claudia?'

His body slackened again as I closed my eyes for a moment, the better to listen to the music. When I opened them, I focused on the frescoed ceiling, then the flashing of the firelight in the cavernous fireplace and finally on nature's noisy rumblings outside. 'We are divorcing. We decided on it last week in Los Angeles.'

'Though I love the woman,' he said calmly, 'and find her and her throaty voice most fetching, I could never live with her . . . 'Bout time, laddie. Though fun to play golf with.'

'She finally admitted to herself, and me, that she was hiding behind her cross. I also finally acknowledged . . .'

He waved a hand and cut me off. 'Don't want to know the details – to know the dust-up is over is sufficient, isn't it?'

'You're right, but just one more comment, given what we've been through together over the years. Unlike some of the scathing, machete-mouth conversations I've heard between you and Sarah, when her face goes Durham-dark with rage, there was none of that with us. Irrational comments were made, of course, but they weren't hateful. None; though as I mused when flying over here – and as her easy smile was starting to become a realistic shadow in my mind, and our goodbyes had been whispered – I sensed a secret, of some kind, hidden behind the dampness of her eyes.'

'Hmm, intriguing. God bless. Aye, the well-documented rage of Lady Sarah.' He set the magnifying glass down and then spoke more softly as he changed the subject. 'A fulcrum for ideas, she is: the Hut, this icon that lets people be taken out of themselves, as she has done to you. I've read some articles on how people have been using her, I have, almost as a bloody fantasy, to escape to somewhere else – perhaps with someone else, he, he – a 9/11-aided fantasy, perhaps: the myth, as we say in the Highlands, of the stravaiger, the wanderer, the explorer of life. 'Tis best to be aspiring, but wary of the precarious nature of pleasure.'

As a swallow of whisky noisily slid down his throat and was met by his bobbing Adam's apple, he straightened himself in his chair and became more formal and theatrical – as if telling him of the divorce had given him an energy boost. 'Aye, the Box has the power to part people of their pounds because of the golf, as well as because of the passion people feel for her. The luxury of two separate paths for convincing someone to buy something they didn't know they needed. Along with compatibility of purpose, which she possesses and oozes.' He chuckled. 'All of life is marketing, isn't it?' He took another gulp of whisky. 'I have also defined a man and his relationship with a woman, have I not?' He laughed again.

I looked at him, understanding from his smile that he was primed for a long night of conversation and philosophising – with me as his attentive foil. 'That happens, doesn't it, when an icon triggers something, in our case, a striving to return to the Links and play the career round of golf.'

'Aye. Now, what you wanted me to ask a wee bit ago is: how long have I known it was inevitable with you and Claudia? Correct?'

'Well, yes . . .'

'Before your marriage day. 'Nuf said.' He turned to me with a genuine smile of relief and offered a handshake. 'Everyone struggles with the pain of moral decisions that won't solve their problems.' He looked at me again. 'Yes, you're right. Even on the Links. Aye, the *golff* is but a wee slow death, but everyone knows someone who loves golf. A paradox. The clouds of 9/11 confirm it more poignantly.' A muffled guffaw rose from his chest. 'Perhaps I should not wait to read the obituary of Lady Sarah. Perhaps murder . . .' His voice shook a little.

'There is not a jury in the world that would convict you,' I answered sincerely.

'Hmm. Perhaps. But mine is a marriage of family interests. Business. There is no room for murder in most businesses. Is there?' he quipped, as he topped up our glasses. 'Varieties of craftiness, yes.' He nodded. 'Wee tumblers, these.'

'Any glass looks like a thimble in the grasp of your freckled chops.'

'Aye.' Angus smirked at the joke and fixed on me with a withering glance. 'There are lessons to be learned here, solid lessons,' he said, as he scratched his leonine head vigorously. 'In the end, what are people searching for?'

'Not knowledge, that often, I don't think, generally speaking. I would say a simple life with happiness, laughter and love comes first, even if it means the risk of taking a fresh direction in life – within or without their community, or clan, as you would say. Doc preached this, and I do applaud her for saying it so succinctly – that we're not meant to live by ourselves, that life is generational and a part of man's basic emotional truths. Happiness is what we want, and we want to share it. Period.'

'Aye, Claudia is right about that. Strivings and ambitions fulfilled only in dreams for most. Love . . . hate . . . fear . . . loyalty . . . renewal . . . tenderness . . . justice. Living successfully involves constant attention to the assumption you will not live for ever. You must conduct the daily life on the belief that death will come at day's end.'

'Except in the case of Will,' I said.

'Except in the case of Will, of course.' Angus's eyes softened.

We were interrupted by the butler, who set down a silver tray upon which lay an ice bucket and what looked to be pint bottles of ale.

'What is that?' I tried to read the labels.

'Aye, Fraoch Heather Ale. Been brewed in Scotland since 2000 BC,' he answered with a royal tone in his brogue as his eyes brightened. 'Not know it? No Scot, ye.' He nodded disapprovingly. 'One for each. As an aperitif, as the French would say. In ancient times, fruits, herbs and flowers were used to flavour fermented drinks, before hops were imported into Britain.'

'I'll pass.' I sensed he was about to deliver a history lesson. He didn't disappoint.

He snapped the cap off one of the bottles with a bottle opener I hadn't seen used in years and filled one of the frosted glasses. 'Church keys, we call the can- and bottle-openers.'

'A sarcastic euphemism, laddie. Hmm. I have a conspiracy theory on the nation's first purity laws,' he said, taking a sip, 'which required brewers to use only malt, hops, water and yeast in the brewing process.' He scratched an ear and paused a moment. 'Because taxes were raised from the sale of malt, it meant income for the House of Lords. Lords owned the hops farms. A tidy bit of good financial planning, but as it's been passed down they ruined the taste of a proper Scots ale, from what I've read and remembered my grandfather telling me.'

He finished off the glass and opened the other bottle. 'Fraoch's is still flavoured, if slightly, with heather flowers, to recreate the heather ale of the tribal Picts, who were in the Highlands before the Celts. Aye . . . the Picts' heather ale was the first beer brewed in Britain.' He took another swallow. 'It was intensely bitter, they say, with hallucinogenic properties.' His eyes narrowed in seriousness; his brogue thickened. 'The secret died with the Picts in a war. Fourth century, I think. Now it carries a sagey bite that tickles yer tongue. Aye, too much of a good thing can be wonderful. Try it now?'

'Enjoy. No wonder some of your ancestors practised witchcraft.'

'Spot-on,' he acknowledged in his typically nonplussed fashion. 'Some were burned at the stake – midst the poisonings, insanity . . . others pickled in salt . . . Hmm.'

I tried not to laugh. 'Long ago when men cursed and beat the ground it was called witchcraft. Now it's called the *golff*.'

'Aye.' He mumbled approvingly, pulled up his mink-covered sporran and took out his gold pocket watch. He flipped the cover open, checked the time and tidily pushed the pouch back in his lap. He closed his eyes for a moment. 'Time for the meal and a fine claret. We're to have sea trout, grouse and venison tonight. I had a fine shoot in the moors, near a copse, at first light.' He paused. 'Sometimes it is possible to have a good time without scandal or a lady present: seldom, but possible. He changed the subject and his voice became more emotional. 'How is Claudia doing?'

'I have no clue. I only saw her when we worked things out. We were brutally honest with each other and didn't allow the mundane or personal personality traits to enter the conversation. Cliché aside, we will remain friends. There is too much sophistication between us for that not to continue. We never should have married – the "dating" philosophy should have remained in place. Some aren't meant for marriage: Claudia and me included, I think. Of course, for some, like you, marriage was never a matter of personal choice.' I hesitated. It seemed so eerie to discuss my personal life as I never had before. 'She sends her regards and wants you in California for some wintertime golf after the Bing Crosby or, rather, the AT&T.'

'Aye. Only at Pebble Beach. Too hot everywhere else.'

I remembered Rob Donaldson, my undertaker, and his comment about hot weather.

As we made our way along the long corridor to the dining room, Angus resurrected his train of thought. 'The decisions and burdens that come with the quenching of our thirst, as you Americans say it, are the fuse of the bomb of life. Not the match that lights the bomb. Not the bomb.'

'That sounds like something Doc would say.'

'Aye. She did. Tell Claudia Fraoch ale qualifies as an icon.'

'You tell her.'

'Aye. Must change my thinking. Claudia understands our burdens and the decisions we foolishly make in the name of short-term gain, which only lead to long-term suffering – and the precarious nature of pleasure. That I assure you. With all the secularism in the world today, the cleric just has a harder go at getting through to wee mortals because she has to use the good book as the reference point. Her fulcrum.' He stopped to nod respectfully and reverently at an oil painting of his grandmother hanging prominently in a niche of the wall. 'The icons in the Bible are not very convincing.'

'Her crutch,' I said firmly. 'Most seek to associate with a mentor, a celebrity icon, a sports idol . . . as if doing so is assurance something interesting will happen in the margins of their everyday life.'

'The Box is teaching you well, laddie, about many things. There is an old English proverb: "Danger and delight grow on one stalk."'

Completely sated by the long, heavy meal, I begged relief and a walk on the grounds. Angus agreed. I took our brandy glasses and went to the mud room to find the wellies and quilted hunting parka I kept at his house. He went to get cigars.

The crunch of our rubber soles on the pea-gravel road was a fine music that mixed in well with the mist and noise of the crisp wind working its way through the stand of pines that followed the coursing of a hill. It was all a strong counterpoint to the night's uninviting shadows and a foreign whirring sound I heard coming from somewhere in the distance – a sound I knew, but couldn't place. We stopped to light our cigars.

'Aye,' Angus said as he looked to the east and the faint lights of St Andrews, visible through the patches of haar. 'A night for clans and rendezvous, 'tis.' His head jerked, uncharacteristically, as if some idea had been ignited in his brain. 'That explains it. All of it. I have it.' He adjusted his tam, stabbed his umbrella into the earth, turned to face me and took a theatrical stance. 'The hunter crouches, hidden and anxious, in a thicket at the bog's edge, awaiting first light. He hears the dogs barking and then the music of beating pheasant wings. His pulse races as he raises his shotgun and takes aim at a cock. I know my lands, laddie. I know the animals and the poachers and tinks who trespass. I know when things are right or wrong, and with the tinks, they're mostly wrong, though good field workers they be at harvest time.' He slapped his belly, spilling a little brandy. 'My men work hard to make sure the land can sustain the shoot and the angling. Do you understand?'

'"Tinks"?'

'The gypsies from the north who travel with everything they own and much they don't own. Aye! Those who regard the sports as being destructive don't understand the hard work we do to improve the habitat. We don't *own* the land. The animals do. We are only the *custodians*. They are rarely a feature at the sharp end of affairs! They don't understand that preserving resources and enhancing the bogs and forest and barley fields is vital to the ecology of the Neuk of Fife – as are windmills.'

I was a little surprised at the intensity in his voice. Surely a nerve had been fractured by something or other that had come up businesswise earlier in the day, or while he had been studying the maps, before I arrived. Perhaps he was crusading for wind farms again?

'There's a parable or a rule here for me and icon marketing, I'm sure?' I said lightly. I felt humiliated that I even questioned the working of his mind. 'Why shoot birds when you can buy them oven-ready at a supermarket? Why go to a football game when you can watch the edited highlights in ten minutes on television? Why eat in a Michelin-starred restaurant when you can get all the nutrients you need in a handful of pills? Why visit the butcher Murray Mitchell?'

'Aye, ye understand.' He looked back to the house and its windows, bathed in a warming light, the same colour as the brandy. 'Why? Hah! The number of birds bagged is never a measure of the quality of the shooting day. The joy of the hunt lies in our passion for adventure and experiences and emotions, the thrill of the sport in working the dogs and the satisfaction of providing one's own food, the beauty of the countryside. Like golf, laddie! Like life, without the barriers of class or age or sex. The bloody Hut is a metaphor for it all.'

I looked up. The haar had blown to sea and the stars were twinkling. A shooting star, and then another, raced across the sky and disappeared.

Angus turned back to return to the manor, but I was restless and didn't feel like going back indoors just yet. I told Angus I was going to take a walk, alone, for a while. He flipped the cover of his pocket watch open again and furrowed his brow.

'Given the very early morning hour, 'tis, and your pre-dawn flight from Edinburgh Airport, I may as well have my driver take you back to the hotel and wait for you. You're leaving your car here in the barn anyway, aren't you?' he asked.

'You're right: good idea. I didn't know it was after one o'clock. I can sleep on the plane.'

While Angus made the arrangements, I continued down the land towards the main road under brilliant moonlight. I heard the sound I couldn't place earlier; then I heard it again, mixed in with the music of water running over stones at the bottom of a burn. Before long, I came to a silhouetted figure alongside the road. It was Will. He was pushing a lawnmower, the old hand-pushed kind of lawnmower, cutting the broad band of grass between the lane and the hedge and the trees in between. A wooden-handled hedge-clipper was anchored at the small of his back, between an old, tight-fitting leather gardener's belt and his anorak. Typical Will: working without respect to the time of day or night. The whirring I had heard was from Will's mower as he pushed it, cutting the grass, and pulled it back, priming it for the cutting of another swatch. This was what I had heard and couldn't place: a sound that had been foreign to me since I'd mowed lawns for summer money in the 1950s.

He looked up and we smiled at each other. An empty phrase sputtered from my mouth: 'Good night, Will.' A 'dear, dear Will' followed, but only from my heart. It was all I could think to say to this wonderful human being, who personified what Angus and I had been talking about.

'Aye!' he answered with gusto, almost speaking to himself. ''Tis a lovely clear night now with a fine moon – most useful for stayin' ahead of the chores!'

CHAPTER 26

CALIFORNIA BANKING

WEDNESDAY, 24 OCTOBER 2001: MORNING

If you think it is hard meeting new people, try picking up
the wrong golf ball.

Jack Lemmon

LAX remained in a confused, nervous state when I returned to Los
Angeles from London. The bulletproof vests and machine guns
of the helmeted, protective soldiers in their camouflage combat
fatigues said it all. Passenger drop-offs and pick-ups were severely
restricted and many of the air-traffic corridors across Southern
California remained closed.

A friend had kindly agreed to pick me up at a remote drop-off
point a few miles north of the main terminals and take me to the
Hyatt in Century City. It added to the loneliness I felt after the
long flight as the hotel was only a mile or so from what had been
my home.

'Long flight?' my friend Rick asked, knowing my mind was on
Claudia. 'How many hours?'

'Bad winds. Thirteen hours, about. I was ready to take out a
canoe paddle and start the J-stroke. Food?'

'Good idea. Spicy and Asian.'

'I'm driving to La Quinta in the morning. Come along and you
can play some golf at PGA West while I have my meeting at the
Country Club of the Desert.'

'I thought you would never ask,' he said expectantly as he drove
into the car park of Typhoon, a Pan-Asian restaurant housed in the
Santa Monica Airport's administration building on the south side
of the runway.

★★★

Myself and my exploits were the first items on the agenda of the Country Club's marketing meeting. Jack Franks was noticeably absent. I passed out the souvenirs I had brought back: a sample cutting of the Trust's official tartan, miniature bottles of Old Course single malt with the Box's image on the label, ball markers, golf towels, postcards and an excellent CD written by Peter Mason and narrated by Alan McGregor on how to play the Old Course.

During the meeting, a staff member said he had discovered that relationships between the Box and the Country Club already existed. Pete Dye had told him he remembered the Box when he'd played in the British Amateur on the Old Course and was sure he had a first-tee photograph filed away somewhere as a memento of the tournament. One of the construction managers was sure Clive Clark must also have his own memories from his days of being a European Tour player and, before that, an accomplished amateur.

'It all seems to be coming full circle,' Nancy Aaronson, the project manager, said, adding, 'I believe this legend will like her new home, here, and our winter weather.' (The Box was to be positioned between the first tee and eighteenth green of Pete's course, and would be visible from Clive's course.)

Later, I went to the bank to wire Rob Donaldson his first-draw and mobilisation monies. The woman on the platform, wearing a starched white shirt under a masculine, tailored black jacket, started our conversation by asking me, in an overly inquisitive manner, which I attributed to the fallout of 9/11, the reason for the 'requested' transfer. The fact the money was going to the account of 'Donaldson & Co. plc Undertakers' in an unknown (to her) Scottish bank probably didn't help either. Logically, I sprinkled the conversation with the words *Old Course*, *Starter's Box*, *artefacts* and *icons*. I took out photographs and sequentially arranged them on her desk as I glanced at her beautifully sculpted Japanese facial features.

Perplexed, she had no clue what I was talking about. 'Scottish pounds or British pounds?' she said, reading from her well-worn procedures manual. 'Different rate.'

'The United Kingdom only deals in pounds sterling as far as I know.'

'Huh?'

'When was that manual written, before World War II?'

'Huh?'

I decided to be nice. 'Do you play golf?'

'No. No golf.'

'Have you ever been to Fife?' I asked drily as I toyed with her somewhat contemptuously. Before she could react to the word *Fife*, another officer came over, excused himself for interrupting and asked her a question as his eyes scanned the photos.

'Old Course Starter's Box? You buy Starter's Box? I saw on television and in paper. These photos are of Old Course Starter's Box? Right? I have picture of me at Starter's Box, with sign. In Hell Bunker also, deep, ten-foot crater in the middle of fourteenth fairway – a religious experience. Ah, so! You Mr Hagen? I saw article in paper. You buy Box, right?'

I felt relieved.

'I handle, Miss Takeda. Come to my desk, please, Mr Hagen.' He gathered up the photos. 'Why you buy Box?' he asked.

'To guarantee she will be preserved as the universal symbol of sportsmanship she is,' I said, 'and also for real-estate marketing reasons.'

'Ah, global marketing. Very wise.'

I smiled. 'I agree with you. Now there are at least three people on the planet who believe in the concept.'

'Huh?'

'You, Jack Franks – the developer who owns her – and me.' I took some additional photos out of my briefcase and handed them to him. 'Inside joke . . . as is . . . when all else fails . . . there are only really three alternatives.'

'Huh?'

'Yes, one is to commit suicide; but forget it. It is so selfish. The others are to consider moving to either St Andrews or Paris.'

'Huh? Interesting global opportunity for golf marketing. Box should be in Japan. Asia big emerging market. Jack Nicklaus big in Japan. He icon. Big celebrity. Tiger Woods big, too. Big icon. Arnold Palmer.' He sat down at his desk, wiped his eyeglasses vigorously with the bottom of his tie and flipped through the photos.

Signing the documents to process the wire transfer took only a few minutes. Listening to his experiences in Scotland consumed half an hour. As I was leaving, he told me he had a jam jar on his desk that was filled with Hell Bunker sand.

CHAPTER 27

LOCH LEVEN AND GOLF PLACE

FRIDAY, 2 NOVEMBER 2001: AFTERNOON

It came with a lass and it will pass with a lass.

> *James V, king of Scotland, on learning of*
> *the birth of Mary, Queen of Scots*

It was Friday, 2 November. While in the Friday noon line of traffic waiting to pay the toll for the Forth Road Bridge, gold and russet leaves swirled through the air on a golf course to my left. The colour was close to the warm hue the sun had splashed across the Old Course on my last trip, when I was with Iain. It was an appropriate welcome.

I crossed the bridge and entered the Kingdom of Fife, a place of ancient castles, sea mist, wind- and rain-lashed expanses stretching to the horizon. A fast-moving squall half a mile in front of me streaked across a tilled field randomly peppered with enormous rolls of baled hay, grey as the clouds. It seemed as if some mythical giant might have laid them out as a part of some mystical game. Rain blew in gauzy, translucent sheets, like scrims of lace across a stage.

A little further north and to the east, as zephyrs cut across Loch Leven, I glanced over at Castle Island and its crumbling ruin. Most of the times that I had driven by this famous Kinross-shire landmark, it had been appropriately shrouded in centuries of historical mist, for it is the castle that housed Mary, Queen of Scots as a prisoner in 1567 and is where she was forced to renounce her throne before being sent down to London for her beheading in 1587. (Rumour has it that she played golf in East Lothian, south of Edinburgh, a few days after the murder of Lord Darnley, her second husband, in 1567. If she did, she was surely the world's first golf widow!)

Lowest first 36-holes score in the 2004 US Open at Shinnecock Hills Golf Club (Phil Mickelson)

For some reason it all made me think of General Custer, his last stand and the business lesson to be learned in not being afraid to swallow your pride: stem the financial haemorrhaging if you've made a bad business decision – because everyone does – and move on, learning from the experience. The black humour is that Custer was 'out-Custered' by Sir William Kirkcaldy of Grange, who had held the castle for Queen Mary but after its honourable surrender 'suffered death for devotion to her cause'. (Grange, a small hamlet on the outskirts of St Andrews, is under the ownership of one person and is known for its excellent restaurant.)

BBC Radio 4 was playing Elgar's *Pomp and Circumstance March No. 3*: perfect music for driving through the countryside. I was comfortable driving on the left again, and I let my mind wander and meld with the rhythm of the rolling farmland and the lazy, if annoying, pace of a farmer ahead of me, driving his tractor and pulling a manure wagon from one field to the next.

It was late afternoon when I passed Grannie Clark's Wynd and turned onto historic Golf Place, the street that runs north off North Street, in the centre of St Andrews. Early twentieth-century five- and six-storey buildings, with ground-floor shops and offices above, line both sides of the street. Among them are the R&A offices, which house the Open staff (the oldest of golf's major annual competitions, dating to 1860) and, in another building, offices that administer the rules of golf in 123 countries throughout the world (except in the US and Mexico, where the rules are administered by the USGA).

A 200-foot wall of joined buildings on the west side of the street ends at The Links, where the vista opens in all its grandeur. Golf Place continues, with a small shop of the Links Trust and the Playfair memorial on the left, behind the eighteenth green of the Old Course, before it threads its way between the R&A and the British Golf Museum. As it turns west, following the sea wall behind the Starter's Box and Caddie Pavilion, the street name changes to Bruce Embankment.

At the Himalayas, it changes its name a third time to West Sands Road. There it turns north, passes the Links Clubhouse and dead-ends half a mile out on the outer reaches of the peninsula, where most of the holes of the Old, New and Jubilee Links lie (and where the fisher wives harvested the mussels). Beyond, the

Eden Estuary and the Firth of Tay separate the courses from the Royal Air Force base in Leuchars, the Sidlaw Hills and, further east, along the northern shore of St Andrews Bay, the links of Carnoustie. (Who can forget the image of Jean Van de Velde with his trousers rolled up, in the burn of Carnoustie's eighteenth hole on the seventy-second hole of the 1999 Open Championship, and the burlesque that followed?)

I parked the car next to the Caddie Pavilion as three people with hiking staffs (one a ski pole), wearing drab quilted parkas and tam-o'-shanters with flat crowns of bright tartan, walked up from the beach, their dogs close behind. Little had changed from my visit a week before.

I stood there, lonely and cold, in the day's final, leaden light. An east wind carried the smell of decaying kelp. Focusing on the view, it occurred to me that the intent of any panoramic-vista photograph taken over the years was to capture the Swilcan Burn and the Swilcan Bridge, the double fairway, the Valley of Sin, the R&A Clubhouse and, perhaps, the fencing. The fact that the Box and Caddie Pavilion were included in who knows how many millions of personal photographs, postcards, calendars, advertisements and television impressions was probably a coincidence or an afterthought. (As was inclusion of the Martyrs' Monument on The Scores, which commemorates the local Protestant reformers who were executed or burned at the stake in the 1500s.) I felt sad that this lady was to be no more in this mystical, passionate place in a few days. Coincidentally, in the same month, I was soon to confirm, her construction had been completed in 1924, 77 years before.

Year, plus 1800, Alf Padgham won the Open Championship at Hoylake

CHAPTER 28

....

'PLAY AWAY PLEASE':
THE FINAL ROUND

SATURDAY, 3 NOVEMBER 2001: 12.30 P.M.

It will always be the greatest because nowhere else is there
the turf that you have here.

Peter Thomson

On Saturday, 3 November 2001, a warm, sunny 53 days after
9/11, my body filled with an embalming fluid called jet lag – I
was now well into my third trip to Scotland from California in
20 days – the last foursome to check in at the Box did so after
another Passing of the Keys ceremony. This ceremony was real:
Alan had confirmed the wire transfer for the purchase of the Box,
and so I was presented with the actual sets of keys each starter
had been entrusted with over the years. Historic, emotional and
melancholy as the occasion was for the four of us, the mood was
festive because the weather was perfect for golf. The foursome
included Alan McGregor, chief executive of the Links Trust;
Alistair Nicoll, chairman of the St Andrews Links Management
Committee; Dr Duncan Lawrie, chairman of the St Andrews Links
Trust; and myself, my nervousness and dour mood guarded and, I
hoped, under control. As the starter announced over the tannoy the
simple time-worn phrase 'May the 12.30 time *play away please*,' I
wondered, 'Why *me* . . . here . . . now . . . with all the fresh pain in
our world?' On 10 September, nobody in America seemed to know
anything about Islam. Two days later, everybody seemed to know
everything about Islam. Now, almost two months later, people
who would not know if a page of Arabic was upside down or right

side up were expounding . . . I tried, really tried, to put my sadness aside and focus on the round.

There was little fanfare and no special mention of the occasion, except that the starter did break from tradition after he announced our tee time by calling out our names and titles. (His mispronouncing my name underscored the level of indifference the 'event' received.) A smattering of applause from Peter Mason; our photographer, Mike Joy; a photographer from *The Citizen*; and Glyn Satterley, a professional golf photographer who had chosen the day to photograph the Old Course, was the only formal confirmation of the event. A few tourists and townsfolk who happened by took it all in casually, without any special interest or emotion other than that someone commented there was an unusually large number of fighter aircraft taking off from Leuchars that day.

In a true personification of public golf, Alan and Duncan carried their own bags; Alistair and I pulled dollies (pull carts), my clubs a rented set. The photographers ran out ahead of us on the first fairway of the 370-yard hole named Burn (after the Swilcan Burn, which loops around to guard the front edge of the green) and took photos as we approached the landing area, all four balls remarkably close together.

Alan, apologetically, asked me if it would bother me if he, Alistair and Duncan conducted a little business during the round. 'This annual round that we're finally having, courtesy of you and her,' he said, nodding towards the Box, 'was first scheduled for March. As life goes these days, it's been cancelled, rescheduled and cancelled, well, I don't know how many times since.'

'Given your title and authority, you don't play three days a week?'

He did not think I was funny.

'Bother me? Of course not,' I added selflessly. 'I welcome a solo walk on the Old under *any* circumstances.' He looked me square in the eyes, without a smile, without a gesture. A unique, knowing, honest bond of respect had been solidified between the two of us.

There is always an agenda when you play a round of golf, whether played alone or with friends, your children or a partner. Often it is for the solitude, or to pay back a social obligation, or for business, because golf, and certain card games, may be the best vehicle known to mankind for collectively measuring the moral strength and mental capacity of a human being. Most of the time, however, a round of golf is about relaxation, fellowship and the outdoors, and is a reason to forget, or ignore, the pressures of daily existence.

With no one playing behind us, and the others already discussing something quite seriously, my mind flashed to another realisation: how fortunate I was, at this moment in time, to be here in this sacred place. I remembered simultaneously a friend who, because he had innocently missed his morning train into Manhattan, and his office in the Twin Towers, on 9/11, was alive to tell the tale, and that I effectively had the Old Course, in perfect weather, to myself, without any pressure from players behind me.

By the fourth hole, I had unexpectedly numbed most of my 9/11 thoughts and was focusing on the *golff*. (It is often said you can best understand yourself and see the history and mystery of Scotland in a round of golf on the Old.) The afternoon warmth was making me thirsty. My mind turned to Old Daw Anderson, and I wished that he was still alive and operating his concession. (Old Daw had a mobile refreshment stand on the fourth hole during the nineteenth century where he sold ginger beer and, it was rumoured, an occasional gin or whisky on the side . . .)

Coming off the fifth green – the huge, more than 1.5-acre double green also serving the thirteenth hole – I remembered that during the Open, when the green was cut with a hand mower, like Will's, it took a green-keeper an hour and a half, and a seven-mile walk, to complete the job.

The difference between the lowest point of the Old Course and the highest is around 25 feet, but there are few pieces of ground anywhere with more undulations. Players steering away from the deeper bunkers in the middle of the course find their shots being turned away from their targets by contours at the front of the greens serving as a part of each hole's defences. The result is the most complicated course in the world – one of the few I have played where your game plan must be revised after every shot. Also, don't forget that to discuss the sand in the bunkers is a misnomer. It is all sand, from three inches down to thirty feet, as Peter Mason likes to remind anyone who will listen.

Standing on the tee of the sixth hole, named Heathery because the original green was made up of a mixture of earth, crushed heather and shell fragments, Alan said, 'You're right about the Box. It does bring people together.' He laughed as he told Duncan and Alistair how the Box had become a catalyst for making people smile and unwind and temporarily forget about 9/11 and, morbidly, had even allowed the three of them to finally have their annual round of golf together.

When I hit my tee shot on the ninth hole, End, into the gorse on the left near Mrs Kruger's bunker and lost the ball, I really didn't care. Losing a golf ball was irrelevant to the day compared to the pain and sorrow that continued to consume the minds of almost everyone in the Western world.

'Not to worry. I'll birdie,' Duncan snickered confidently, patting me on the back. He knew where my mind was.

Later in the round, as we left the sixteenth green, Duncan gestured to me as he walked over to the Wig bunker, which is to the left of the sixteenth green, near where it intersects and loosely defines the second hole's green. (The second and sixteenth holes share the same green.) I didn't know why he'd gone that way so I followed him, happily knowing I was about to learn something new, as few golfers know the Old Course as well as Duncan.

'How many times have you played the Old Course?' he asked, taking my putter from my hand and making a few deliberate, sure pendulum motions.

'Oh, I don't know,' I replied casually, not really thinking about it. 'Thirty or forty, I suppose. Maybe more.'

'Look back to that foursome we played through on the fifteenth hole, back on the tee. I can tell from the way they're gesturing and pointing that they're all about to commit the classic driving sin.'

'Huh?'

'Where did you try and hit your tee shot?'

'Why, to the left of the Principal's Nose bunker. Obviously.'

His eyes laughed, knowing I had hit a poor shot right of the bunker, nearly driving it out of bounds. Luckily for me, the ball had hit the wall and bounced back onto the course to a perfect lie, and I made my second birdie. 'Nicklaus said, famously, that where you hit it was "strictly for amateurs". He is absolutely correct, as you know.'

'That reminds me of a classic Nicklaus story,' I said. 'Five or six years ago, I was with him in Florida because we were contemplating a golf resort north of Malibu. One afternoon, he said he was going over to Loxahatchee, a course he had designed, to practise. Being the perfect host, he asked me along. When we got to the back of the driving range, I kept my distance and my mouth shut and watched him masterfully carve one shot after another – high, low, soft, hard. It was magical. A half-hour or so into his practice, he took a break and handed me a club. I took some jittery practice swings and hit some range balls. Mind you, it was difficult because the club's shaft was so stiff it might as well have been a length of plumbing pipe. After I made a particularly poor pass at a ball, I let out a quiet expletive. Jack looked at me seriously, as his patented piercing eyes drilled through my skull, and said: "John, you're not good enough a player to get mad. Relax and enjoy the game for the walk and the fellowship."'

Duncan belly-laughed as three of the four golfers behind us took aim on Principal's Nose, or just left of it, and hit their balls with high fades only to land over the wall, out of bounds. 'There isn't any room there,' he said. 'It's foolish to try and knock it over the bunker with an afternoon breeze in your face. It may not feel like it, particularly today, but there's always an afternoon breeze. Always, though it may be timid. Plenty of balls over there for the juniors.'

We played a customary, to Scotland, better-ball match with Alistair and Alan playing against Duncan and me. We lost two and one, though Duncan shot seventy-three, which I had to believe was a lesser number than his age. The match was over on the seventeenth hole but, after a discussion, we played out the eighteenth, named Tom Morris. (Old Tom claimed that the green was his finest work.) We all avoided the Valley of Sin and made pars. Duncan's par came from making a spectacular, twisting, fast-running 40-foot putt after he missed the green long right with his second shot and then was barely able to nudge the ball onto the green from a terrible gnarled lie with his third.

'Sometimes I miss those left,' he said nonchalantly as he reached down to take the ball from the hole.

'Thank God they made a club called the putter,' Alan chimed as the tourists standing behind the fencing applauded. We shook our heads. Nothing is surprising when Duncan has a club in his hands. Indeed, he is the perfect personification of the old adage 'putting is an indication of someone not happy, or happy, as the case may be, with their game and their life'.

We did not cross the Swilcan Bridge as we left the eighteenth tee, which meant no ceremonial photograph was taken on it with the Box in the background. Instead, we walked across the simple flat bridge to the left used by maintenance vehicles and the rangers. Why? None of us remember. Perhaps it was because, we all admitted later, 9/11 was subconsciously on our minds due to the large number of fighter jets taking off from Leuchars. Or that we really were common men on a public course and the fellowship was important, not the ritual.

I tried to lighten our mood. 'Or maybe it's because this is your last round of golf until April.' No one laughed.

Darkness was arriving as I pulled a mobile phone from my golf bag. We had played the round in three hours and twenty minutes in an almost warm breeze and clear skies. I dialled the Country Club as it was about 8 a.m. California time. The plan was to have Alan wish the Country Club all the best as it was, coincidentally, the morning of the first day of play on their Pete Dye course. An answering machine interrupted the call, so he left the message: 'May the eight thirty tee time, the first tee time at Country Club of the Desert, *play away please.*'

That evening, the Links Trust hosted a dinner that included the four of us, and Peter, with wives, at a wonderful seafood restaurant in Anstruther. Alas, Claudia was there in spirit only, which was just as well, because had our marriage been intact, she would certainly have pulled rank and, being the better golfer, taken my spot in the final foursome. (Had I complained, I knew Alan would surely have suggested a vote be taken. No question about it: I would have lost 3–1.)

CHAPTER 29

··

KINGSBARNS

SUNDAY, 4 NOVEMBER 2001: MORNING

Is there a man with a soul so dead it doesn't stir at the sight
of a brisk breeze and winter sunshine and the knowledge
he has a fair chance of getting in a round before a coming
deluge?

Anonymous

On opening the curtains of my hotel room the next morning, dawn
presented a gift in the form of a calm sea, a clear sky, little wind and
the same hint of warm air that had been in the air the day before.
My room overlooked a golf course designed by Sam Torrance and
Gene Sarazen. The course, which circles the St Andrews Bay resort,
has stunning sea and panoramic views of the River Tay estuary, the
North Sea, the Fife countryside and the burgh of St Andrews. The
flagsticks were barely ruffling.

Malcolm Campbell, who wrote the text for the Kingsbarns
yardage guide, had arranged a round of golf on the two-year-old
Kingsbarns course a few miles down the road, in a spectacular
setting beside the sea. Among the pearls of Scotland's seaside
courses, Mike Aitken, a journalist for *The Scotsman*, once wrote:
'Perhaps only Turnberry has as much charm or a greater sense of
theatre.'

Gordon Moir, one of the Trust's managers, joined us. Gordon
possesses one of the thickest combinations of brogues and burrs
you're ever likely to encounter; during mornings, especially, the burr
that rides along on his words becomes particularly impenetrable.
(In certain areas above Aberdeen, where he was raised, around the
old fishing villages of Fraserburgh and Rosehearty, a few people

still speak the Doric dialect. I have only heard it spoken once, but I've been told it is almost incomprehensible to those unfamiliar with its idiosyncrasies.) In Gordon's case, I'll be overly polite and say the way words fall from his mouth suggest that his tongue has been coated in a thick syrup, or maybe even glue. He may be speaking the Doric. I certainly can't tell.

By the time we were on the tee at eight thirty, the weather had turned. The wind had strengthened and was beginning to gust. Gordon, standing on the opposite side of the tee from Malcolm and myself, said something. Between his brogue and the noise of the wind, he was impossible to understand. Malcolm and I looked at each other and shrugged our shoulders.

I walked over. 'No offence, but, with this wind, why don't we enjoy the round and only try and talk to each other when we're on the greens? I can't understand you with the wind.'

'Fit are ye spikin' aboot?' he said. 'Ah canna hear naethin' fir the win'.'

The head professional at the time, David Scott, who had been watching us from the clubhouse, came out to the tee. 'Forget it,' he said jovially. 'Hit the ball. You're holding up play.' He knew Gordon well.

CHAPTER 30

....

PRINCE WILLIAM

SUNDAY, 4 NOVEMBER 2001: AFTERNOON

If you can meet with Triumph and Disaster
And treat those two imposters just the same

Rudyard Kipling

Whatever the weather, Sunday afternoon is strolling time on the Old Course for the local residents and university community, as it was for the 'burgess and cleric' in years past, in Raymond Lamont-Brown's phrase. Sometimes it includes strolling across the soothingly named Grannie Clark's Wynd and out to the West Sands, as the fisher wives did, or taking a four-mile jog along the fairways. The Trust's security personnel, who constantly roam the course on small motorcycles, prohibit walking on the greens, though, unfortunately, it often happens. You would be surprised how many people who visit St Andrews, including Scots themselves, don't play golf, don't know the difference between a fairway and a green, and lack respect for protocol when it comes to footwear.

This afternoon was no different, except that it had become unusually warm and the shifting, blustery wind of the morning had found a home elsewhere. *The Citizen* reported the next morning that it may have been the mildest autumn day on record. The sky was cobalt blue but for a few pockets of high pinkish clouds. I parked my car next to the Box again as a flock of shorebirds sitting on the roof of the Caddie Pavilion welcomed me with a refreshing cacophonic pealing.

Rob and his crew had delivered a forklift and other heavy equipment, and had enclosed the area around the Box in the chain-link fencing he had rented from the organisers of the Dunhill

Links Championship. I took one of the starter's keys, said a word of thanks to the good Lord and asked that he continue the fine weather. Then I unlocked the door to an 'amen'.

The Trust's computer, telephone and walkie-talkies had already been removed. I inventoried what was left and put it all in my car, including the scorecards; a driver mould from Laurie Auchterlonie's golf shop, used as a paperweight for who knows how many years; the starter's clock; Saturday's final ballot; and some rather simply made signs that said *Preferred Lies Today*, *Course Closed on Sunday* and *Today's Weather*.

Hanging from a nail was a clipboard holding a few months' stash of letters of introduction with handicap confirmations for golfers from around the world. The top letter carried the crest of Philadelphia's Merion Golf Club, one of America's greatest courses.

While shooting a final series of photographs from the middle of the fairway, and only a few feet off the ground, as Iain had suggested, two couples walked onto the eighteenth green. One of the ladies, in high heels and a pencil skirt, was oblivious to the holes she was punching in the green. I cringed as I bolted towards them. 'Get the hell off the green!' I yelled.

My arm-waving and explosive voice had its effect. Startled, she stopped, steadied herself, took off her shoes and started loping down the fairway in half-steps, not pausing to catch any of the other expressions of wrath I had prepared for her. Laughing to myself, because I could not believe what I had just seen, I made a mental note to tell Eddie Adams I had discovered a new way to airify the greens.

A mother pushing a wide-wheeled pram came up from the West Sands and stopped at the Box. I took a peek inside and saw happy, laughing twins.

'They're adorable. How old are they?'

'Wee ones 22 months,' she said with pride, in a wonderful rolling brogue. 'Lesley and Laurie.' Her cheeks were windburned red, as was her nose, which was too large for her face, but it was a beautiful nose that complemented her stature. 'Birthday's January the tenth.' The warmth and width of her smile said she wasn't concerned that I, a total stranger, was playing with a foot and finger of one of her children. 'Bought the Hut, did ye?' She noticed her words had startled me. 'Saw your picture in *The*

Citizen, I did, with the lasses and lads from Madras College. My son's in junior golf; he's a golfin' now at Strathtyrum with his daddy, 'tis.' She paused, perhaps to let the image of her husband and son bonding together over a Sunday round of golf settle in her mind. 'It's wonderful, 'tis, what the Trust's doing for junior golf.' The burr in her voice dragged both *junior*s out for a wonderful eternity.

The explosive roar of two fighters igniting their afterburners swallowed our conversation. We turned towards Leuchars. Two delta-winged aircraft rose and disappeared into the cloud cover.

'We're all sorry for America.' She closed her expressive eyes for a moment. 'It's us, too . . . freedom for us and the wee ones in the future.' Her hands mechanically folded a tartan blanket. 'Sale of the Hut is not an issue to get overly worked up over, is it,' she added parenthetically; 'there are more important things to worry 'bout in life.'

I mentioned Claudia and her eulogy after 9/11 – when she said we must find a way to be thankful for what is in our world and in our life today. We must rest knowing that we will see more pain turn to joy, and sorrow into gladness.

'Difficult, 'tis.'

'Yes,' I said. 'Life starts anew when you say it does. We must be gentle with ourselves.'

The girls were beginning to stir. 'What's going to happen?' She picked up Lesley and stood her on the grass. 'Her Majesty had your national anthem played at Buckingham Palace during a changing of the guard, she did.' A hint of resignation remained as she picked up Laurie and set her down next to her sister.

'Go along with them. Enjoy your daughters and the day. I'll mind the pram.'

'Thank you. Barely walk, they can.'

The wee ones bounded in circles and scrambled down the fairway, waving their arms in the air. Both fell but laughed it off, stood up and continued on. Their mother went after them, but slowly, letting them enjoy their freedom. Maternal pride was showing, of course, but so too the reality and impact of 9/11, and her family's future.

I ignored another roar from across the estuary as I put my cameras and jacket in the pram and pushed it across the first tee and into the Valley of Sin. I wanted to take more low-level pictures of the Box. As I finished, I started laughing to myself, at the incongruity of it all: me pushing a pram on the Old Course, through the Valley of Sin, with America at war . . .

The twins and their mother were nearing Grannie Clark's Wynd. It reminded me of a caddie incident when I'd played the Old Course with three friends. When our foursome stood on the first tee that day, one of my playing partners, Jim Lange, of the American TV show *The Dating Game* fame, noticed a woman pushing a pram across the Wynd as he was preparing to hit his tee shot. He backed off. She was certainly in range of being hit by his ball if Jim made a poor swing. A caddie, undeterred, motioned to him to play on as he uttered a memorable caddie statement: 'You've got the right o' way.'

He was also the same caddie who, later in the round, when we were at the tee of the eighth hole, the furthest point out on the course, unceremoniously dropped the bag he was carrying and announced he was finished for the day. The four-star NATO general he was caddying for was shocked; so were the rest of us. 'Where are you going?' he barked as the caddie jogged away. Our caddie-abandoned playing partner was not accustomed to such a level of insubordination, nor carrying his own clubs. No golfer he.

'The pub,' the caddie called back over his shoulder. 'My birthday.'

I pushed the pram down to the twins and their mother, said goodbye and walked back to the Box for one last – private – nostalgic look. The fact the weather was holding did not go unnoticed. I paused and again asked the Almighty, in case he hadn't heard me the first time, to continue this fine weather for another five days.

Two new visitors wandered by. We chatted, and I casually asked one of them to take a photo of me with the Box. (Where was the pram when I needed it?) Darkness was setting in. I invited them to join me for hamburgers and ale as it was obvious they were university students, which meant, by definition, they were hungry. The tallest (at over six feet), most handsome lad politely declined.

The other also thanked me but also said no because he was heading down to Edinburgh to have dinner with his parents. He added, nodding towards his friend: 'He can't. He's an overnight with his gram.'

Prince William

There was extra emphasis on the burr that suffused the word *gram*, but I had no reason to give it or the black Land Rover that had stopped on the Wynd any consideration. Later, it occurred to me the tall lad was Prince William, a student at the university, and he was off to Balmoral Castle, a little over an hour's drive north, to spend the night with his grandmother, Her Majesty Queen Elizabeth II.

CHAPTER 31

··

BRICKS, FLUES AND
THE GANG OF SIX

MONDAY, 5 NOVEMBER 2001: MORNING

The only time my prayers are not answered is on the golf course.

Billy Graham

My prayers of 16 hours before went unanswered. Or, if they had been answered, there was a terrible misunderstanding, because the chariots of wrath that arrived brought weather that had turned foul overnight. It was cold, foggy and rainy: not only the worst possible weather for dismantling the Box, but also for Guy Fawkes Night, or bonfire or fireworks night, as it is sometimes called. (Celebrated across Britain, the night commemorates the anniversary of Fawkes's 1605 arrest for his, and his fellow Catholic conspirators', attempt to blow up London's Houses of Parliament.)

When I arrived at the Old Course, British Telecom was there, on schedule (which is mostly unheard of), disconnecting the power and telephone cables. Rob Donaldson and his crew had begun the dismantling process, and the shipping company was unloading the shipping container in front of Mike Horkan's curious eyes. The lorry driver suggested that with all the publicity the Box had received, his company was not about to be late in delivery of the container. 'An event certainly to be noted in the press,' he said in a barely coherent brogue. He lowered the rabbit-furred earflaps of his hat and tied the string under his double chin. 'She's respected by some as a national treasure.'

| 150 | Amount, in pounds, spent to increase the Jubilee Course from 12 holes to 18 holes in 1905 |

He added he wanted to pick the container up on Thursday afternoon instead of Friday to ensure its on-time delivery by rail to the Port of Felixstowe, in south-east England, from where the freighter would sail on Sunday to California, after stops in Germany and France.

Rob heard him and nodded an 'aye', which seemed to come out as a question. As foul as the weather was, he was only clothed in a jumper and plain, rather thin twill trousers. He hadn't bothered with a hat.

'Pleasant day, Rob,' I said mockingly. I pulled up my jacket's hood to block the wind and keep the rain from running down the back of my neck. 'Need sunscreen, I suppose?' I looked up at the heavy clouds.

'Sunscreen?'

The way he sloughed the word suggested he might not have known what sunscreen was. I shook my head, waved him off and walked over to the Caddie Pavilion, where I stood under the protection of the roof's overhang and studied Rob's interaction with his crew. It was clear he had thoroughly thought out the take-down and packing process, and had devised a schedule that made the best use of everyone's talents. I decided to privately name the crew after Chairman Mao's Gang of Four (the now long-dead, most powerful members of the Chinese Communist Party's radical political elite). In my case it was the Gang of Six, with them all having well-defined responsibilities – though slightly more modest than did Mao's Gang of Four. I would later commend Rob for having an enforcer (problem-solver), an advance man (due diligence), foot soldiers (executors of ideas) and a facilitator (ambassador).

The biggest, and strongest, who could easily qualify for reincarnation as a bulldozer, I nicknamed 'Ox'. Burly, compact and built low to the ground, he had a high forehead and a steady gaze that was not easily averted when he walked – no, waddled. He never wore a hat or gloves, never laced up his brogans and always wore his rather filthy parka indifferently – either unzipped or wrapped around his waist. Weather conditions were never an issue. (I preferred being around him when he wore the parka because it masked the smell of his omnipresent body odour.) When he walked, his arms slowly swung out from his body, there being little room for a hinge where his trunk and shoulders merged. He had no neck. Most of the time he carried himself as if he were playing the part of a 'death machine' in a James Bond thriller.

Two others were middle-aged, tall and muscular. Both had full heads of red hair, large pointy ears and prominent beaked noses. Obviously twins, they were the kind of workers that ensure every business operates efficiently. Soft-spoken and thorough, they took Rob's usually strident orders without hesitation or question. Rob called one 'Ringo' because he was a drummer in a heavy-metal band (a *terrible* heavy-metal band, Rob told me as an aside). The other he called 'Oban' because he drank a lot of whisky. 'Aye, Ringo,' he would call out. 'Move that further tae the east.' Or, 'Oban, 'ey, Oban, clear a path for the backhoe . . . here by the wee box.' I was never to know their real names, not even when I finally shook their hands at lunch on our final day together.

A fourth, who looked to be well into his 30s, was never called by a name and never appeared to be doing anything specific, yet he was always in the centre of whatever activity required the most manpower. I nicknamed him 'Shadow'. Three or four times a day, Rob would take him aside and speak to him, while gesturing with his arms and hands. Was he tutoring him? He was slightly built, with a nondescript face, but it was hard to tell as he always wore a quilted parka and never lowered the roll-top hood of the sweatshirt he wore underneath. Near the end of the job, I mentioned to Rob that he seemed to be on track for becoming a foreman. Rob shook his head. 'Nae, he's tae young fer that yet. An' he's got tae learn tae drive.' It turned out that Shadow was only 16 years old. What kind of life had he endured to age so quickly? Child-labour laws in Scotland? I did not ask, nor did I want to know.

The fifth member of the crew I dubbed 'Fleet Foot'. He was a lanky-looking young lad with feet much too large for his body (or maybe it was that his steel-toed work boots were cast-offs and several sizes too large). He was Rob's 'go-fer' and 'go-to'. He always ran from one task to another, even if it was only a few feet, much as a young child does when learning to walk.

I refocused. The Dunhill signs had been set aside, and I considered – but pooh-poohed the idea because it had nothing to do with the Box – of going over to the Dunhill trailer to ask for one as a souvenir because the rumour around town was that next year's event was going to be cancelled. A tragedy, I believed, now that Kingsbarns was in rotation with Carnoustie and the Old Course for hosting the tournament. (Are there a stronger three courses used for any tournament, anywhere? I doubt it.)

The door had been removed from its hinges, the tannoy taken down and much of the casework spread out on the first tee. (Some staging area.) Shadow was standing on scaffolding inside the Box, carefully taking the deep-blue tongue-and-groove wooden ceiling apart with a crowbar. By 10 a.m., the roof's perfectly joined framing timbers had been exposed. Remarkably, there was no dry rot. Rob's brogue softened out of respect: 'This joinery's better than the Grade IV restoration-o'-a-kirk job we just finished. An', good news: nae termites in Scotland.' As another squall blew in off the sea, he ran to his lorry for his woollen-stocking hat and a parka.

Fraser Smart arrived, his hair playing in the wind. Rob warmed his hands in the pockets of his parka and watched Fraser work his pipe. 'Men,' Rob said, 'I'm worried we're goan tae hae a week o' changin' weather, given last week's conditions.' Bored by Fraser's pipe-lighting and relighting, he focused on me instead. 'Forget the weather in the papers. Saw you readin' *The Courier*. 'Tis a waste of money, newspapers are. Concentrate on the farmer's forecast on the radio at noontime an' hope the north-east weather holds away.' (The farmer's weather forecasts in Scotland are the most reliable, and few challenge what is predicted.)

'Why the north-east?' I asked.

'Aye. Menacin',' he said, with ominous conviction. As he walked us through the morning's work, he said the crew had experienced some surprises. 'Two, so far.' He gasped a little and threw a playful, mocking glance at Fraser. 'The walls o' the Box are actually double-walls, made o' brick. Ye usually just get them in buildings wi' height, no a wee one-room hut. Didnae plan on it. Assumed the wood frame and lathe and old plaster and the horsehair they used as binder back then. Aye, I'll need a masonry saw tae cut the walls intae proper panels. Big surprise.'

Without fanfare, and without even remotely suggesting a contract renegotiation, he made a few calls on his mobile. When he finally put the phone in his pocket, he said there were only two saws of the type he needed in all of Scotland. One of them – a unique, portable, gasoline-powered model that was water-cooled

– was to be delivered by morning bus from Edinburgh. He also told me he had decided to rent a larger 'brick grab' than the one he had in the construction yard alongside where he lived.

'Can't you modify the strapping on the one you have?' Fraser asked.

'Naw, dinnae think so. Thought about it a moment ago, but dinnae think she be steady 'nuf on the forks after the section's cut. Lot o' mass and dead weight now.'

Fraser nodded approval to his statement.

'I don't think the ship she'll be riding on cares about the weight,' I said.

Rob ignored me. 'The second surprise is she had a hearth an' a flue.'

We wondered if the starters had put in a makeshift hearth and built a wood or peat fire to keep warm.

'Certainly not with peat in Fife back then,' Fraser said, posing thoughtfully. 'Around Dornoch or further north to John o'Groats, perhaps, but not this far south.'

'With no flue, what did they do?' I asked. 'Open a window or the door for ventilation to prevent asphyxiation?'

'Aye,' Fraser answered, double-drawing his pipe. 'I think so. Certainly the Lowlands way.' He picked up a sill brick and studied the kiln stamp. 'Made by a brickworks north of Dundee out of business 30 years or more.'

It quickly dawned on me that Mike Horkan's comment and concern on my previous trip with respect to college pranks was probably a little more prophetic than I wanted to believe. I wrote a few anxious notes in my journal about the brick walls, the saw and the flue.

'Aye?' Fraser said. 'The Trust didn't provide a fact sheet before the auction, as you know, and they wouldn't let me break into a wall to check the construction technique after the auction, either. A true phantom woman, the Box is, I should think.' He raised both his eyebrows slightly as he tried to downplay the situation. 'What you see is not always what you get.'

'True, Fraser, true. Or, as they say, quality is almost always better when it is somewhere else,' I countered, 'when automobiles and women are involved.'

'Automobiles? My passion is Formula One. There are a number of mechanical devices that increase sexual arousal, particularly in women. Chief among these is a flaming-red Mercedes Benz SL600 Roadster.'

Rob took off his hat and scratched his head. 'Dinnae know about that.'

Fraser emptied his pipe of dead ash, which the wind seemed to vaporise in an instant, and flashed a mischievous smile. 'There is an actor, voyeur or exhibitionist in us all.'

Rob looked at us, blank to Fraser's words.

I broke out laughing as he again tried to light his pipe. 'I like your attitude, Fraser. It really didn't bother us that no one was checking her framing because first and foremost we were buying an icon in which the passion and history associated with her, not her architecture, would rattle the nerves of the public. The architecture of her – or the lack thereof – is almost incidental.'

He turned from the weather and squinted.

Rob excused himself as the foreman on the R&A job came over. When he returned, he said, 'When I was preparing my bid for ye, I came over wi' a half-bar to poke about. Heard echoes when I rapped her pretty hard, so assumed she was wood. Obvious now what I hit happened tae be a chance cavity.'

'Do you have the Three Stooges over here?' I asked.

'On the telly.' He nodded with a smile. 'Sundays, in the pub before the football. Curly and the Box?' His facial expression was lighthearted yet confused.

'Aye,' Fraser interjected. 'Due diligence, I think he's referring to. The Stooges had great ideas, but most of the time the execution was not the best. I remember the time they posed as plumbers . . .'

'True,' Rob said seriously, not quite understanding the analogy.

A few curiosity-seekers happened by, as did some of the Trust's staff, and then Duncan Lawrie in an R&A blazer, club tie and grey woollen trousers, but no raincoat. He surveyed the scene as his hair scattered in the wind, and he rubbed his hands together. Shaking from the cold, he quickly left, signing off with a worried, 'Good luck.'

Rob and I spent some time with a reporter from the *Fife Free Press*, while Ringo and Oban reworked the scaffolding as a ladder to climb up onto the roof. The intent, if the framing allowed, which we now knew it did, was to cut the roof into two symmetrical sections. After all 82 slate tiles were removed and numbered, Ringo turned on his power saw. Half an hour later, the roof was in two pieces. Rob carefully measured the unwieldy sections, then manoeuvred the forklift and carefully lowered them in a jerry-built but effective sling the crew had constructed from cables and belting. Within an hour, both sections were on the ground.

'Simple work, this,' Rob said, with a short shrug.

When he puffed his cheeks, I took it as a sign he didn't believe the job was going to continue this smoothly. 'No more surprises, please.'

His smile back was more of a sneer. 'Aye. Hope not.'

Eddie Adams pulled his stocking hat low over his ears as he walked over from the Caddie Pavilion. The wind was stiffening and the temperature dropping. He congratulated Rob on his dexterity with the forklift and added, 'A few biscuits and some Marmite still in there for you.'

Ever shy, Rob waved a gloved hand 'thank you' from the cab as he spun the wheels of the forklift and drove down towards Bruce Embankment. I wondered if his shyness and modesty, which are so atypical of people in the construction business, were a conscious action because he was working on such a politically active project? Or, perhaps, was it because of me, the first foreigner, Fraser had told me the day before, Rob had had a conversation with in his lifetime?

I would discover that he would take the lunch break, and the morning and afternoon tea breaks, in the lorry with his crew. The two times I suggested he join me in a pub or the Links Clubhouse for lunch, or the Caddie Pavilion for tea, as Eddie had just done, he had declined, not even smiling in appreciation of the suggestion. 'Must stay with my men,' was the answer.

Fraser, his hair blowing unprotected, squinted in surprise as we turned and made our way to the Caddie Pavilion for elevenses and tea. In the short period we'd known each other, a respectful relationship had developed. I acknowledged the glint in his eye.

'Aye,' he said, confirming his approval of the accolade Eddie had bestowed upon Rob. 'Rightful choice with him. A well-grounded man. Doesn't play golf, either, so no way to consider his worth over a round on the Links, the Scots way of measuring the ability of a man.' He had been correct in suggesting Rob was the right man for the job.

'What do you think, Fraser? Any other potentials for the unknown?'

He unzipped his parka, pushed up his sleeves and manipulated the electric kettle as I upturned two foam cups and set tea strainers across their tops. 'I doubt there are foundations. Just a wee slab on the sand, I should think. But the contract bears no responsibility below the turf so no need to fear the severing of utility lines, wherever they may be. The power clearly is taken from Golf Place.'

'True. She's quite naked now. Not much else to bare.'

'I don't think we have to worry about any increase in fee coming from Rob Donaldson, given the small footprint. He's quite good about that. Often too good, I think.' He took a spoon and swirled the tea leaves a final time, then poured us each a cup. 'White?'

'Please. Thank you.'

He added a splash of milk to both our cups as the door opened and a large-framed, well-proportioned, youngish woman walked in, carrying a double-roll of drawings under an arm. She was attractive in an artsy, mysterious way. The hair slides that held back her waves of curly wet hair added to the composition, as did her unbuttoned floor-length grey coat, worn over a cabled black polo-neck sweater. Big silver necklaces danced across her full-figured torso.

'Heather, good morning,' Fraser said. 'Just in time.' He poured her a cup of tea and introduced her as a staff member, as he told her about the morning's surprises. We sat down on the wooden caddie benches.

A big Scot without an ounce of mousiness about her, she gave me a firm handshake. 'I'm Heather Paterson,' she said with strength and conviction. I guessed the amused grin spread across her face was permanent.

'The Three Stooges have also been in our conversation,' Fraser offered with a laugh.

'Well, as my father told me,' Heather said, 'the input of lawyers and accountants is important, but they often hae limited imagination. Their motives are strictly on the side of the sterling, and the sterling has nae conscience.' Her eyes quickly studied me, somewhat inquiringly. Then she said, 'I'm an Aberdonian, a Granite City lass, born and raised – schooled here, then architecture at Westminster, doon in London.'

'Oh really? I've had the pleasure of visiting Aberdeen, years ago.'

'Have ye played Royal Aberdeen?' she asked proudly. 'It dates from 1780, though it's believed the Queen's Hole dates tae 1625. The Balgownie course was designed by the Simpson brothers of Carnoustie and later lengthened and rebunkered by James Braid.'

'I have. Wonderful golf course. Home of the "five-minute" rule for finding a lost golf ball, I believe.' I smiled and studied her in return.

'Aye, know yer golf, ye do. Some members still complain about the rule.'

'As well they will when the wind off the North Sea attacks the ball and carries it into the dunes. I remember a difficult day or two up there.'

'D'ye know the story o' the green-and-scarlet uniform coats and the black velvet cap to be worn when playing the game?'

I didn't really, but said 'yes' because Fraser seemed bored by it all.

She seemed unnecessarily stoic. 'My father had a very dangerous job. He was an oil geologist. Mum used to say he'd be better off if he was tae spend an evenin' in the kitchen cookin' with his high-falootin' advisors tae unearth their value and level o' humility. Better o'er a pot o' bilin' tatties than a table in the pub. They argued about it some.'

'Or,' Fraser added, 'sometimes it's better to play a round of golf with them. If it becomes unpleasant, you can walk away more easily.'

'No a golfer, Dad wasn't. Didnae hae the patience. That's whit drove me to the game, I must admit. It got me away frae the hoose and the arguin'.'

I glanced outside to see that Duncan had returned and was talking to Rob, who gestured from his seat on the forklift. Duncan dashed over, while trying to protect himself from the rain with a half-bent umbrella. As he struggled with the door, he said a quick hello and asked if I would join him for lunch at the Woollen Mill.

'Of course.'

'Good, twelve thirty then.' He was gone as quickly as he'd arrived, driving his feet into the turf as anchors against the hunting, chilling wind that swept across the eighteenth fairway.

CHAPTER 32

LUNCH AT THE ROYAL AND ANCIENT GOLF CLUB'S WOOLLEN MILL

MONDAY, 5 NOVEMBER 2001: NOON

The national dish of Scotland is something called haggis, the specific ingredients of which I won't go into other than to say that if you can visualise boiled, inside-out road kill, you're pretty close.

David Grimes

The R&A purchased the old Woollen Mill behind the eighteenth green in the mid-1990s and refurbished part of the building for members' use during restoration of their storied clubhouse. It is a modest building, but one in which a high level of sensitivity was exercised in the renovation. (The Woollen Mill now serves as a second, 'mixed' clubhouse; as a member so tactlessly said it, 'where women may be entertained'. It is a misconception that women are not allowed in the R&A Clubhouse. Indeed, the wives of members often entertain in the dining room.)

On The Links, the R&A's ground-floor entrance and reception area are located next to a separate entrance that serves as a Links Trust retail store, which also opens onto North Street. The retail space was originally the factory where Robert Forgan operated one of the earliest St Andrews golf club- and ball-making shops. (A classic photo shows an employee holding a man's silk top hat, with its narrow brim and tall, cylindrical crown. The cavity is said to hold the quantity of feathers required to make a 'feathery' golf ball

– which cost five to ten pounds in today's money.) At its height, his business had close to 40 employees, maybe more. Robert was club-maker to the Prince of Wales, later Edward VII. Following this appointment, in 1863, the Prince's feathers were impressed on all Forgan club heads. The company went out of business in 1962, but the name is still visible from the pavement outside the entrance.

The first floor houses meeting rooms, dining and lounge areas, and a balcony overlooking the Old Course. In many ways, it is a better place from which to view the iconic scene than the balcony off the Secretary's office in the main clubhouse. (When the Open is played on the Old Course, the balcony is reserved for the use of past captains and their wives.)

I kept a jacket and tie in my car for spontaneous press and photo sessions as there were one or two scheduled for every day of the week. The clothing I had worn at the Box was hardly suitable for lunch at the Woollen Mill. It was bulky and unattractive, and, I knew, it would be mostly filthy and wet. That day, for instance, I wore a thick woollen stocking hat, rain trousers and jacket, a heavy cashmere sweater, thick corduroy trousers, fur-lined leather gloves and sand-encrusted trainers. Wellies would have been more appropriate. Rob, a sometime jokester – if a surprising jokester, when the quirkiness of his personality was added in – told Eddie Adams he had never before seen anyone wear all the clothes he owned at the same time.

At noon, I changed in the Caddie Pavilion and walked over to the Woollen Mill in rain that seemed to be coming down in solid lumps.

The porter stopped me because I was wearing trainers. I hadn't left a pair of dress shoes in the car because all the photo sessions had been scheduled onsite. As trainers aren't allowed in the R&A, I had to drive back to the hotel to get my leather shoes. When I returned, I was surprised to see almost a hundred people standing around, chatting, playing construction superintendent while watching the crew, and taking pictures. I was later told that an 85-year-old member of the R&A who lived in a flat along the eighteenth fairway was in the crowd. He remembered the Box being built when he was a youngster!

Duncan ordered us each a glass of claret and introduced me to a number of the members, and to Peter Dawson, the Secretary of the R&A, who had recently succeeded Sir Michael Bonallack. Politely, with Scots honesty, they all offered condolences on 9/11. We joined the other members who were at the window, excitedly commenting on the crew and the now roofless Box. A member friend said, 'No tam.' Despite the laughter, there was a certain feeling of melancholy floating around in the overheated, cigar- and cigarette-scented, stagnant air of the room.

Someone asked me how 9/11 had affected life and business in America. After giving him a grim report, I lightened my tone and said, embellishing Alan's words on Saturday, 'The Box and her fairy-tale life, in this magical setting, seem to bring a smile to everyone's face when the auction and what you see going on out there off the first tee are mentioned.' I remembered a phrase that Lucy often used in the Sweet Shoppe, and answered with it because it seemed appropriate: 'As a friend says: "'Tis a mood boost."'

As if on cue, as another member collared me and said seriously: 'Ye know ye bought the London Bridge? Only a Hut, ye know – no air-conditioning for California . . .' It was an obvious reference to the company who bought the London Bridge for Lake Havasu in the mid-1960s and may have thought they were actually buying the more famous Tower Bridge.

More hip-hips and bantering followed, with subtle name-calling and innuendo mixed in, until Sandy Rutherford, an R&A member known for his often acerbic wit, called out in his inimitably bristling fashion: 'Aye, next ye know the money-grubbin' Trust'll be sellin' the Swilcan Bridge!' Duncan looked at me solicitously and led a hasty retreat to the dining room.

After we were seated, Duncan looked at me closely and said, 'You're a marked man, I'm afraid.'

'I know. You're not the first to warn me. Some have been so impolite as to suggest I'm stealing a national treasure from the shadow of Saint Andrew.'

'Not the last of the nasty talk.'

'Sometimes I have fun tying business rules to people and incidents.'

'Oh?'

The waitress delivered our wine and a basket of bread. We clicked glasses, exchanged nods and sipped.

'This time it's about Sherwood Forest and Robin Hood. For me, now, it seems wise to assume I have an archer's target stitched to my back, with many in Scotland, and particularly Fife, taking aim on the bull's eye.'

'Quite accurate, I'm afraid. But as I've noticed from reading the papers and listening, you're capitalising on the controversy by answering all the questions with the truth. It gains respect, doesn't it, and it disarms those who want to bring harm.'

'Very good. Shakespeare?'

He managed a weak smile. 'Aye, I don't think so.'

'In Hollywood, they say there is no such thing as bad publicity.'

'I wouldn't know about that.'

'I have news for you: neither does Hollywood.'

We laughed as the waitress brought our plates and ladled steamed vegetables.

'I've already been cursed as a buccaneer instead of being applauded a preservationist.'

'One minute you're the matador hero with the cape. The next you're wearing the horns.'

'Aye,' I said, mocking his baritone brogue. 'Rather good, that – as is the question am I on a runway or a gangplank?' I touched Duncan on the arm lightly and whispered, 'Little does that good old boy playing bridge in there know the Box will be rebuilt a little over 120 miles from where the London Bridge now spans the Colorado River.'

Duncan's sudden sharp gasp brought stares from the others in the room.

'I'll tell you two other interesting facts,' I said quietly. 'The Coachella Valley – or the Palm Springs area, to most tourists – where the Box will be rebuilt, is about the same size, in area, as Fife; the populations are roughly the same also.'

The lunch consisted of fish soup, mixed salad, boiled meats with potatoes, turnips, carrots and cauliflower – a proper British public-school lunch. At least that's what I guessed the vegetables were. I wasn't sure, as every last bit of flavour, and certainly nutritional value, had been purged in the steamer. Liberal applications of pepper, butter and mustard hadn't helped. But who was I to care? It was a hot meal, and the company of Duncan and other R&A members – and the Stilton, oat biscuits and port – were wonderful.

Haggis was not served.

CHAPTER 33

SAW BLADES AND SNAKES

MONDAY, 5 NOVEMBER 2001: AFTERNOON

Man blames fate for other accidents, but feels personally
responsible when he makes a hole in one.

Anonymous

I left the Woollen Mill to the porter's ominously sounding 'We
wish you good luck, sir,' as he held the door and waited for me
to change back into my trainers. 'Leave the leathers here. We will
have them brightened. You can collect them later.'

'Why, thank you.' I scanned his emotionally drained, red-tinted,
cherubic face and walked outside, while asking myself why the
faces of all British butlers looked as if they shaved themselves
every hour.

As the rain passed, the wind assumed control. It was a cold, true
winter wind. Rapidly rolling clouds sailed across the skies under
the brilliant but lifeless sun. It was clear on the other side of St
Andrews Bay, and a spectacular rainbow arched out in the water
towards Arbroath.

I stood upwind of the billowing dust as the crew cut the
first 600-pound panel of brick from the south wall of the Box.
Plumes of reddish dust and chunks of brick swirled in the air.
What organisms might there have been incubating in the cavity
all these years? I asked myself. If this were the US, the Gang
would be wearing goggles, masks and protective gloves, and
a lurking presence from the Occupational Health and Safety
Administration would be a certainty. Ox didn't bother with any
of them. Who knew what his lungs were inhaling?

A little later, a high-pitched, screeching explosion announced a snapped saw blade. The gods were with us: no one was injured. Rob made a hurried telephone call. 'Aye,' he mumbled when he finished, 'two saws in Scotland and only two blades as well.' The burr in his voice betrayed his annoyance.

'How many?' I asked, hoping I had misunderstood.

'Two,' he said. 'Here's one.' He held up the twisted blade with his gloved hands as if it were a dead snake. 'Other one here by coach from Glasgow in the mornin'.'

I looked to the sky. A hawk hovered against the wind, searching for prey.

CHAPTER 34

THE UNIVERSITY LIBRARY AND MASCARA

MONDAY, 5 NOVEMBER 2001: AFTERNOON AND EVENING

Never give your reasons, for your judgment will probably
be right, but your reasons almost certainly will be wrong.

Lord Mansfield

A Links Trust receptionist called to relay my messages. One was
from Carolyne Nurse to tell me my credentials for use of the
Special Collections Department in the university library had been
arranged.

Cilla Jackson, a senior curator, met me at reception at 2.30 p.m.
'I hope you're dressed warmly?' she said demurely. 'It's cold in the
cellar. You will need a jumper, I should think.' My eyes followed
hers as they focused on a dreary staircase behind glass doors. She
was wearing a fitted, long, pleated tartan skirt and two cashmere
sweaters.

'It can't be any worse than over at the Box.'

'Yes, it can – and may well be.' She smiled meekly and handed
me my library pass and computer codes. 'Eight months should be
long enough,' she said, showing me the expiry date. 'Not to be
troubling, but I don't think you'll find much to your benefit. Then
again, you may.'

More ominous words – as from the porter at the R&A.

Mrs Jackson was right. The temperature in the basement
research room had to be near freezing. Sharing a long layout table
with me was a student in a kilt, a brilliant red-and-black tam, an

open-hooded fur-lined parka that went to his knees and heavy, thick-soled motorcycle boots with an American logo.

I logged on to the university's computer network and began searching the archives for Box-related material and photographs. I found little narrative material but a number of superb images, including many from the Cowie Collection, a historic collection of photos that had been gifted to the university.

After little more than an hour, I logged off because my feet and ears, which had been frozen during my college years in Minnesota, were cold to the point of being painful. Katie Cadigan, the attractive graduate assistant who had been assigned to assist me, took the list of books and photographs I wanted and left to cull them from the stacks. When she returned, pushing a trolley, her breath was visible though she was bundled in an ankle-length black-wool coat, wore woollen gloves and had a scarf wrapped around her neck.

She studied the list. I studied her because she was certainly a truly beautiful woman, though something about her face was out of place. Plus, I was able to catch the welcoming scent of her wonderful perfume. When I stole another glance I realised it was her mascara. It had frozen and cracked from the cold.

'Would you like these in the room reserved for you?' she asked.

'Down here in Siberia?' I asked, as I realised the scream of Ox's saw blade was still ringing in my ear.

'Yes.' She forced a smile.

'How about joining me for a coffee first?'

'I'm assigned to you. For whatever you require. I can lock the books in your room.'

'Good. Let's leave.' I helped her with the books and, as we went up the stairs, we debated whether to go to the student union or elsewhere. Elsewhere won out. It started to rain again as we crossed North Street near to the police station and walked along College Street towards Market Street. 'Sweet Shoppe or a pub?' I asked as I unfurled my umbrella.

'They serve coffee in the pub,' she answered quickly. 'The Sweet Shoppe would be closed now.' I detected a questioning and suspicious edge to her voice, as in 'how would he know about the Sweet Shoppe?' and 'is this crazy American really considering a coffee or tea at four thirty in the afternoon when wine and whisky are an option?'

'I haven't paid attention. I only see Lucy and Sophie first thing in the morning,' I said playfully, looking at her without, I hoped, any suggestion I was studying her again. 'Ale and food at the front of your mind – always.'

My knowledge of the shop and the girls seemed to give me credibility. 'Claret and food,' she corrected me, her eyes innocently dancing, 'and ale and a margherita pizza occasionally. I'm sure it was the same for you.'

'It was White Castle hamburgers, or "gut bombs" as they were affectionately known. I rarely drink beer. I really don't like the smell of it. Wine was almost unheard of in Minnesota in the 1950s, and McDonald's was still someone's bad dream.'

'Ugh. I hate Big Macs. But the fries are OK. There isn't one in town, anyway.'

'I have a good idea,' I said. The rain was getting heavier so I guided her to the Vine Leaf.

'This is not a pub.' Her arched eyebrows and smile confirmed that the restaurant was one of the better in town.

'I know, but the roof doesn't leak and there's no reason to walk another block in the rain.'

She did not object.

As we were seated, Katie took a small spiral notebook from her handbag and set it down on the table. 'As you were told,' she said professionally, 'I'm doing a paper on icon marketing. Is it all right if I take notes while we talk?'

'Of course. A benefit to working down in Siberia?'

She laughed. 'Definitely, I suppose. I hope you may be of help to me.'

As we started to sip our wine, she opened her notebook to a lengthy agenda. 'I'm impressed. You're prepared.' Having practised architecture and reading plans from either side of a conference table, I was still pretty good at reading upside down.

'Thank you.' She started by asking the normal academic questions. I didn't complain as I found her very bright and her questions well ordered and sophisticated. Plus, it was genuine conversation and I really hadn't had any with anyone, except Duncan, at lunch, since I'd left Los Angeles.

The bottle was finished quite quickly. 'Do you have dinner plans?'

She seemed a little embarrassed. 'No, but I have to study.'

'Would you like to join me?'

'Yes, but . . .'

I held up the empty bottle. The waiter caught my signal and went to fetch another. 'With the weather as it is, it makes no sense to leave. Agree?'

'Of course, but . . .'

'Katie, I have no plans for dinner. Eating with you will be more interesting than sitting in the hotel dining room with the day's newspapers and overhearing golfers retelling the story of their rounds of ten years ago. A good dinner and you can be off.'

She laughed refreshingly. 'Thank you. I used to be a waitress. Golfers are sometimes boring when they talk about their games.'

I told her I didn't have any pressing California business waiting for me, even with the eight-hour time difference, other than to call the Country Club. 'What about the books?'

'They're under your signature. There is no problem.' Her glance was awkward. 'Special Collections closes in an hour, anyway.'

'I apologise, but I've never spent time in a restricted library environment researching before. I don't know the protocol.'

'Oh? It's one of the great privileges of being a scholar. If you want to, you can keep anything you want hidden from your competition, almost for ever.'

'Interesting. Even with the Internet.'

'Yes. Scholars want to control the source, just as business people want to do. Now, can I ask you another question about the icon phenomenon?'

'Of course.'

I caught the awkward turn of her head. This time it was to acknowledge a fellow student who had walked in with his parents. 'Are we now fodder for gossip?' I loved the potential innuendo.

'I'm sure.'

'Does it bother you?'

'No. It reminds me of my father, when he was alive and took me with him on business trips to London. He loved introducing me as his daughter and getting the smirks and knowing-otherwises . . .'

'I did the same thing with my nieces. It was very exhilarating.'

We laughed together, both knowing how truthful we were being.

As the second bottle of wine was being decanted, we agreed on first courses of finnan haddie bree (smoked haddock, leek and potato soup) for her and a Scottish sea scallop with Balbirnie black pudding and a rocket salad for me.

I looked at the happiness in her face as she read the rest of the menu. What Claudia had often said was so true: that the building of a friendship and making someone happy is the most rewarding of good attributes. My mobile vibrated, and I read a text message.

'Don't worry about courtesy with me,' Katie said. 'Go about your business. I've never been here before. I'm having such a good time.'

When I finished replying to the message, she put the menu down. 'There are things on the menu I've never heard of. You order for me.'

I laughed. 'Do you eat haggis?'

'Not if I have a choice: not brains or tripe either. Given a choice, that is.'

I scanned the main courses, set the menu aside, firmed my smile and waited for her to speak.

'This business of celebrity endorsement and hiring golfers to design golf courses. It sounds like there is so much vanity involved.'

'Welcome to the world of ego and celebrity worship,' I replied. 'When Nicklaus's playing career began to wind down and he accepted the challenge of becoming involved in the design of a golf course, he started with the participation of some of the well-respected designers of the time. He worked very hard at it. He had to. He had to protect his persona as a bulletproof icon. Even the most sophisticated businessmen are still in awe of him – as well they should be. Sure, he's made design mistakes, as we all make mistakes – it's part of the process of living and maturing – but he's learned how to rise above them. But that doesn't necessarily mean any professional golfer can become a good designer. Few do. Or, look at it this way, Katie. You're very bright; you know that if you get 95 per cent of the answers correct on a test you will earn an A. It's the final 5 per cent that really matters and is distinguishing, isn't it?'

'What about someone like an Anna Kournikova, who doesn't seem to be able to achieve her potential in tennis?' Katie clapped her hands quietly as her steaming bowl of soup was set in front of her, then picked it up and looked at me, her classically proportioned face giving a questioning look.

'Begin, begin,' I said. 'In Anna's case, she was marketed for her sex appeal first and her prowess on the tennis court second. But she's a bit of an exception. You have to realise that almost all of these iconic gals and guys were raised as athletes, not business people. Which is fine; the public has to understand that they're not invincible. But back to the example of Nicklaus. He is no slouch as a designer, mind you, but he can be repetitive at times, as were Alister MacKenzie, Harry Colt and even Old Tom Morris. Again, it goes with being creative. Think of Monet and his "haystack" paintings. All unique and yet similar. The real questions are, for the Nicklauses of the world, does the additional fee paid to these icons – and it is most often many additional millions of dollars – help sell real estate and can you realistically amortise the cost?'

'Well, does it?' Katie eyed my sea scallop as the waiter refilled her bowl from a tureen.

'Go ahead, begin. Enjoy.'

'Thank you,' she said, batting her thick eyelashes.

'Does a Nicklaus, or Norman, or whoever's design help sell real estate for the developer? The answer is "yes", but a case can be made that they eventually dilute themselves and diminish their marketing power. How many Nicklaus and Arnold Palmer courses does the world need? When does their creative energy exhaust itself? Is there a benefit to the member and homeowner? Perhaps, but ultimately the owner is saddled with the big designer fee. A case can be made that the "budget-out-the-window" designer golf courses are more expensive to maintain, so the trade-off may be, at the end of the day, not all that much.' I looked at Katie again. She was writing furiously, barely pausing for a sip of wine – but when she did sip, it was more a gulp.

The waiter came by. I ordered us Caesar salads, with extra anchovies; Scottish lamb, rare; Highland beef, rare; and mixed vegetables, lightly sautéed with garlic. 'Approve?'

'Perfect.'

'As for the Box, no matter what she costs in terms of buying, shipping and reconstruction, it's an awful lot less than the fees paid to a celebrity architect for what you hope, in the end, is a respectable golf course you'll have fun playing on a regular basis. Remember, as you write your paper, that in the marketing of icons, rational decision-making has no value. It is all about the potential buyer's perception and passion for celebrity.'

170 Approximate capacity, in number of seats, of the restaurant of the Links Clubhouse

The waiter returned and refilled our wine glasses. 'Another?' he asked me.

'Why not?' I smiled in reply.

'Well, OK,' she answered with her silvery voice. 'This is like being with my dad. I can read in the morning. I haven't had wine like this since before he died. Or food, either.'

I sensed the grief she had for her father, and it was interesting that she had never mentioned her mother. 'But it doesn't only happen in golf, Katie. Think of the "wee Scot", Scotland's great Formula One driver, Jackie Stewart, and his shooting schools. There's one over in Perthshire, at Gleneagles. He's done a great job. Don't forget Wimbledon and its skill in selling a lifestyle in its off-site shops at Harrods in London and in Japan. A lifestyle of white woollen cable-knit sweaters with piping, pleated skirts, cuffed trousers, wooden racquets, strawberries and nostalgia.' I paused for another long sip of wine and continued. 'What you need to focus on and evaluate is a realisation that the Hollywood celebrities and athletes all have their own agendas. Many are not very bright by what I think your definition of the word might be. Most are terribly one-dimensional. You read about how their immaturity and agendas can negatively impact a marketing programme overnight – drunk driving, drug arrests, relationship betrayal and extreme political leanings come to mind. Instead, focus and consider the known quantity of a large-as-life celebrity who has died, something from nature or an inanimate object – a Marilyn Monroe, an Eiffel Tower, a London Eye, a Starter's Box – instead.'

'I had never thought of celebrities as icons in this way,' Katie said.

'I apologise. They are all, in the end, simply human, aren't they, even though millions don't want to admit to the fact and prefer to believe their personal perceptions of Hollywood and sporting celebrities and their lifestyles – whether they are accurate or not.' I re-crossed my legs and readjusted my body across the seat of the wicker chair. 'At the end of the day, we all have to take stock and privately judge our quests. With me, as I share it with you, it is because of my passion for contributing to golf's heritage and legacy – the preservation of the Box – and understanding and accepting the logic, the rationale of it all, some of which, at times, seems irrational to almost everyone. You package it with mystery and the *perception* word, the way they do at Wimbledon, which has correctly realised that England has become a fast, transitory society and that there are more foreign players of substance than ever before. So Wimbledon has positioned itself against that, dressing itself up in illusions of integrity and the spirit of a pre-war era. Have you been to the US?'

'Yes, I was an exchange student in what you call the junior year.' Her eyes lit up and she pushed her notebook aside. 'I was in Omaha, Nebraska. Wonderful people. Plenty of wind there. Scotland without the lochs and mountains.' She smiled a fresh, silly smile, the kind that comes after a few glasses of wine. 'I can't lie,' she said, catching herself and giggling from embarrassment. 'Not quite Scotland.'

'Well then, I'm sure you were on a farm or two?' I caught her nod as she reached for her water glass. 'I have a simile for you. You may remember the "back forty", the farmlands away from view where the Nebraska wheat farmer was probably experimenting with a new strain of wheat or barley, without prying eyes? Mystery sustains marketing and all your good efforts. You don't buy a banana already peeled.'

'That's good; I like that.' She wrote it down.

'Flesh may be a garment, but as a courtesan once said: "I want to leave some of my clothes on, at least for a while . . ."'

'Mr Hagen!'

The shock and surprise she yelled out in a soprano's high pitch over the top of her food, and the coupling of her mouth with a hand, jolted me from the sullen, lethargic – thinking-about-Claudia – mood I had unknowingly slipped into. I sat up in my chair. 'Enough of icons and the Box tonight, lassie. I apologise. Let me summarise and give you something to dwell on before I see you in the library tomorrow.'

Her smile released a tentative charm of acceptance as her nose stopped its wrinkling. The shock and semi-disgust had worn off. 'It is a funny line, now that I let it rattle around in my head.' She dropped her pen on the table and with a clumsy motion picked it up again.

'She embodies *hope*, Katie, the Box does. No politician could ask for a better endorsement.'

'I will remember that.'

Later, a taxi drove Katie to her hall of residence and then me to my hotel. My car could enjoy the night camping out on the first tee. Walking to the room, my moral compass advised me it was not a good idea to call anyone with my questionable speech pattern, except the Country Club, where I would probably be connected to voicemail anyway. Any doubt I had was dispersed by a cryptic, milquetoast text message left on my mobile phone that floored me: 'Hi, J.P. up & out. 2 cedars. last rites. Our dear friend Bruce. Dxo.' Bruce was a very close friend, who had passed away.

CHAPTER 35

BALLET, ROBOTS AND SLEET

TUESDAY, 6 NOVEMBER 2001: MORNING

There are two seasons in Scotland: June and winter.

Billy Connolly

It was a treacherous taxi ride down into town the next morning as hail and rain were blowing from every direction. Even with the help of dim daylight, it was more dangerous than the week before, when I'd had dinner with Angus. The entire putting green and first tee, under normal American soil conditions, would have been a quagmire and flooded. But true to the linksland's sandy soil and its ability to drain, Rob was able to manoeuvre the forklift without difficulty, and there was very little standing water except in the Valley of Sin and some of the larger depressions out in the fairways. He made a note of the sharp temperature drop of the past hour as he and the Gang went off to the protection of their lorry for the mid-morning break.

I stopped at his lorry while sprinting to my car. He rolled down his window a couple of inches and said, 'Fife winter weather greetin' ye now.' He also said we'd need a second container. The oddly shaped roof sections weren't allowing him to pack the container as efficiently as he had planned. He looked at me with the same quality of eye contact we had made when he told me about the saw blade.

I stood under the limited protection of my umbrella, called the Port of Felixstowe and made arrangements for a second container to be driven up overnight.

Ox, whom I had never heard speak before, leaned forward and said: 'True weather now. 'Tis the Scotland where men are men and the sheep are in trouble.' His laugh came from deep in his throat and was hoarse. He was missing a number of teeth.

Cracking a falsely set smile of acknowledgement, I detoured to the warmth of the Caddie Pavilion as Rick McKenzie, the caddie master, was in his office. A pot of hot tea would surely be brewing.

In the early afternoon, I stood at the inside edge of the eighteenth fairway – if there is such a place – to take progress photographs. I had outlined a small square in the turf with golf tees, because before we had begun the takedown, I had decided to take a photograph every hour of the working day from the same spot as a form of time-lapse archival record. I intended to use one of the photos, along with a shot of the vista, both with and without the Box, and a few with the Box in place in La Quinta under palm trees, in a commemorative poster that could be sold, with the profits going to junior golf.

The rain started to mature into an almost surrealistic, chilling sleet. The Gang was forced to manoeuvre their equipment, and themselves, with unnatural, unsteady gestures. It was slow motion, ballet-like. First they would plant their feet, then slowly begin to work, then replant their feet again, as if they didn't trust their reflexes. Their exposed skin and hair, and parts of their coarsely woven woollen clothing, were matted and caked with rust-coloured dust and flecks of brick that had been mixed and solidified by the rain.

The noise was deafening, sinister-sounding and menacing as the saw blade was forcefully driven through the bricks by Ox with a deep whirring sound until it caught and jammed. It was deafening again in a high-pitched whine as it was partially pulled from the groove just cut, before it changed to an anguished grating and exploding racket when driven down again through the groove until it found another pocket of resistance.

The men might have been on another planet. Ox, lumbering now and showing almost savage qualities, continued to ride one end of the saw with his full body weight as Oban and Fleet Foot steadied the other end of each panel with their arms and shoulders as it was gradually dislodged. Tedious and dangerous in dry, warm weather, it was certainly a questionable activity in rain and sleet. I changed my mental description of their motions from being ballet-like to robot-like. Certainly the crew was cursing the hallowed linksland, the Box and the madman California Yankee who had bought her.

Within another hour, the weather had deteriorated to such a state that the only worthy adjectives were *absurd* and *frightening*. The fronts were sweeping through every half an hour, it seemed, and the sleet was mixed with a heavy, wet snow. Rob evaluated the working conditions as he had, as usual, listened to the farmer's forecast during the noontime news. The weather forecaster, as only a Scot can phrase it, with a heavy dose of the ominous, had said to 'prepare for worsening conditions into the weekend'.

I glared at Rob. The wind was so sharp it felt like it was sawing at my ears.

He knew what I was thinking. In the understatement of the week, he said: 'I think it best we start tomorrow afore first light.'

176 Bob Martin's winning score in the Open Championship on the Old Course in 1876

CHAPTER 36

••

BRITISH GOLF MUSEUM

TUESDAY, 6 NOVEMBER 2001: AFTERNOON

Scotland, thank God, is not for everyone.

Robin Douglas-Home

The crew ran to their lorry and left for Lower Largo at 4 p.m. as I ran across Golf Place to the British Golf Museum to meet Peter Lewis. In addition to being the museum's director, he is Golf Heritage Secretary of the R&A. I had called him from California the previous week to ask that he check to see if there was any information on the Starter's Box in the R&A archives.

'I can confirm the Hut was built in 1924,' he said, unceremoniously. He handed me a letter on R&A stationery, signed by Fiona McDougall, Assistant Curator, Golf Heritage Department, which summarised what she found in the R&A's archives.

From the evidence in the archive of the Royal & Ancient Golf Club and the St [*sic*] Town Council, it would appear that the most recent Starter's Box for the Old Course was built in 1924. At the R&A's Green Committee meeting on 2nd July 1924, Charles Grace, the Honorary Secretary of the committee, 'was requested to obtain a sketch and estimate for a larger Starter's Box at the Old Course'. At the next meeting on 30th July, there was submitted to the meeting an estimate by Andrew Thom & Sons, joiners, for supplying a new Starter's Box for the Old Course at a cost of £21/10/ (about £21.50), and after discussion it was agreed to write to the Town Council stating that the present box is in a dilapidated condition and ask them whether they would join with the Green Committee in providing a new box.

At the Town Council in Committee Meeting on 4th August, there was a letter, dated 31st July, from the Joint Honorary Secretary of the Green Committee, pointing out that the present Starter's Box at the Old Course is in a very dilapidated condition, that the Green Committee consider that a new box must be obtained and have received an offer by Messrs Andrew Thom & Sons, Joiners, to supply this box for the sum of £21 10s and requesting the Town Council to join with the Green Committee in defraying the cost. It was agreed that the Town Council should pay one half of the expense of the new box on the condition that the present box is handed over to the Town Council, who can make use of same.

At the next meeting on 18th August, a letter was read from Mr C.S. Grace, Hon Secretary of the Green Committee, agreeing to the proposal made by the Town Council that they should pay the sum of £21 10s, being the cost of the new Starter's Box at the Old Course, on condition that the Old Box is handed over to the Town Council.

The new box was finished before the end of the year because the Green Committee accounts on 13th December 1924 show a payment of £21/10/– to Andrew Thom & Sons amount of the estimate for Starter's Box [sic].

Peter apologised for the museum being closed for its own renovation and for not being able to give me a walk-through. I asked him if he cared to join David Joy, Mike Horkan and me for a pint. He declined as he wanted to get home before the weather made driving unsafe.

'We respect the farmer's forecast,' he said simply as he shook my hand and walked me to the door. 'Most surely if thunder-snow is to occur.' Brevity has always been a part of a Scot's nature. Peter is no exception.

'I haven't heard those two words used together before.'

'It is when sleet and snow occur along with thunderstorms.'

'I can't wait.'

CHAPTER 37

DAVID JOY

TUESDAY, 6 NOVEMBER 2001: 4.30 P.M.

DANGER! Golf in Progress.

Sign alongside the lane leading around the rear of the Links practice
facilities to the Eden Clubhouse and offices of the Links Trust

David is a fourth-generation St Andrean. Indeed, three generations
of his family are currently members of the St Andrews Golf Club.
Being the author, thespian, historian, painter and playwright he
is, he has an extensive and unique knowledge of St Andrews and
the Links. He is also a founder of the charitable organisation
Keepers of the Green. Ask him a question about the Links, and
the dates and names he rattles off come so effortlessly you think
he is either faking it or making up what he says. But he's not.
He has been committed to the preservation of St Andrews and its
history his entire life. As an actor, he's known around the world for
his compelling portrayals of Old Tom Morris on stage (CDs are
available that memorialise the act) and, most recently, in Titleist
adverts.

'Aye, yer Irish?' he said in his baritone brogue as we shook
hands in the Dunvegan.

Pausing for an extra breath after my second sprint – this one the
hundred yards or so from the museum to the Dunvegan – I smiled
and looked around at the walls and interior columns, completely
covered by golf-themed photography, and the golf bags with the
name of a Tour professional attached. A copy of David's new book,
The Scrapbook of Old Tom Morris, was sitting on a table.

'All Norwegian blood,' I said, signalling the waitress. 'My
grandparents lived in Stavanger and Trondheim.'

He nodded politely. 'Live in California?' He was a cautious Scot, but he seemed to begin to warm to me after the obligatory preliminary mental jousting had ended. This was our first meeting, other than the chance introduction by Iain, though we had exchanged emails and had telephone conversations after the auction.

I told him about my background in architecture, the arts and as a real-estate developer in San Francisco and resort areas such as Carmel, and I explained, as I had to the Trust, how serious a matter the Box was to us, though many suggested we were borderline insane.

'Takes the subjective thinking of a Yankee to see the marketing potential, I suppose,' he said, with a wry smile. 'But it is sad, isn't it?' He coughed almost immediately, a mannerism I soon learned to expect. 'Nowhere for it to go here.' The irritation in his eye from his cigarette's smoke passed. He looked at me, squarely this time. 'You're all right.'

Any tension between us was gone. I asked if anyone had been in the pub asking for me. He said no and changed the subject. 'I have an 1890s replica Hut up at my studio in the Grange, with cast-iron wheels.'

I let the comment stand, unable to tell if he was being informative or, I hoped, about to invite me to visit. We talked for a while about the Links and St Andrews in a general way before focusing on the Box and the rumours that had been going around before the auction as to who was prepared to buy it and at what price. I told him a golfing friend in England said one pub rumour in the City, London's financial district, was that the Japanese were prepared to pay £300,000. Another rumour floating around suggested a large American corporation – namely Pebble Beach or Pinehurst – had been prepared to bid millions because of the Box's marketing and branding possibilities.

David shook his head in disbelief at the thousands of pounds being bandied about and took a long draw of ale from his glass. 'I heard the same rumours. You said someone was coming by?'

'Yes.' I took out my mobile and called Mike Horkan. 'Where are you?'

'At the driving range. Hitting balls.'

'Horkan, it's freezing outside. It's snowing. The street's a skating rink.'

'Aye, sleeting over here. On me way.'

A few minutes later, Mike walked in as I was showing David the letter Peter Lewis had given me.

'There's a reason so many pubs are close to golf courses in Scotland,' Mike said, rubbing his hands together.

'Well, the magnifying-glass exercise turned into a waste of time,' David said. He chuckled roughly.

'What is he talking about?' Mike asked, as he ordered.

I told him Rick McKenzie had been trying to date the box from an old photo he had found that had a car in it. It involved Rick using a magnifying glass to read the registration plates and trace their numbers and letters back to the year of issue. 'We have proof from the plate on the car in the photo that the Box was there in 1931,' I said, 'but that's the best we have been able to do – until I met with Peter Lewis this afternoon.'

The three of us chatted for a while longer. I was content to listen to the two of them discuss local politics while my eyes focused on the sizzling and cracking sounds coming from the bricks of peat burning in the fireplace. After a polite period of time and a few yawns, I pleaded jet lag, time zones, a business day about to begin in California and a need to get back to my hotel and on the Internet.

I went to the bar to pay the bill. While waiting for change, my eyes focused on a photo to the left of the till. I took a closer look. The photograph was of David, as a young man, along with his father, Arnold Palmer and Gary Player.

David stood next to me. 'It was taken in 1961, before the Open at Royal Birkdale. Arnold and Gary were in town for a "Shell's Wonderful World of Golf" match on the Old Course. Palmer won the match and collected £20,000. Then he went down to Birkdale and won the Open later the same week. The purse was £1,250.'

As we walked out of the pub together, he kindly offered to have some of the classic old photographs in the Cowie Collection copied for me. His offer was genuine, and I thanked him for his kindness. I didn't tell him I felt I had frozen to death doing the same thing the day before – or that I didn't care because I had had a most enjoyable evening with young Katie.

CHAPTER 38

SNOW SQUALLS AND RAINBOWS

WEDNESDAY, 7 NOVEMBER 2001: 6.30 A.M.

Harrington's 63 (in The Open) would have upset him. He always wanted the golf course to win, especially his golf course.

Jeremy Watson, Scotland on Sunday

When Fraser Smart met me at 7 a.m. in the Links Clubhouse for breakfast the next morning, he politely described the morning's weather with the words 'a fresh level of deterioration'.

'Fresh? I can't see the first tee of the Jubilee Links for the fog and rain – it's only 40 yards away. When I passed the Gang of Six driving here, I could really only tell one from another by the colour of their clothing.' The rain was spattering across the windows with a sound like buckshot hitting metal.

He glanced outside. A threesome was actually considering teeing off. 'Now I know why I don't play the game.' He shook his head in disbelief and pulled up his sleeve to check his watch. It featured a barometer. 'We ought to hasten the process or misery will certainly be our company. The weather is uncaring now. I'm fearful of a violent storm and what may lie ahead.'

We hurried our breakfast and started the quarter-mile walk back to the Box without talking, our backs turned to the sea to soften the onslaught, now, less than 20 minutes later, a fresh mixture of sleet and snow. I turned a little to get my bearings and adjust the hood of my rain jacket. No Fraser. Then I saw flashes of flame-orange. Barely ten yards away, he was almost totally blotted out by the heavy snow.

By the time we reached the Box, the weather – surprise – had changed again. The sun had broken though the clouds in a few places and there was another rainbow out at the end of the Eden Estuary, its pot of gold probably anchored on the ninth green. The snow on the eighteenth green was melting and reflecting the rays of the sun in a blazing white light. I laughed at the misery of the moment because it was all so very beautiful.

Fraser pointed towards the West Sands with his pipe and nodded disbelievingly. Two people and their dogs were making their way down to the beach from the car park.

The Gang of Six had finished loading the first container with the two roof sections, the all-important *Links Trust St Andrews Old Course Starter* sign, the casework, bulletin boards, fencing and other miscellaneous items. I sealed the container with the metal customs banding and took a photo of the lorry. The Gang stopped what they were doing and seemed to watch with a reasonable sense of respect as it passed by the R&A.

The sun disappeared as quickly as it had appeared. With it came another sudden drop in temperature and a heavier, more persistent wind. Then the rain and hail began again, this time blowing briefly in sheets before it turned into a heavy, wet snow.

Rob came over to us. 'Wee bit nippy now,' he said, a little too indifferently, while pulling up the collar of his parka. 'Severe lack of sunshine today, 'tis.' He grimaced for the first time as he added, 'A rather typical late autumn day. No worse than usual. Good day to be on the pond awaitin' a duck. Oft get pelted by hail.'

'Now, what's your answer to the question of coming to California and rebuilding the Box?' I asked, twitching from cold, as I looked across the fairway. The water in the Valley of Sin had turned to a frozen pond.

'Nae,' he said. 'Thought aboot it, but tae hot.' He raised a sleet-encrusted eyebrow and glanced towards the sea, which was churning and whipping up whitecaps. The couple was only a foot or so outside the surge of the pounding surf.

(I later continued to casually needle Rob about the possibility of his coming to California and supervising the reconstruction. He always declined – even when I added the bonus of a few days on the beach in Malibu – without the guarantee of *Baywatch* girls. He wasn't able to fathom the desert's high summer temperatures and at one point said he didn't think he had been in weather much above twenty-five degrees Celsius (about seventy-seven degrees Fahrenheit).

'Farmer's forecast says it'll worsen later.' For emphasis, he stood a little more erect and continued: 'We'll work late. Tomorrow will be bad. The weather'll switch to the nor'east during the night.' He looked at me as seriously as he ever had. 'Bone-chilling miserable it will be, even to a Scot. Thought of often as an invasion.' For the first time since we had met, he spoke without a brogue. Was it for emphasis? Was it another omen?

'This is very bad.'

'No. Tomorrow will be bad. This is the weather god's rehearsal for the nor'easter, I think.'

It was dangerous to be outside, let alone working, around what was left of the Box. The patches of snow and ice were pink-tinged from the dust. Three of the five sides had been taken down. The two that remained were barely four-foot stubs of wall. The occasional boot print reminded me of those from the moonwalks. The darkening skies and lack of daylight didn't help. After the lunch break, Rob moved his lorry so the headlights lit the work area, and I, fearing the wrath of Eddie Adams, but really not caring, followed his lead and drove my car up the first fairway, pointed it north on the first tee box, turned the headlamps on and left the engine running. Between our two vehicles, it helped to light what was left of the Box. Finally, when a section of wall fell from the brick-grab that was recklessly swaying from the boom of Rob's forklift about ten feet in the air, just missing Ox before it crashed on the turf and exploded in a plume of dust, I took it as a bad omen. I told Rob to shut the job down.

Unbelievably, he protested.

'No argument this time, Rob,' I yelled. 'Too many bad omens.' The familiar pattern of rain to hail to sleet to snow to blowing sleet reasserted itself.

'Fife's finally tired o' California weather.' His eyes told me he had considered what I'd said and agreed. He flicked the ice off his gloves in disgust and called the Gang to his lorry. 'Finish the job tomorrow, we will. One way or another.'

'You sure?' I asked, somewhat surprised.

'Yup. Leave Lower Largo half five, in the dark of night, we will. Cannae count on the weather now. Be here half six, we will.' He ran to his lorry and drove off with the crew, wiping the windscreen with his cap as he drove up Golf Place.

I looked back at the Box as I ran to my car. The Gang had rushed to the lorry without storing their tools. The comparison was to a retreating regiment in a winter war zone somewhere in the Crimea, leaving behind their cannon, muskets and dead horses as they fled the opposition. Here, instead, it was power saws, hammers, crowbars, the forklift with its brick-grab swinging in the storm, and what was left of the Box. I called Mike Horkan to tell him we were starting work very early the next morning.

I exhaled, wondering how the weather could possibly worsen. When I had done the due diligence, I allowed for unknowns. But I hadn't been prepared for the Box to be built of brick instead of wood. And only two saw blades in Scotland? I had set aside a 'third-column' contingency for a second and third shipping container, though I hadn't told anyone, so that tempered my miscues a little. And the weather? Never in my wildest dreams did I think it would be such a factor. All I could do was laugh.

As I drove down the first fairway to the Wynd, the scream of the saw was still echoing in my head. An Arctic blast slammed in from the sea and a snow squall followed, riding sideways on the wind. As I turned the corner at the R&A, I barely managed to get around a snowdrift in the middle of Golf Place.

CHAPTER 39

....

OLD TOM MORRIS

WEDNESDAY, 7 NOVEMBER 2001:
LATE AFTERNOON

Golf is a game invented by the same people who think
music comes out of bagpipes.

Tomarty Larkin

By the time I had driven the few miles from the centre of town to
Grange, the skies had cleared again – if only briefly. It was still
bitterly cold.

Joy! (No pun intended.) I was visiting David Joy in his studio
as he had called in the morning, offering an invitation. His iron-
wheeled hut was parked in a corner of his garden under a tree.
I raised the hinged window and glimpsed inside. A number of
articles and historical references were either hanging on hooks or
tacked to the walls, and a putter and some yellow golf balls lay on
the small nearby putting green. One of the plastic-clad photos was
of an old droopy-moustachioed starter of the late 1800s named
'Wingy' Radley, standing inside his box, smoking his pipe and
sipping something. (He was called Wingy because he was missing
an arm.)

David's studio was what I expected from someone with
interests as diverse as his. There were photographs and news
clippings tacked or taped everywhere, including parts of the
ceiling. So many, in fact, that it was nearly impossible to tell the
colour of the wall paint – if, indeed, the walls had ever been
painted. It was neat and tidy, and the large north-facing window
presented a wonderful view of St Andrews: the cathedral grounds
and the remnants of the more than 350-feet-long nave; Cathedral

Year, plus 1700, Horace Hutchinson won the British Amateur
on the Old Course, when it was played in a clockwise direction

Tower, which dates from the twelfth century; and the square St Salvator's tower.

David chatted on about the Box and the political issues that were still floating in the wind. He had nothing new to report, so he went into some detail on his Old Tom Morris scrapbook project, which, he said, he 'compiled' as opposed to 'wrote'. As we were leaving to visit The Grange restaurant, just along from David's house, he opened a wardrobe and said, 'Aye.' An eye closed as he passed me a hanger holding Old Tom Morris's coat and plus fours: the costume for his one-man show. The ensemble was heavier than my golf bag. The deep-green fabric was heavy tweed, thick and coarse, almost like the felt I had seen being 'cured' in a steam vat in Ireland before it was cut and sewn into military overcoats that would reach down to the ankles of a boot-wearing soldier, Napoleon-like. Its most distinguishing characteristic, however, was the smell. Perhaps something organic might have been stashed in its pockets for a too-long period of time and forgotten?

'What's the odour?' I asked, holding the hanger away from me and quickly passing it back to him.

'I've been wondering about that a little myself,' he said. 'Something's gone ripe.'

'Have you checked the pockets?'

'Nae, I'm afraid to know now,' he answered. 'Once I found a mouse living in a pocket.' He coughed a few times and hung the hanger back in the wardrobe.

The weather became wretched again, and by the time I neared the entrance to the hotel, three miles up the A917, the conditions were those that play with one's mind and senses. The sky patterns kept changing as the fronts passed through with pelting rain before moments of total darkness occurred, followed by clear skies featuring stars and a sliver of a quarter moon. It was as if a gauzy scrim kept being lowered and raised across the landscape. A few minutes later, the haar was so thick I missed the turn-off from the road into the hotel's grounds – and it is marked by monumental signage and intense lighting.

CHAPTER 40

THE GOOD, THE BAD
AND THE UGLY

THURSDAY, 8 NOVEMBER 2001: 6.30 A.M.

Scotland and God and golf – the meeting of triumph with
disaster and fate – are not for everyone.

Anonymous

The bone-chilling, even more miserable weather did arrive during
the night as Rob and the farmer's forecast had predicted. While
driving into town, the music on the car's radio was interrupted
by a BBC announcer who reported wind gusts of up to 40 miles
an hour in isolated locations. It was suggested people curtail
driving and wait out the conditions in sheltered areas. Overnight
drifting snow had closed the roads near Braemar in the Cairngorm
mountains, a two-hour drive north.

I knew the Sweet Shoppe would not have opened yet, so I drove
straight to the Old Course and up the first fairway. Coffee and
the papers could wait. Rob's lorry had arrived ahead of me and
the Gang of Six were working, their pace a little quicker than
normal.

'Delay the hot noon meal,' Rob called out as dawn began to
break, at about 8 a.m. His brogue and shivering body accentuated
urgency. 'The good we've had is goantae get tae be the bad and
then the ugly – sooner rather than later. Or we winnae finish and
be ready for the lorry.' He looked pained, like a member of a hastily
assembled wedding party unsure of his role.

I was shocked by how he used the words *good*, *bad* and *ugly*. It
was so foreign to his use of the English language and the way he

Year, plus 1000, that Hugh, excommunicated as Chaplain of
William the Lion, died in Rome

composed his sentences. 'Where did you pick up that . . . ?'

He cut me off. 'The telly: ITV,' he said. 'Clint Eastwood.'

I laughed at his ability to keep a sense of humour.

Fraser and Eddie walked by on their way to an R&A construction trailer, their heads lowered away from St Andrews Bay and the North Sea. 'Aye,' Fraser uttered indifferently. Eddie said nothing, including making any comment on my car being parked on the first tee.

The Gang finished loading the second container at 2.30 p.m. This time, the ceremonial act of photographing and securing the customs bands went unnoticed. The lorry went off as another squall slammed into the Links.

'Let's go!' I yelled, which meant to the Links Clubhouse for the hot lunch I was hosting for Rob and the Gang, and Fraser Smart and Mike Horkan, when the job was finished.

The men sprinted over through the stinging wind and rain, except for Ox, who walked, or almost waddled, as fast as his short legs in unlaced boots allowed.

I drove. As I opened my car door in the clubhouse car park, a blast of wind snapped it from my hand, bending a hinge. The loan of a roll of duct tape from the R&A undertaker would seal the door for the rest of my trip.

Sensing the crew might be intimidated by the clubhouse, I had us seated in the grill instead of the closed-off, more formal dining room. I also pre-ordered the meal to make sure they wouldn't see a menu or the prices.

When I had planned this all out with the restaurant manager early in the morning, I had warned her the workmen were, well, workmen. Their clothing would be filthy, and their language salty. 'Not to worry. It *is* the Box, isn't it?' she had answered with a warm smile.

Lunch included large bowls of very hot vegetable soup, plenty of double cheeseburgers with raw onions, chips, pints of ale and sodas. Nothing steamed. I took a quick glance at the crew when I returned from taking a call at the reception desk. Except for Fraser, no one had removed a jacket or hat to eat. I don't remember that any of them had stopped to wash their hands before going into the grill, either. I was surprised that only Ox and Oban ordered ale, but they made up for the rest. Ox had three pints. Oban bested him with four.

Fraser and I took pictures as a sheet of paper was passed around the table. Each of the crew was free to write a note, if he wished, and sign it, for archive purposes, as I had done with the junior golfers at the Passing of the Keys and with my Saturday foursome. Ox signed his name, breaking the pencil as he added an exclamation mark. Fleet Foot scribbled something unintelligible and hurriedly passed the paper on, as if he were embarrassed and desperate to get rid of it.

At the end of the meal, I shook hands with everyone. It was a struggle. Ringo and Oban nodded politely, their eyes cast downwards, avoiding eye contact. They were clearly uncomfortable with the clubhouse's setting and being among people they must have perceived as of another ilk.

After they left, Fraser and I had a quiet chat. I gave him a gift, a monograph written by my friend, Richard Meier, the architect, on his design for the Getty Museum in Los Angeles.

He blinked at the incongruity. 'I'm not sure the Hut isn't more satisfying,' he said. 'Certainly better people to work with here.' He winked uncharacteristically, and his face rippled.

We vowed to meet again, in Europe, at a Formula One race. He said he would be happy making plans around the Monaco Grand Prix.

I walked him to the reception area. On the way, he reminded me that sophisticated open-cockpit cars were raced on the West Sands well into the 1950s, and the private planes of wealthy golfers were even allowed to land on the beach. After we paused and shook hands again, I bought him a bottle of Old Course whisky as another gift. As he raised the hood of his parka and ran to his car, Alan McGregor came up the stairs from the golf shop.

We went back into the grill, ordered red wine and sat down at a quiet corner table, well away from the staff and other guests. 'Well, how did it go?' he asked politely, not really wanting an answer. 'It is certainly a historic day on the Old Course. You've done it.' We toasted, and he continued. 'Peter tells me you've made some solid strides with the Friends of St Andrews Links project?'

I nodded.

'And I hear you'll be working on the Friends project over the holidays?' He looked at me and answered his own question. 'Good; we can discuss it during the Orlando PGA Merchandise Show, in January.'

'I'll be ready,' I answered just as curtly, knowing that the Christmas and New Year weeks that Claudia and I almost always spent alone were now completely unbooked and available. I was emotionally exhausted. 'We'll continue to keep the project among the three of us. I understand from Peter Mason that not even Carolyne is to know at this juncture.'

'That's right. If I know one thing about you by now, it is that you can be entrusted with confidence and silence, when needed.'

'Thank you.'

'John, I have one more item to discuss with you,' he said, 'and this is in strictest confidence.' He looked around, then waved off the waitress. We instinctively moved our heads closer together.

'Yes?' I said, intrigued.

'We are serious about building a seventh course on a parcel along the coast, on the way to St Andrews Bay. Do you know where the go-cart racetrack is?'

'Of course.'

'I don't have time to go into all the reasons with you now. They can wait until Florida.' He took out a piece of paper that had the names of a number of golf-course architects written on it in his handwriting. 'I can't linger. I must get home to Jane, before the storm worsens.'

'Give her my best.' I had truly enjoyed meeting her at dinner after the 'final round'. I looked at the list. Some of the names were obvious and internationally well known, others were emerging stars. There were a few names I did not recognise.

'Do the Links Trust a favour, will you? See what you can find out about them, particularly those who have recently worked in the States. How they are to work with, the ego issues, sticking to budgets, that sort of thing.' He took a good swallow of wine, looked towards the bar and signalled for two more glasses.

'I'd be honoured,' I said with hesitation, shocked he would confide in me with such an important and politically explosive issue. I swallowed the last of my wine as the fresh glasses arrived.

'You must understand, John, that I'm also asking you to gather press clippings, snapshots and anything else that you may find of import . . .' He looked at me meekly.

'And, I have to do it . . . because I'm there and you're here . . . and Carolyne Nurse, whose job it would be . . . ?'

'Exactly. You told us the Old Course Hut was a part of your give-back to golf, and . . .'

I took a sip of wine, excited by the challenge. 'I have the feeling the "Friends" project is going to wind up costing me a lot of start-up money. And now I'm also a part of the grass-roots work on a seventh course . . . ?'

'Indeed, John, indeed.' He said the words deliberately and quietly. 'I must go. Sorry to surprise you like this. Safe journey and all that. Let's talk next week. Secrecy, John, secrecy. Bye for now.'

We stood up, shook hands firmly and smiled privately, each of us knowing full well the political and financial consequences of building another golf course – especially in view of what we had experienced with the Box. He was out of the room in a flash.

I felt giddy, adrenalin replacing the exhaustion. I drank the rest of my wine and let my rubbery legs guide me to the bar. 'Let's try a negroni again,' I said to Jim Sandell, the bartender I had come to know quite well because of his rather poor attempt at mixology the past Sunday. He paused a moment, then poured a week's ration of vermouth and Campari in a shaker. I kept my mouth shut, except to have him add more gin to the glass when he was finished. I took the concoction back to the table, where I sat in silence and listened to the wonderful misery of the weather. The obscured landscape and its stark contrasts came in and out of focus as the cloud banks opened and closed, reflecting the lights of Dundee and darkness of Carnoustie.

Other music suddenly began dancing through my head. It was the music made by the engineers of the ScotRail trains as they blasted their distinctly sing-song alternate tones of E and G-flat on their horns as they passed the ninth green of Carnoustie at 70 miles an hour. More exhilaration.

CHAPTER 41

···

FAREWELLS

FRIDAY, 9 NOVEMBER 2001: MORNING

Bide a while traveller, here ye'll find – sustance baith fae belly and fae mind – guid ale fae sillar, and a free muckle ill-rede' philosophie.

Anonymous frieze high on the wall of the
Magnum Pub on Albany Street in Edinburgh

I started my morning rounds for the last time in a rather pleasant drizzle, stopping first at J&G Innes for the newspapers, being the newspaperaholic I am. I had the *International Herald Tribune*, *The Scotsman*, the *Northern Times*, the *Press and Journal*, *The Times* and the St Andrews papers saved for me every day. The clerk and I had our normal guarded, polite conversation. I thanked her for opening for an hour the past Monday, Guy Fawkes Day, so the locals could buy the papers.

'Thank you, and good luck with the Hut,' she said dutifully, and bashfully, communicating more with her smile than with her words.

I smiled quietly, knowing I had never told her who I was. The soft tinkling of the shop's bell followed me as I closed the door.

Heather Paterson, the young architect I had met who worked for Fraser Smart, nearly walked into me as I was about to cross the street.

'Mr Hagen,' she boomed apologetically as my papers fell to the pavement.

'Good morning, Heather . . . no matter,' I said, picking them up and tucking them under my arm. 'What brings you to St Andrews on a Friday morning?'

Her face flushed from embarrassment as she adjusted the roll of drawings she was carrying. She casually offered words I had not heard before. 'University meetin', Raisin Sunday an' the Kate Kennedy pageant.'

'Huh?'

'Aye, a lot o' tradition at the university. The Kate Kennedy pageant is in April. The students dress up as distinguished, and not so distinguished, town an' university authorities. All in honour o' Kate Kennedy, who, so legend has it, was the beautiful niece of the university's founder. Early students supposedly swore her everlasting loyalty an' fidelity.'

'Interesting. Would you like a coffee?'

'That would be nice, but I am in a wee time-bind. I'll walk with ye an' order a takeaway, if I may?'

'Of course.'

We walked towards the Sweet Shoppe. 'This Rite of Spring, as some call it, was banned in 1881 because o' rowdiness. It came back tae life in 1926. Kate is always played by a first-year male student; we call him the *bejant* – which means he's in drag.'

'Two years after the Box was built,' I interjected.

'Really? University dates from 1410, I think. Students were admitted in medieval times at the age of 13. Church needed priests.' Her voice was uncaring. 'Raisin Day is this Sunday, though usually ignored except as an excuse for a flour-and-egg fight, a toast tae the haggis and getting drunk on whisky – as is our national day, St Andrews Day, on 30 November.'

'Oh?' I caught the smell of peppermints and tobacco on her breath.

'It is supposed tae be the day the third-year students become academic parents. Ha!'

'I have happened to be here on the May Sunday morning of the Pier March. The students walking along the seafront in their red robes is quite impressive.'

'Ye've noticed the tradition with the scarlet gowns, have ye?' she said, her eyes crinkling in amusement.

'I have, but I don't understand the lackadaisical attitude . . . or should I say "slovenly"?'

'Oh, that's university tradition; tradition is revered. First-year students always wear them prim and proper, whether in class or town. In the second year, one shoulder will be bare o' the robe,

First-round score, minus 130, of Craig Stadler in the Open Championship, Royal Birkdale, 1983 in the third, both. By the time of graduation, the gown is mostly tied around your waist and draggin' on the ground, if worn at all.'

'I thought it might be the dons who . . . ?'

'Nae. Tradition also says there is supposed to be a dawn swim in St Andrews Bay preceding Sunday services, but that doesn't happen so often any longer. Bloody cold, the North Sea is.'

'Any other titbits for me?' I asked, as I opened the door to the Sweet Shoppe.

'Need a month's time to tell ye o' the pranks,' she said, implying she had plenty of stories – with herself involved – to tell me, in due time, if I was interested.

The four questioning eyes of Lucy and Sophie greeted us as Lucy laughingly said: 'Mr Hagen. You naughty. You naughty laddie!'

Embarrassed, I introduced Heather as she ordered herself a hurried cappuccino.

'What do you mean?' I asked, putting the papers on the counter as I ordered a highly illegal Highlands coffee for the first time.

'Why have you avoided us for two days?' Sophie teased, as she brought me my soda rolls and an extra pat of butter. 'You're famous!'

Heather looked at me inquiringly. 'Better be off before the authorities are called,' she kidded, 'and ye hae me choking on me biscuit. See you soon. Till then.'

'Bye.' I waved as she left the shop, smiling impishly at me as she did so. 'Wha . . . ?' I stopped to think as I turned back to the girls. 'Well, yesterday we started work at six thirty, before you were open, and Wednesday . . . I had a breakfast meeting with the Trust's architect at the Links Clubhouse. And, Tuesday . . .'

'Of course you did,' they teased. They told me Katie had been waiting at their door on Tuesday morning when they arrived. 'Hurry,' she had said. 'I need a double Highlands to take with me to the library.'

'Katie blamed it on "the bloody Box, the bloody Box",' Sophie said, laughing.

'Aye, and we worked out the rest, we did,' Lucy added. 'Had shrapnel in her stomach, she did.'

'You would know, Sophie. Better than most,' I said, assuming the worst.

She put her hands on her hips. Lucy followed with the same motion, as only women can do when they assume a suggestive stance. 'Thanks for inviting us, Mr Hagen,' they chimed again. 'Thanks a lot. No spot-ons for you!'

It was impossible to keep a straight face. After things calmed down and they had tended to other customers, Sophie made herself a coffee, reached up to a shelf for a tin of biscuits and plopped herself on the stool next to me. Lucy took the tin and with a practised hand pried open the cover to a musical-sounding *twang* as the metal was twisted. The wonderful crunching of waxed paper being unfolded was next. She held it out.

'Ah, the joy of shortbread – slathered with chocolate and caramel – and a "corrected" coffee at nine in the morning,' I said, taking a biscuit.

'A wee mornin' sugar-load.'

'The added wee dram is a nice touch, is it not? Yummy,' Sophie added, bobbing her head in pleasure. 'Dinnae like ye leavin' us. If I may ask, who were the other bidders at the end?'

'It's interesting you ask,' I said, 'because in the twenty-three days I've been here dealing with the Box, over the past four weeks, no one else has, including the media. There were five or six of us still in the bidding in the last ten minutes, I think, but at the end, only two. The Danes – a Danish golf club – and us. The Japanese and American conglomerates and golf resorts weren't in the bidding at the end; actually, I really don't know if they were in the bidding early on.'

I looked to Lucy, who was opening a large bag of vacuum-packed coffee beans. The aroma was overwhelming. 'I must tell you that I was terrified at the end. My fingers weren't able to type a bid raise on my computer's keyboard fast enough. I kept missing keys and was worried about the time lag between my hitting "send" and the Trust receiving my bid, or about my dial-up connection being dropped. I finally called the Trust near the end to ask if we could bid by phone.'

A gaggle of Madras College pupils came in for coffees. I scanned the front pages of the papers while they were attended to. When they left, I took a bite of shortbread. 'After Mr McGregor announced I had won the auction, he congratulated me and told me to celebrate. I was slumped in my chair, exhausted and sweating – wearing only a bathrobe, mind you. As I think back on it, I told him that even in

California, at four in the morning, on a warm September day, there were few options if one wanted to celebrate.'

'In Hollywood?'

'Well, Lucy, I'm sure you could find some interesting trouble at that hour.'

'Not sure,' she beamed, 'but it would be fun tryin'.'

I laughed, then went on with my story. 'You are funny, Lucy, you really are. I called the project manager of the Country Club, Nancy Aaronson, and woke her. At first she didn't believe the news. I didn't blame her. Then I went back to bed. The birds outside in the trees started chirping. Sleep was not an option. I read some more of the morning newspaper and finally called Mr McGregor back, but he was at lunch – and celebrating the sale, I was sure. When he called me back, I told him to expect me in Scotland in two days' time. Of course, that didn't happen. The next day was 9/11.'

She passed the biscuits again, obviously wanting to hear more.

'I don't want to pry, but how much higher were you prepared to bid?' Sophie said.

'Another question I have not been asked. At the beginning . . . £55,000 ($110,000), or £4,000 less than my final bid; I went over. Guessing the character of the developer, Jack Franks, I gambled that a few thousand pounds more wouldn't matter – in the grand scheme of things – if I had to up the ante and bluff my way a little longer. How much higher would I have gone? I have wrestled with that question. At the time, probably another four or five thousand. As I look back at it, in the grand plan of marketing, probably another five thousand above that. So, probably up to £70,000 or £75,000, which would have put it in the $150,000 range.'

'Aye.' She blushed, accentuating what was running through her mind. 'His money; your instinct. How do you justify the expense?' she asked. 'Katie started to tell us, but her head was . . .'

I laughed, thinking of the evening with Katie. 'It is all for marketing, lassies – evaluating her as an icon as opposed to the use of an eccentric celebrity. To us, it's all about capitalising on Scotland's wonderful history and heritage of golf and exploiting it through the Box, the totally unique, only-one-in-the-world icon she is. She will draw golfers to the project and sell memberships and home sites and generate a level of positive publicity that's unobtainable at any price.'

'Hmm. Still need a photo of you, we do.'

'Oops. I'm glad you said that.' I opened my briefcase, took out a photo of Mr McGregor and me and the juniors – the same photo that was in the newspaper – and signed it.

Sophie found a tack and on the wall it went, next to the tacked and taped business cards and student want ads.

Lucy put the cover on the tin and handed it to me. 'Our gift. Visit us again soon.' Their smiles lit up the room.

'I shall.' We hugged and kissed each other naturally, the kiss of Lucy being a little more elaborate than necessary. My takeaway Highlands coffee and newspapers in hand, I started to leave. 'By the way, ladies, a night out on me during my next trip is a given.' I caught the glow of their beaming faces once again. 'Tell Katie it wasn't the bottles of claret and the rusty nails that did her in. It was her dessert. It was the double order of Key-lime toffee cheesecake and the trifle.'

The tinkling of the door's bell followed me into the street. I looked in the window one last time. Sophie was holding her hands to her throat, mimicking gagging.

I had breakfast in the Links Clubhouse, then walked to Grannie Clark's Wynd to take final photographs of the vista, barren of the Box and with nothing there but roughly graded mounded earth that looked like a grave site. The very gut and soul of the vista had been stripped away. A heavy, dense haar floated in from the sea, without a breeze to hurry it along. I blinked. Did I see the shadow of Old Tom Morris pass through the Valley of Sin and down the fairway, his head bowed? Did I hear a solitary drum banging slowly? Did I hear a piper somewhere? I shuddered. The R&A was barely visible. Any picture-taking was futile. Perhaps it was fitting. The theatre that held golf's greatest stage had gone dark.

I drove back into town and passed by the offices of *The Citizen*. They had enlarged the photograph of the Passing of the Keys ceremony and prominently displayed it in their window.

I parked the car, put my parking card on the dashboard and went to the photo shop to pay my bill and collect my Christmas cards. (Mike Joy had never asked for a deposit and never asked me to pay up whenever I was in his shop and needing one thing or another.) 'When we've finished the job,' he always said. I looked at the bill. Something was missing. He hadn't included a fee for all the time he had spent taking photographs for us. I pointed it out.

'Film-selling and developing I do here. It's my only business. Remember?'

We shook hands. I left to the sound of his shop's ringing bell as a tear drifted from my eye.

In the window of a spirits store across the street, there was an enticing display of single-malt whisky. I walked over to take a look. Twenty-three days in St Andrews, spread out over a month, with much continuing ceremony, and not one dram of whisky consumed, except by me in the Sweet Shoppe – and by Oban, I found out, when I paid the Gang's lunch tab. (He had had the waitress bring him quick double gills during the lunch while I was called to the telephone at reception.) Not even in a toast. No bagpipes heard, either. I decided the music of St Andrews may well be the sound of weather, the tinkling of shop bells, the pealing of shorebirds and the sharp *whack* of a golf ball when it leaves the club face and rises up over the linksland.

My next stop was at J&T Rodger (now shuttered), on South Street, to buy oats. The little shop was surely singularly unique in retailing as it sold cat and bird food along with many styles of shortbread, oatcakes and' other made-from-grain products. I know nothing about the quality of the cat and bird food, but their oats made the best oatmeal and oatcakes I've ever had: ever. (Ah, the oatcakes . . . when spread with a room-temperature Stilton cheese.) I left, as I always did, with an assortment of biscuits and cakes and four two-kilo packages of thick-cut oats for myself and friends in the US. Think of the joy of explaining to a US Customs official, in the aftermath of 9/11, why you're travelling with nine pounds of oatmeal, when he notices that Rodger's packaging is nothing more than a hand-stamped simple white-paper bag that has been sealed with a piece of adhesive tape.

My final piece of business was to pay my bill at Luvians Bottle Shop – the independent drinks specialist, as opposed to Luvians Ice Cream Parlour and cafe. Both are on Market Street, near the fountain. They had courteously offered me the same credit relationship as had Mike Joy.

I was surprised to see Angus standing outside the shop, talking to a hunter who held a fine brace of ducks. He called me over and introduced us. The smell of the man – and his spent shotgun-shell cartridges, still in his pockets, dried duck blood, grain stalks and caked mud on his boots – took me back to my youth and hunting with my father and friends. The smells of the earth.

'Aye, where were ye this mornin'?' Angus continued.

'A pond, near Ladybank, on the spinney side,' the hunter said coyly, without adding even a hint of the location. 'Now they're going to Murray Mitchell for a proper dressing.'

'You'll do well to leave Murray's butcher shop with a haggis or two,' Angus suggested. 'They looked mighty fine when I passed by a wee bit ago.'

'Aye, two for the Sunday hot meal,' the man answered, as he doffed his cap, shook my hand and walked across the square.

Angus's eyes followed the hunter until he paused at Murray's window and then disappeared into his shop. 'Autumn hunting in Scotland: 'tis a cause for excitement, laddie, though I'm in no mood for a walk on the moors today.'

'No?'

'Nae, but shooting is very good for business. Today should be a £3,000 day for us between the Scottish moors for grouse and the Cotswolds . . . on Lady Sarah's farm down there.' A disdainful nod was directed towards England.

We went into Luvians. Three cases of wine and a case of Hendrick's gin were stacked near the till. 'Weekend provisions,' he said, grunting a little and smiling. Angus was wearing a heavy-wool hunting kilt.

'Thanks for inviting me,' I said glibly.

'Aye, not enough lassies to go around,' he answered, without missing a beat. His rolling eyes betrayed his attempt to be serious. 'You're welcome to a wee nosy, however. If it suits.' He straightened his tam. 'But I'll tell, er . . . I was going to say Claudia. Sorry.'

'No offence. I have to get used to it.'

Then, as if it were premeditated, he tore open the cardboard flap of the case of gin, took out a bottle, cracked the seal with his thumbnail and twisted open the cork. We toasted the Box with warm gin, poured neat and drunk from paper cups.

'Thank you,' I said to Angus and the bottle shop's staff. 'Thank you.' I held my cup in the air.

'Don't think you'll be celebratin' this way in the States,' he said, as he locked his eyes on mine, understanding my loneliness without Doc there to share the occasion with me.

I laughed recklessly in acknowledgement.

'Aye, a perfect reason for a wee nip at ten on a Friday mornin', 'tis.'

We went out to his Land Rover together, a shop boy following with the order on a trolley.

'Take good care of her, and her label,' he said, with a hint of remorse mixed in his brogue. 'You've got a bloody national treasure on your hands, you have. A sporting icon that can't be duplicated. Enjoy the next chapter of your crusade.'

'How well I know.' I promised him her safety.

He shook my hand. 'Keep workin' hard enough to stay ahead of the next surprise.' He laughed. 'I'm off to the Jubilee Links. No Hut on the Old. A sacrilege. A bloody sacrilege.'

He opened the door to his Land Rover slowly, as if he were thinking about changing his mind about where he was going next. 'The autumn season in Fife is the last time the pace of country living is lively, ye know, before the miserable winter weather arrives. Speakin' of the autumn, the rolled-straw bales you asked about that are out in the fields? Near a half-ton in dead weight, they are. Dry. Wet is another issue entirely. Hmm . . .' He looked to the sky. The drizzle had turned to dull grey penetrating rain.

I knew him well enough to know that he was wondering and questioning if this day was to be the last good one for both hunting and golf. 'Do both, my lord,' I said. 'A walk on the Links, and in the fields and moors for pheasants or a stray mallard, are always a fine way to spend the day – to paraphrase Will, who says it so much more eloquently with his brogue and burr mixed in.'

'Aye.' Angus smiled, fired the engine and lowered the window. 'The treatment the game gave me yesterday, the *golff* may not be an option. Some days it's a bloody waste of beautiful land to have it serve as a madman's sport. Don't want to lose my sense of humour for the weekend.'

I offered a hand. Angus took it in both his hands. 'Thank you, Angus,' I said. 'Thank you.' My eyes started to tear.

He tightened his grip and looked me square in the eyes. 'Aye, ye only live once, laddie; but if you work it right, once is enough.'

CHAPTER 42

··

PARIS AND GALLIC AMBIVALENCE

SATURDAY, 10 NOVEMBER 2001:
LATE AFTERNOON

We are Boston, Glasgow is Cleveland.

John McKay, Lord Provost of Edinburgh 1984–8

On the way back to California, I detoured through Paris for a few days of decompression and reflection. To me, that means seeking adventure and assuming the role of the stravaiger, as they say in Scotland's Highlands: one who strolls or wanders aimlessly. Or, the word the French use, thanks to Charles Baudelaire: *flâneur*: as in to wander and discover the city. (Somehow the work *trek* does not have a nice 'ring' to it in Paris.)

The city and its citizens, as they are so practised at and capable of doing, were managing once again to ignore any events, local or international, that did not have an impact upon the availability of their regular morning chair in the neighbourhood *café*. Classic Gallic indifference.

It was difficult to fathom that freedom was at war with an unknown adversary and have most of the rest of the world call it 'our' war. At least that's how French television was to ascribe it on the Saturday-night news – *their* (America's) war. The 9/11 story was the third item on the television news. Bad weather in Algeria was the lead story; another toe-stumbling by Lionel Jospin's government was second. A disturbing amount of ambivalence was floating through the democracies.

One night, under the late glow of the southern sky, I happened to be passing the George V hotel as I walked towards the Seine and the Left Bank. It brought back the memory of Claudia and our having Christmas dinner there one year. Seated in the bar at a table near us were the infamous televangelists Jim Bakker and his wife Tammy Faye. We had laughed about it as we sipped our aperitifs. A little while later, I happened to be in the men's room attending to business when Jim came in and stood at the stall next to me. I couldn't resist.

'Business must be good,' I said, laughing, as I commented on how expensive the hotel was. He did not think I was funny. His face turned beet red, and he left without washing his hands.

CHAPTER 43

....

US CUSTOMS

MONDAY, 10 DECEMBER 2001

It requires a surgical operation to get a joke well into a
Scotch understanding.

Sydney Smith

The shipping containers arrived in the Port of Los Angeles, on 9
December, nearly three months to the day after the auction, but
because they were not 'Military Priority', they would be delayed in
customs processing.

In anticipation of potential customs-clearing problems, caused
by 9/11, Alan McGregor and I discussed the language of the
manifests and Bill of Sale at length. In the end, we used similar
language to what I had used for the full-size wood replica of a
NASA Shuttle that my company purchased during my Mitsubishi
joint-venture days, and we shipped from Canada to the US. The
Bill of Sale stated the purchase was:

> disassembled and salvaged, used building materials with no
> reuse value and limited historic value. The building materials
> are not for resale and are promotional items only . . .

On 13 December, I received a telephone call from a customs
inspector who wanted to ask me a few questions. I answered
simply and cautiously. In passing he said the contents had survived
the voyage 'in good shape'. None of the windows was broken and
only a few sections of banded bricks had split. The brick panels
had been individually strapped together with metal bands. He
asked about the grass.

'What grass?' I responded. My mind focused on the final loading, in near darkness and terrible weather. I remembered Eddie Adams had taken his crew off the Old Course early that day and that the R&A undertaker had sent everyone home at noon. I also remembered the putting-green sod was neatly stacked out on the first fairway. Had the lads at the last minute included a few pieces of sod in the container – to consecrate the Box and give California a bit of living Scotland?

They had. The inspector told me that his agents had taken one of the squares of sod, filleted it lengthwise and tested it to see if there were drugs hidden inside. He wanted me to come down and inspect the containers with a fellow officer. I asked if he was a golfer.

He said, 'No; hate the game. Why?'

I did not like the tone of his voice. 'Are any of your fellow officers golfers?' I sensed a problem.

'Mmm. Ya, I think Fenton is. Why do ya ask? Hold on a minute.' (Ah, the humanity in this man.) He yelled, 'Hey, Fenton, you're a golfer, ain't ya?'

I heard a muffled, 'Absolutely, why?'

'Fenton is.'

'May I speak with him, please?'

'Ah, ya, I guess so . . . Fenton, talk to this guy Hagen, will ya? Something's strange. Here are the papers.'

'Fenton here.' The tone of voice was no-nonsense, as you'd expect given what had been going on in the world over the past few months.

'You're a golfer?'

'Love the game.' He warmed. 'What can I do for you?'

'Ever been to St Andrews?'

'Only in my dreams.' He paused. I heard papers rustling. 'Are you the guy that bought that thing in Scotland?' There was excitement in the voice; suddenly he had a reason to cast off the routine humdrum of his job. 'Un-effin'-believable.'

'That's me, and that's why I was called by your assoc–'

He interrupted. 'Hey, Charlie, I'll handle this. This is great stuff. Well, Mr Hagen, what have we here?' He spoke directly into the phone.

'Apparently the crew in Scotland decided to have a little fun with me.' I held my head in my hands and spoke as clearly and calmly as I could.

'Ever had anything like this happen to you before?' I heard papers being shuffled again.

'Well, yes, as a matter of fact,' I said, seizing the opening. 'Do you recall Ocean Trails a couple years ago, when they had their little problem?'

'Oh, ya, hee, hee, over on the Palos Verdes Peninsula, wasn't it, when the eighteenth hole fell down the palisade and into the ocean? The one Donald Trump owns now.'

'Yes. I was co-chairman of the Nordic Cup charity tournament that was to be the first event on the course. I've never had a tournament cancelled on me because a hole fell in the ocean before. Sometimes you need more than a Plan A and a Plan B.'

Fenton laughed. 'That's a funny one. Nothing is ever what it seems to be, is it? Not in business and not in sports, with all the drugs they're takin' these days.'

'Not in sex either.'

Fenton laughed again. 'You're right about that. There is no such thing as ordinary sex, is there? Murphy's in the bedroom, too. I just hope not mine, if you know what I mean . . .' He guffawed at his own joke.

'Actually,' I said, laughing with him, 'I believe a divine order will sort out everything in life eventually, though the way people today live their lives, it seems unlikely.'

He hissed and said nothing more as I heard pages being flipped again. He asked a few questions about Scotland and St Andrews.

I told him he would be invited to the Country Club when the Box was dedicated. 'Bring your clubs with you.'

'Much obliged.'

The Box and the sod cleared customs without further incident. In passing, I thought I should give him another piece of information, so I said: 'In casual conversation, the Old Course green-keeper told me none of the Old Course Links had been treated with any fertilisers or chemicals – for at least the last ten years, anyway. In case California's Department of Agriculture wants to know or has to sign off.'

'Don't worry. You think I'm gonna call the farmer boys on this? They'd think I was effin' nuts!' He let out a belly laugh.

Address on South Street where Robert B. 'Buff' Wilson, a professional golfer, sold used golf clubs for 2s. 6d. and up

CHAPTER 44

JACK FRANKS – REPRISE

FRIDAY, 14 DECEMBER 2001

We often find out what will do, by finding out what will not do; and probably he who never made a mistake never made a discovery.

Samuel Smiles

Nancy Aaronson and I met at the Port of Los Angeles the next morning. Inspector Fenton joined us as we walked into a quarantine area, where he unlocked and swung open the heavy steel doors to the Box's two containers. Nancy and I excitedly peered into the caverns. 'You two look like kids about to enter a toy store,' he said.

'In a way, you're correct,' I said, as my eyes adjusted to the dim lighting conditions and my mind raced back to the final day of loading.

With officious flair, he helped Nancy climb a ladder up to the floor of one of the containers. She stepped inside. 'This is it?' she asked, as she turned and looked down at me, a bewildered expression on her face.

I laughed as I scanned what I could see of the masonry pallets, a half-section of the roof and the banded roof tiles. 'This is part of it, Nancy. There *is* another container. I warned you she wouldn't be pretty.'

'I suppose it would be impolite to say that I have been in construction yards that are more organised than this.'

'I told you working and packing conditions the last day were close to impossible.'

'Thank God for stucco,' she said with a shaking of her head, as

Fenton helped her back down the ladder. 'The desert's answer to ivy.'

'Actually, she has been packed very well,' Fenton interjected. 'A couple of split pallets – minor stuff, really – but look over there, Miss, against the wall of the container. The sign is in perfect condition. Not a scratch. None of the sash has been damaged and all window glass has survived without so much as a crack. Very unusual, not that I've had a lot of huts come through the port to compare her with.' He cackled at his comment and reached up for a square of sod. 'Hairy mass of turf, isn't it? Needs a good mowing. Sorry we had to tear it up a bit . . . the drug issue, as you know.' He nodded to Nancy. 'Without it being listed on the manifest, we had no choice.'

'It will all grow back normally,' I said assuredly.

'Right. Some water and fertiliser, and in a few months, good as new.' Fenton ran a hand over the grassy surface, then held it out to Nancy. 'Go ahead, touch it. It won't bite. This is sacred turf.'

Nancy eyed him as she slowly ran her hand through the grass. 'This is centuries of history.'

'You're right, Miss. Not many people can say they've done what you just did.' He flipped the square back into the container and wiped the dirt on his hands off on his trousers. 'Well, that about does it for me. I must get back to my office. Stay as long as you like. Just sign out with security at the gate. And thank you for inviting me to the rededication. I'll be there.' He shook our hands and left.

Nancy looked back up at the sign. 'Amazing to think we own all this . . . all this "stuff". Amazing.'

'Rob and I blanket-wrapped the sign before we duct-taped it to the wall of the container behind the roof section. It will be as important to your club, as a label and validation of your connection to St Andrews, as the Box will be, over the long run. It's priceless as a graphic, especially with the Links Trust logo smack in the middle and prominent. Your members and their guests will mention it every time they prepare to play golf. They'll never tire of boasting about it. It's a validation like that of ancient kings when they dripped a bit of hot wax on a document and then stamped and sealed it with the crest of their rings.'

'No one knows if Geoffrey Beene is dead or still designing clothing, but they do know the label. Same with Yves Saint Laurent.'

JACK FRANKS – REPRISE

'You are absolutely correct,' I said with emphasis. 'The same with the labels of René Lacoste or Jack Kramer in the tennis world.' I put my foot on a ladder rung as a gentle sea breeze blew across the container docks, and I again strove to comprehend what had been accomplished.

Nancy's mobile phone rang. She unhooked it from the holster attached to her belt and said in her jolly voice, 'This is Nancy.' Slowly, her usual smile froze – and her face became ashen and despondent-looking. Then her mouth became contorted and twisted as the phone fell from her hand to the weed-speckled pavement, and she started sobbing. I heard a faint, 'Nancy, Nancy,' coming from the phone as I picked it up.

Two short knockout sentences sputtered from her mouth as if fired from a shotgun. 'Jack Franks was arrested this morning! The FBI and our lender have shut down the project. They've locked the gates!'

I was stunned. 'What the f . . . ?' I couldn't believe what I had heard. 'You gotta be fu . . .'

She cut me off. 'Fucking kidding?' She grabbed her phone from my hand. '$5,000,000 is missing!'

'Fuck!' My foot slid down from a ladder rung of the container.

'They want me back: now.'

Her sobbing slowed as her mind raced. Instinctively I offered my handkerchief. 'Any inkling?' I asked meekly, the question clearly out of place.

'None.' Her raven-black hair was caught by an eddy of air, accentuating her open, dry mouth as if it were an image from Munch's *The Scream* or a Francis Bacon 'Pope', when he realises there is no God.

'The Box?' I asked tritely, with black humour, as I felt my body shudder.

'At least you and I were smart enough,' she said with tears in her voice, 'to prepay the shipping and delivery.' Her tongue twisted in dismay. 'If the Feds allow her onto the property.'

'They will,' I said, thinking quickly as I collected myself. 'It's an asset. If Jack is as smart as I think he is, I'd bet a nickel he has it on the books for what he believes is a *true* value.'

'Huh?' She steadied herself on my shoulder.

'Who knows? The Box has to be a private joy for him in this

scenario, doesn't it?' I answered my own question as I started shivering from uneasiness. 'If he doesn't know the value, no one does. No one can dispute him. Crafty!'

'Fuck you.'

CHAPTER 45

··

NOSTALGIA

SEPTEMBER 2002

O Scotia! My dear, my native soil!
For whom my warmest wish to heaven is sent;
Long may thy hardy sons of rustic toil
Be blest with health, and peace, and sweet content.

Robert Burns

Peter Mason was in California in September 2002, nearly a year to the day after the auction, visiting Links Trust licensees. 'She is,' I said to Peter when he inquired about the Box as we drove away from LAX, where I had met him, as he was staying in my home, 'still locked in a barn, still in a coma – still a Rip Van Winkle.' I added that I had also heard that Jack Franks was on an extended 'vacation' courtesy of the Federal government. (During Jack's trial and conviction, it became clear that Nancy was squeaky clean. She was never involved in any of the incendiary activities of Jack. Her reputation remains untarnished.)

'All this means there is no reason to visit La Quinta?'

'That's right. Instead of golf, consider Philharmonic tickets.'

'Less aggravation,' he answered with a smile.

'Nationwide Realty Investors, the lender, and the new developer, Discovery Land, are rebranding the project as the "Hideaway". Unfairly to the new developer, the local wags, in jest, have already renamed the project "Club Takeaway" because the rumours have been that, in addition to the misappropriated monies when it was the Country Club of the Desert, stockpiled plumbing and electrical supplies also seemed to vanish – often the night of the day they were delivered.'

'How do you think this will impact the Box? We're concerned for her "safety", as you have often said.'

'Privately, I am working to ascertain the viability of having the City of La Quinta purchase the Box and grant the developer a tax consideration. The city is building a municipal golf course, named SilverRock, which will be a rota course for the Bob Hope Desert Classic. I think it a perfect fit. It would put the Box back in a public facility similar to St Andrews, and it will be available to all golfers, including juniors.'

'Interesting.'

'So far my idea is falling on deaf ears. I don't mean it as a bad omen, but don't get your hopes up. The city wants any reconstruction to include a sprinkler system, handicap access, earthquake-code recognition . . . all totally unrealistic for the Box, given her size, historical value and usage.'

The next day I took a picture of Peter standing alongside my XK8 Jaguar, holding the keys in a 'mocked' simulation of the Passing of the Keys ceremony. 'Just like you and Alan at the Box,' he said, before wryly adding irony to the equation, with: 'They both cost about the same.' Spoken like a true Yorkshireman. He was right.

After he finished mocking me and my personalised licence plate – STAOCSB – I told him I was replacing it because I was tired of being stopped, even by the police on one occasion, and asked what it meant. Few, even in the creative capital of the world, were ever able to put meaning to the letters. (The new plate – FIFEHUT – didn't stay on my car very long, either. It was stolen from the car one night while I was having dinner in a Beverly Hills restaurant.)

I returned to St Andrews in November 2002, for a Links Trust meeting that formalised the formation of the non-profit organisation the Friends of St Andrews Links. (The purpose of Friends is to raise tax-deductible funds from golfers and sports enthusiasts around the world. All proceeds go to aiding the Links Trust in the restoration and maintenance of the Old Course.)

When I drove into town from my hotel, I detoured onto Grannie Clark's Wynd. Nostalgia was a reason, of course, but I also wanted to see the new box from the middle of the fairway. I was shocked and appalled. It looked as if a building had been constructed, then whacked in half by Ox and his power saw. Ugly. I felt chilled: the same chill I had felt when Nancy received the telephone call about Jack Franks. The images of that scene suddenly unfolded again in my mind, but in slow motion, as if I were watching a duel being played out on a dusty street in an old Western movie.

Angry, I instinctively drove to the Sweet Shoppe, anticipating the fresh conversation and the gossip of Lucy and Sophie, but also because I felt a definite need for a Highlands coffee, properly corrected.

Alas, the Sweet Shoppe was no more. A retail shop was in its place. Neither the shop manager, nor those of the adjacent shops, knew where the girls had flitted off.

In a pub with Peter Mason later that day, however, near the West Port of South Street, the only fortified gateway to survive in Scotland and which had been rebuilt in 1589, the barman said he understood Lucy had moved to Edinburgh with a freshly found boyfriend who had a bit of money, and that Sophie was in Australia. (One travels to Australia to 'dry out'? I asked myself.) I am still so disheartened by their disappearance that I, to this day, don't remember what the new shop *sells*.

(The recession has caused the shuttering of other shops since November 2002, as well. Ian Joy's photography shop is gone, as I noted earlier, after 60 years in business, as is J&T Rodger, though the company's shop in Cupar remains open for oats-buying. Murray Mitchell, the butcher in business in St Andrews for over 80 years, has also closed. Ill-health is said to be the cause. Luvians? Open for business, of course.

Alas, Prince William and his friend Kate Middleton, who were often familiar figures in Murray's queue, as the prince was said to have enjoyed Mitchell's steak pies, have now graduated from university.)

Epilogue

4 DECEMBER 2009

The shortest way out of Scotland is a bottle of whisky.

Anonymous

Passion is what lifts us above daily life. It makes us more open, more human, more refined and, sometimes, even more intelligent. It is a way to go forwards and accept that, to do so, we must often go backwards first if we want to clear our hearts.

It is the beauty of the tango: the opposition – the push and pull – the stop and start. It is the song of sex and death and how we say goodbye to one and prepare ourselves for the other.

It is the seeking of the perfect round of golf on the Old Course.

It is all this before I mention the weather.

Indeed, the Old Course Links sod survived the five-week journey by lorry, railway and sea-going freighter to California without watering. It did not die in transit. Instead, it grew over four inches. (I made a note to email Malcolm Campbell and tell him he needed to revise his definition of linksland. He needed to work in the phrase 'tenacious and drought-resistant'.) It was replanted in an area around the first tee of the Pete Dye golf course at the Hideaway in 2002. It flourished and now, seven years later, it is mostly indistinguishable from the other fescue.

Portions of the Box are finally being integrated into an 18-hole putting course at the private and upscale Madison Club in La Quinta, California. It is due to open in February 2010. This will be, in Old Course-speak, their 'Himalayas'.

'Portions of the Box?' you ask.

Yards, plus 7,000, of the 2002 US Open at Bethpage State P ark, Black Course

Yes, because, Scott Birdwell, business manager of the Discovery Land Company, developer of the Madison Club, told me, some time between 2002 and 2006, the roof was mysteriously 'gifted' to a local church. (Don't ask your next obvious question because I don't know the answer either.) For now, let's just say it may have been part of the 'Club Takeaway' programme. Much of the brickwork and the slate roof tiles are intact and will be incorporated into a 'Putter Box', or Hut, for lack of a better name, at the moment. The sign – the label – will be prominently displayed. It will be a shrine to integrity and fair play in sports.

Icons, labels, celebrity, athletes (dead and alive)? As Katie and I discussed at length, consider the alternatives in view of the Tiger Woods stories of December 2009.

The cost of the 'new' Old Course Box, including the piling required because of a ground shift under the R&A, was about £75,000 ($150,000). The total costs involved with purchase, dismantling, shipping and reconstruction of the Old Course Starter's Box have approached £400,000 ($800,000). £475,000 ($950,000) for the icon – and its proven provenance? Minor, I believe, when compared to what Mr Woods may be paying in legal fees, public-relations damage control and who knows what else, at this moment. The potential cost of possible endorsement blemishing? To be determined.

People continue to ask me about my passion for the Box, and whether it has been worth the trauma and sacrifice. I answer: '*Of course!*' My dream of saving the iconic label and Box, if partially, in spirit only, was realised – not the way I programmed it, I admit, but then who amongst us has had their dreams of glory and grandeur fulfilled as imagined?

Yes, I continue to say: 'Go confidently in the direction of your dreams. Indeed, we should all dream more, especially when we are awake – and we should more often go in the direction of those dreams. Kites rise in the sky against the wind. Live the life you've imagined. Life is a magnificent wilderness. Lighten up, put some fun in your life and give of yourself to others and to charity. Be part of a fairy tale. Break with tradition. Push the envelope and, to paraphrase Sophie again – as her eyes sparkled – "*spread some happy dust*".'

Play an extra nine holes, even if it is in the haar, at dusk and in a stiffening breeze. You may even come across Davey, my caddie

when I was in St Andrews with Claudia, out on the Links, looking
for two right shoes.

> Ye'll tak' the high road,
> and I'll tak' the low road,
> And I'll be in Scotland afore ye,
> But me and my true love
> will never meet again,
> On the bonnie, bonnie banks
> o' Loch Lomond.

Anonymous

APPENDIX: THE HOLES
OF THE OLD COURSE

How does one play the Old Course? The answer is, of course, that there is no absolute answer to the question. Even after the golfer arrives at the first tee and assesses the day's weather, his frame of mind and the golf swing he happens to possess that day will affect his game. And then conditions will certainly change throughout the round. On no other course I have played is the game of golf such an uncertain journey.

I highly recommend the hire of a caddie and the purchase of a Links Trust course guide, or, at least reading the Hole Guide on the Trust's website, from which my comments are adapted. A caddie, with his course knowledge, stories and lore, will add an incalculable level of enjoyment to your round. He, or she, will probably also point out the nearly hidden tees that are used for the Open Championship and will be sure to mention Tiger Woods's four rounds in 2000, when his ball never found a bunker!

I hope my general observations will contribute to the enjoyment of your round.

HOLE 1: BURN
370 YARDS, PAR 4

One of the most famous opening holes in golf, the first features the Swilcan Burn, which loops across in front of the green. Heed the advice of your caddie because, depending on the weather, and the club chosen, the burn is often 'in play' from the tee. Place your drive to the left-centre to avoid the out of bounds on the right. Somewhat deceptively, the green slopes from the rear down to the front and the burn. The stroke average on the hole in the Open Championship of 2005 was 3.97.

HOLE 2: DYKE
411 YARDS, PAR 4

Not only is the tee shot blind, but also hidden gorse and bunkers 200 yards out await a shot hit to the right. The percentage shot is to try and play the ball left of Cheape's bunker, which commemorates the Cheape family of Strathtyrum and its contributions to the Links. If the flagstick is on the left, consider pitching the ball short of the green and hoping it runs on. The 'dyke', or wall, forms the boundary between the hotel and the seventeenth fairway. In the 2005 Open Championship, the hole's difficulty ranking was 4, with a stroke average of 4.24. Be aware, as you will now be playing on double greens for the most part, that the incoming golfers have the right of way. White flags identify the outward nine holes and red flags the inward nine holes.

HOLE 3: CARTGATE (OUT)
370 YARDS, PAR 4

The hole's name comes from its being close to the old cart track that crossed the fairway and led to the beach. From the tee, there is plenty of room to the left of the fairway before the Principal's Nose bunker comes into play. On the second shot, take note of the Cartgate bunker in relation to the flagstick. The green slopes away from you. Generally, the hole plays quite easy. Its difficulty ranking in the 2005 Open Championship was 14, with a stroke average of 3.87.

HOLE 4: GINGER BEER
419 YARDS, PAR 4

Named after the more-potent-than-ginger-beer refreshments Old Daw Anderson sold alongside the hole in the 1850s, the tee shot should be aimed over the mound on the left and hit with a fade for a landing in the narrow valley. Greenside, there is a large mound on the right and a cluster of bunkers on the left.

HOLE 5: HOLE O' CROSS (OUT)
514 YARDS, PAR 5

The hole may be so named because some believe there was a cross on the hole. Aim the tee shot left of the Spectacles bunkers in the distance. Depending on the wind, the green can be reached with the second shot. As you evaluate the risk and reward, remember the green is 100 yards deep and may be the largest green in the world. The hole played the second easiest on the course in the 2005 Open Championship with a stroke average of 4.62.

HOLE 6: HEATHERY (OUT)
374 YARDS, PAR 4

The hole is so named because the original green was composed of heather, earth and small shards of seashell. As the tee shot is a blind shot, drive the ball over the market post as there are six bunkers on the right and four on the left. The deep pitch in front of the green will cause you to consider a chip-and-run shot to the flagstick.

HOLE 7: HIGH (OUT)
359 YARDS, PAR 4

Think 'middle' with your tee shot, or if you are driving well and can carry the ball 220 yards, aim over the gorse. The greenside Shell bunker, one of the largest on the Old Course, is to be avoided at all costs. Bumps and dips in the green add to the challenge. Enjoy the beautiful view of the Eden Estuary from the green.

HOLE 8: SHORT
166 YARDS, PAR 3

The name of the hole is self-explanatory. Pay attention to the strength and direction of the wind. On the first day of the 1995 Open Championship, only two birdies were posted and the hole played over par with a stroke average of 3.11.

HOLE 9: END
347 YARDS, PAR 4

The Kruger bunker and the Mrs Kruger bunker should pose no problem, though it did for me in the 'final round'. (The bunkers were built during the Boer War of 1899–1902, when the British were fighting in the Transvaal, an area of northern South Africa, and Paul Kruger was serving as president of the republic.) Avoid the Boase's and End Hole bunkers as they can cause problems. A tee shot on a line over the biggest bush is best. (At times, the green can be driven from the tee.) The approach shot is unique on the Old Course in that you will be hitting into the only green that is flat, round and without any significant greenside bunkers. I have often putted my second shot; you should consider this tactic also.

HOLE 10: BOBBY JONES
340 YARDS, PAR 4

When the great American golfer died, in 1971, St Andrews named the hole after him. Aim the tee ball to land in the middle of the fairway. The difficulty of the hole comes from second-shot decision-making based on hole location, the wind and how well you are striking your iron shots. Depending on the wind, this hole can also be driven from the tee. (Trivia question: what was the name of the hole before it was named Bobby Jones? I don't know the answer.)

HOLE 11: HIGH (IN)
174 YARDS, PAR 3

For good reason, many consider this hole one of the great par 3s in golf. It is also difficult as it played as the fifth-toughest hole in the 2005 Open Championship, with a difficulty ranking of 5 and a stroke average of 3.20. Wind direction and strength are always an issue, and the greenside bunkers, Hill and Strath, are very deep. (Strath bunker is named after the Strath brothers, particularly Davie Strath, who was a friend and golfing partner of Young Tom Morris.) The green's slope to the front is so severe that, depending on the location of the hole, you can, embarrassingly, putt the ball off the green.

220 Length, in metres, of the replaced gabion baskets between the fourth tee of Eden Links and the seventh green of the Old Course

HOLE 12: HEATHERY (IN)
316 YARDS, PAR 4

The key here is to drive the ball left of the Stroke bunker, so called because, once in it, you will almost always lose at least one stroke to par. The hole's location relative to the lateral ridge in the green should be evaluated when planning the second shot. A drive carrying 230 yards is necessary to carry all the trouble in the centre of the fairway.

HOLE 13: HOLE O' CROSS (IN)
418 YARDS, PAR 4

Avoid the Coffins bunkers, about 200 yards off the tee, by driving the ball either to the left or the right. The second shot cannot be hit short. A double green with hole five, the green's great depth can add an element of terror when the putter is in your hands. Walkinshaw bunker, on your left as you walk the fairway, should not pose a problem, though it often did for Mr Walkinshaw, a local golfer whose enthusiasm exceeded his proficiency.

HOLE 14: LONG
530 YARDS, PAR 5

This is the longest hole on the Links and has the Links' largest bunker, the dreaded Hell Bunker. It took Jack Nicklaus four shots to escape from the bunker in the 1995 Open Championship. Other prominent bunkers include Beardies, Kitchen and Grave. The ideal tee-shot line is left of the wall and right of the Beardies bunker. As the green slopes to the back, it makes holding a shot difficult particularly if the hole is playing downwind.

HOLE 15: CARTGATE (IN)
414 YARDS, PAR 4

The drive should be in line with the church steeple in the distance and between the two prominent humps (Miss Grainger's bosoms). The Sutherland bunker, beyond the broad Cottage bunker, refers to Mr A.G. Sutherland, a golfer who, in 1869, when he discovered this bunker had been filled in, supposedly had two cousins go out on the Links one night and rebuild the bunker. Cottage bunker refers to Pilmour Cottage, now Pilmour House, which is the headquarters of the St Andrews Links Trust and also serves as the Eden Clubhouse. For some reason or other, it always seems wise to play it safe and take an extra club for the second shot. The hole played over par in the 2005 Open Championship.

HOLE 16: CORNER OF THE DYKE
381 YARDS, PAR 4

A cluster of three bunkers makes up the Principal's Nose, which is possibly a reference to a Mr Haldane, a principal of St Mary's College in the early nineteenth century, who was blessed with a bulbous nose. Smart golfers drive their tee ball to the left of this bunker. (Remember Dr Duncan Lawrie's comments in Chapter 28.) The green is tight to the dyke. A second shot long is better than one short because of the banked ridge in the front of the green. This hole played the sixth most difficult in the Open Championship, with a stroke average of 4.19.

HOLE 17: ROAD
455 YARDS, PAR 4 (AND A CONTROVERSIAL 499 YARDS FOR THE 2010 OPEN CHAMPIONSHIP)

Famous to most as the most discussed and difficult single hole in golf, it is named after the old turnpike road running behind the green. This narrow paved road, which is a part of the golf course, has proven disastrous for many a professional, most memorably Tom Watson in 1984, when a par on the hole could have sealed him another Open Championship. The correct drive is over the sheds and out of bounds, with a slight draw, to the hidden fairway. (Forget about aiming on a specific letter of the hotel's signage; keep your head down and get through the ball.) The further right the tee ball is hit, the longer the carry to the fairway and the more certain the flirt with trouble in the form of the hotel and its outdoor garden, which are out of bounds. The small but treacherous Road Hole bunker in front of the green awaits those who foolishly believe they can carry it and have their shot hold the green. (Play safe for the front right corner of the green.) The hole played the most difficult in the 2005

Open Championship – as it does in any competition. The stroke average was 4.63.

HOLE 18: TOM MORRIS
357 YARDS, PAR 4

The eighteenth green, which slopes down quite severely from the right rear corner, was considered by Tom Morris to be his finest work. The correct tee shot, with as much club as you dare, is to aim at the clock on the R&A Clubhouse's facade. Avoid the Valley of Sin, the deep, trough-like depression in the front left of the green (which hosted an iced-over pond during the dismantling of the Starter's Box). Grannie Clark's Wynd, the lane that crosses the fairway 125 yards from the centre of the green, is in play, meaning balls landing there must be played as they lie. As this is the only hole on the Old Course with nearby buildings, know the exact yardage for your approach shot as distances appear to be foreshortened. When on the green, try to relax as you grip your putter, even though I know that you know the golf gods will be watching you – as will the strolling tourists and locals, who will certainly applaud as you hole your final putt. In the 2005 Open Championship, the hole played the easiest with a stroke average of 3.54.

GLOSSARY

ACE
A score of one on any golf hole. It most often occurs on a par-three hole.

BETTER-BALL MATCH
A golf match where golfers play in pairs or teams. The 'better ball' of each team on each hole is recorded.

BIRDIE
'The term "birdie" originated in the United States in 1899. H.B. Martin's *Fifty Years of American Golf* contains an account of a foursomes match played at the Atlantic City (NJ) CC. One of the players relates, "My ball . . . came to rest within six inches of the cup. I said 'That was a bird of a shot . . . I suggest that when one of us plays a hole in one under par he receives double compensation.' The other two agreed and we began right away, just as soon as the next one came, to call it a 'birdie'." In 19th-century American slang, "bird" referred to anyone or anything excellent or wonderful.' (Source: http://www.usgaMuseum.com)

BOGEY
'A score of "one" over par on any golf hole. The term "bogey" comes from a song that was popular in the British Isles in the early 1890s, called "The Bogey Man", later known as "The Colonel Bogey March". The character of the song was an elusive figure who hid in the shadows: "I'm the Bogey Man, catch me if you can." Golfers in Scotland and England equated the quest for the elusive Bogey Man with the quest for the elusive perfect score. By the mid to late 1890s, the term "bogey score" referred to the ideal score a good player could be expected to make on a hole

under perfect conditions. It also came to be used to describe stroke play tournaments – hence, in early Rules books we find a section detailing the regulations for "Bogey Competitions." It was only in the late 1900s/early 1910s that the concept of "par" started to emerge – this being the designated number of strokes a scratch player could be expected to take on a hole in ideal conditions. In this way, par was distinguished from bogey. The term par itself is a standard term in sports handicapping where it simply means "level" or "even."' (Source: http://www.usgaMuseum.com)

Broom
A plant that is similar to gorse but without the sharp spokes or thorns. It is really quite beautiful even when your golf ball is embedded in its branches. Broom is softer than gorse or whins, which are prickly.

Bunker
The correct word for the man- or nature-made obstacle on a golf course that contains sand is bunker, not 'sand trap'. At St Andrews, you can never complain and say 'there was no sand in that bunker'. Indeed, the course is all sand, from three inches or so below the grass and the top of the bunker surfaces, down to thirty feet and the water table.

Caddie (or, sometimes, 'caddy')
Historians believe the word can be traced to Mary, Queen of Scots, who was a passionate golfer as a young girl. When away at school in France, she had young men, '*cadets*' (loosely pronounced 'cad-day'), carry her clubs for her.

Captain or Club Captain
A term used to denote the member-elected, non-professional chief executive of a club; similar to a 'club president' in the US.

Castle Course
The seventh course at the Home of Golf, which opened for play on 28 June 2008, and which, like the Links, is owned by the town of St Andrews and operated on its behalf by the Links Trust. The course plays between 5,300 and 7,200 yards. There are currently no handicap restrictions on the Castle Course.

CLARET JUG
The popular name of the Golf Championship Trophy, which has been awarded since 1872 to the winner of the Open Championship.

CLEEK
'A long iron golf club used in bygone eras.'
(Source: http://www.usgaMuseum.com)

DORMIE
'A situation where a player or team cannot lose a match against their opponent(s) because the number of holes left to play is the same as the lead they hold. Historically, the term dormie is derived from the French/Latin cognate "dormir", meaning "to sleep", suggesting that a player who is "dormie" can relax (literally, go to sleep) without fear of losing the match.' (Source: http://www. usgaMuseum.com)

DOUBLE BOGEY
A score of two over par on any golf hole.

DOUBLE GREEN
There are seven double greens on the Old Course; that is, a green which is used by two holes instead of one during the course of playing a round of golf. They are: holes two and sixteen, three and fifteen, four and fourteen, five and thirteen, six and twelve, seven and eleven, eight and ten. (All combinations add up to eighteen.) The four holes with their own green are: one, nine, seventeen and eighteen.

EAGLE
'By analogy with "birdie", the term "eagle" soon thereafter became common to refer to a score one better than a "bird". Also by analogy, the term "albatross" stands for double eagle – an even bigger eagle.' (Source: http://www.usgaMuseum.com)

EMERGENCY ROOM
The closest bar to any given hole on a golf course.

Featherie (or, sometimes, 'Feathery')

Feathery golf balls were made, as early as 1618, from compressed and boiled chicken or goose feathers that were encased in a piece of horse or cow hide that had been shaped and sewn into a sphere. Lore suggests it required a quantity of feathers sufficient to fill the cylindrical crown of a man's silk top hat, or high hat, to make one ball. The balls were very expensive, as even the most experienced ball-maker could only produce one or two a day. (Often they cost more than golf clubs.) The balls were not only hard, but could also fly over 250 yards, though they were difficult to use in the rain, as the stitches that held the balls together would rot and split. Until the feathery was invented, only wooden balls had been used. Various shops in St Andrews made the feathery and all handmade and stamped the ball with their private brands. Among the names were Morris, Allan Robertson, Gourlay and Auchterlonie.

Fore

'The word "fore" is Scottish in origin, and is a shortened version of the word "before" or "afore." The old Scottish warning, essentially meaning "look out ahead," most probably originated in military circles, where it was used by artillery men as a warning to troops in forward positions. Golfers as early as the eighteenth century simply adopted this military warning cry for use on the links.' (Source: http://www.usgaMuseum.com)

Gold Sovereign

A 23-carat gold coin first issued in 1489. Current sovereigns are struck in the same 22-carat gold alloy as the first modern sovereign of 1817. Given the price of gold in mid-2009, a sovereign is worth about £400, or $775.

Golf (or, sometimes, 'Golff')

'What is the origin of the word "golf" or "golff?" The word "golf" is not an acronym for anything. Rather, it derives linguistically from the Dutch word "kolf" or "kolve" meaning quite simply "club." In the Scottish dialect of the late fourteenth or early fifteenth century, the Dutch term became "goff" or "gouff," and only later in the sixteenth century "golf" or "golff." The linguistic connections between the Dutch and Scottish terms are but one reflection of what was a very active trade industry between the Dutch ports and the ports on the east coast of Scotland from the fourteenth through seventeenth centuries. Some scholars suggest that the Dutch game of "kolf" played with a stick and ball on frozen canals in the wintertime, was brought by the Dutch sailors to the east coast of Scotland, where it was transferred on to the public linkslands and eventually became the game we know today.' (Source: http://www.usgaMuseum.com)

GOLF WIDOW
A term reserved, with no endearment attached, for a spouse, male or female, who is abandoned to their own devices on Saturday or Sunday morning – and any available time during other days of the week – while their partner plays a round of golf. Rumour has it that Mary, Queen of Scots, played golf in East Lothian, south of Edinburgh, a few days after the murder of Lord Darnley, her second husband, in 1567. If she did, she was surely the world's first golf widow.

GORSE
Native prickly, thorny, nearly impenetrable shrubs. Also known as whins. The flower, in the spring, is a dazzling yellow. It is almost impossible to hit a golf ball that has become lodged in the gorse.

GREEN(S)
The grassy area on a golf course where the grass is mown tight and a putter is most often, but not always, the club used in an attempt to play the golf ball into the hole.

GUTTA PERCHA, OR 'GUTTY'
Invented in St Andrews by the Rev. Dr Adams Paterson in 1848, it was made from gutta-percha packing material, gutta percha being the evaporated milk juice or rubber-like sap of the Malaysian gutta tree. When heated to the temperature of boiling water, the rubber softened, which made it easy to shape it into a sphere. It was inexpensive to produce and was easy to repair by reheating. The ball did not travel as far as the feathery because of its smooth surface.

Glossary

Heather
A moorland and mountain evergreen shrub that flowers with a beautiful purple-rose blossom in the summer. Like broom and gorse, it seems to strangle any golf ball hit into it.

Hell Bunker
The name of the enormous bunker that menacingly guards the golfer's second shot on the fourteenth hole of the Old Course.

Himalayas
The name of the public putting green adjacent to the Links Clubhouse.

In Reverse
The name given to an annual event on the Old Course in which the course is played in the now-accepted anticlockwise direction, as well as clockwise, as was common prior to the twentieth century.

Keepers of the Green
A Scotland-based charitable organisation that 'promotes the traditions of the game of golf and provides powered mobility for the needy'.

Links
As a supplement to Malcolm Campbell's 'links' description in the text, I add the following, courtesy of the USGA: '"Links" is a term that refers to a very specific geographic land form found in Scotland. Such tracts of low-lying, seaside land are characteristically sandy, treeless, and undulating, often with lines of dunes or dune ridges, and covered by bent grass and gorse. To be a true links, the tract of land must lie near the mouth of a river – that is, in an estuarine environment. From the Middle Ages onward, linksland (generally speaking, poor land for farming) were common grounds used for sports, including archery, bowls and golf. Because many of the early courses of Scotland were built on these common linksland, golf courses and links have forever been associated. The term "links" is commonly misapplied to refer to any golf course. But remember that a true links depends only on geography.' (Source: http://www.usgaMuseum.com)

Links Courses of St Andrews

Some form of golf has been played on the hallowed St Andrews grounds, now called the 'Old Course Links', since the fourteenth century. In the early days, the number of holes often varied, with as many as 18 holes in play up to 1764. Four holes were taken out of play that year because they were thought uninteresting and added to congestion. They were replaced by two new holes, bringing the total to eighteen – which is now the standard in golf courses throughout the world. It is said that a score of 80 was not broken on the Old until 1858, by Allan Robertson, golf's first true professional, who shot a 79. The course contains 112 deep and inviting bunkers, each with a name, and 14 double greens, with only the first, ninth, seventeenth and eighteenth holes having their own greens.

The Jubilee Links began its life as a 12-hole Links when it opened for play in 1897, partly in honour of Queen Victoria, whose Diamond Jubilee was that year. It was lengthened to 18 holes in 1905 at the suggestion of David Honeyman, Tom Morris's assistant. Between 1938 and 1946, further changes were made under the watchful eye of Willie Auchterlonie. The course underwent a Donald Steel redesign in 1989, when it was extended to 6,742 yards.

The Eden Links, designed by H.S. Colt and Dr Alister MacKenzie, opened in 1913. The course is short, at just over 6,200 yards, but with only one par five, it still offers a challenge, though a less testing one than on the Old, New and Jubilee.

The New Course Links, designed by Old Tom Morris, opened for play in 1895. The course has 60 bunkers and thick rough. Accuracy is the premium. The course has just one double green: the third and fifteenth.

Balgove Links, a 1,520-yard nine-hole course, has bunkering and a double green and provides children and beginners with a true golfing challenge. It was opened in 1972 and remodelled by Donald Steel in 1993.

Strathtyrum Links, an 18-hole course, opened in 1993. It takes its name from the Strathtyrum Estate, of the Cheape family, from which the land was purchased. Though a short course by today's standards, and with only 15 bunkers, it offers enjoyable golf and a respite to the tougher championship layouts. It was built in 1993, with the intention of serving juniors, high handicappers and those just becoming acquainted with the game.

GLOSSARY

LINKS TRUST OF ST ANDREWS
The Trust was created by an Act of Parliament in 1974 to manage the Links as public golf courses open to everyone. The email address is: www.standrews.org.uk; the telephone number for reservations and other enquiries is: +44 (0)1334 466666.

OPEN CHAMPIONSHIP WINNERS
The 27 winners on the Old Course from 1873 to 2005 are: 1873, Tom Kidd; 1876, Bob Martin; 1879, Jamie Anderson; 1882, Bob Ferguson; 1885, Bob Martin; 1888, Jack Burns; 1891, Hugh Kirkaldy; 1895, J.H. Taylor; 1900, J.H. Taylor; 1905, James Braid; 1910, James Braid; 1921, Jock Hutchison; 1927, R.T. Jones; 1933, Densmore Shute; 1939, Dick Burton; 1946, Sam Snead; 1955, Peter Thomson; 1957, Bobby Locke; 1960, Kel Nagle; 1964, Tony Lema; 1970, Jack Nicklaus; 1978, Jack Nicklaus; 1984, Seve Ballesteros; 1990, Nick Faldo; 1995, John Daly; 2000, Tiger Woods; 2005, Tiger Woods.

OPEN CHAMPIONSHIP COURSES IN THE ROTA
The Open Championship is currently rotated between nine golf courses in England and Scotland. They are: Carnoustie (Championship Course), Scotland; Muirfield, Scotland; Old Course, St Andrews, Scotland; Royal Birkdale Golf Club, Southport, England; Royal Liverpool Golf Club, Hoylake, England; Royal Lytham & St Annes Golf Club, Lancashire, England; Royal St George's Golf Club, Sandwich, England; Royal Troon Golf Club, South Ayrshire, Scotland; and Turnberry, South Ayrshire, Scotland.

PAR
The number of golf strokes considered necessary to complete play of a golf hole proficiently.

SAINT ANDREW
An Apostle who, like Judas, Bartholomew and Simon, does not have a book in the Bible. In addition to having a town named after him, supposedly because a Greek monk brought his relics to the area in ancient times, he is also the patron saint of Scotland, and of women.

Saltire
The flag of Scotland, one of the oldest in the world, represents Saint Andrew's cross, formed by the crossing of a bend and a bend sinister (from heraldry); or, a white cross on a blue field.

Sand trap
A slang term for 'bunker'. Its use is considered disrespectful to the game of golf.

Shank
There are three words that are never uttered on a golf course. The other two are *divorce* and *alcoholism*. A shank is a golf shot hit where the clubface meets the shaft. The end result is that, for a right-handed golfer, the ball makes a very quick exit off the clubface to the right and generally finds trouble or, worse, is lost.

Swilcan Bridge
One of the most photographed icons in sport, the little Roman-era (it is thought) bridge spans the Swilcan Burn in front of the eighteenth tee of the Old Course. It is much copied by golf courses around the world who hope that a replica constructed on their course will bring them immediate identification with the very public Home of Golf. Also called the 'Roman Bridge'.

Valley of Sin
The name of the menacing deep depression in front of the eighteenth green on the Old Course. It is most recently famous, in competition, from the 1995 Open Championship, when Costantino Rocca holed a sixty-five-foot putt from its surface to force a four-hole play-off with John Daly, which Daly won.

BIBLIOGRAPHY

Alexander, Jules, *The Hogan Mystique* (The American Golfer Inc., 1994).

Allianz Presents, *St Andrews Links from A–Z* (Allianz SE, 2009).

Anon., *The Golf Library of a Gentleman* (PBA Galleries, 2003).

Anon., *Golf Journal* (United States Golf Association, 2003).

Anon., *Masters: The Pocket Caddie* (HM Publishing Inc., 1991).

Anon., *The Official Guide to Golf in Scotland* (Pro-Sports Promotions Ltd, 2006).

Anon., *The Scottish Clans and their Tartans* (Chartwell Books, Inc., 1992).

Anon., *Scottish Golf Union: Official Yearbook, 2003* (Pro Sports Promotions Ltd, 2003).

Anon., *A Year at St Andrews: The Home of Golf* (Highpoint Media Ltd, 2001–09).

Beckwith, Harry, *Selling the Invisible: A Field Guide to Modern Marketing* (Warner Books Inc., 1997).

Billian, Douglas C., *Golf Book of Records* (Billian Publishing Inc., 1989).

Boswell, Thomas, *Strokes of Genius* (Doubleday & Company, Inc., 1987).

Campbell, Malcolm, *The Scottish Golf Book* (Sports Publishing Inc., 1999).

Coffey, Frank (ed.), *Golfers on Golf* (Barnes & Noble, Inc., 1997).

Cohat, Yves, *The Vikings: Lords of the Sea* (Harry N. Abrams, Inc., 1992).

Cook, Helen, *Old St Andrews* (St Andrews Preservation Trust and Stenlake Publishing Limited, 2001).

—— *St Andrews in the 20s, 30s and 40s* (Stenlake Publishing Limited, 2008).

—— *St Andrews in the 50s, 60s and 70s* (Stenlake Publishing Limited).

Cook, Kevin (ed.), *Sports Illustrated: The Golf Book* (Sports Illustrated Books/Time Inc., 2009).

Cornish, Geoffrey S. and Whitten, Ronald E., *The Golf Course* (The Rutledge Press, 1981).

Darwin, Bernard, *The Golf Courses of the British Isles* (a facsimile of the original 1910 edition; Story Communications/Ailsa, Inc., 1988).

Davis, William H., *100 Greatest Golf Courses – and Then Some* (Golf Digest/Tennis Inc., 1982).

Dear, Tony, *Every Golf Question You Ever Wanted Answered* (Collins & Brown Limited, 2002).

Douglas, Ronald Macdonald, *Scottish Lore And Folklore* (Beekman House, 1982).

Duncan, George, *Book of Scottish Golf Courses* (The SMT Magazine and Scottish Country Life, 1945).

Eisen, Armand, *Golf: Life on the Links* (Ariel Books/Andrews McMeel Publishing, 2001).

Els, Ernie, *How to Build a Classic Golf Swing* (HarperPerennial, 1999).

Exley, Helen (ed.), *Golf Quotations* (Exley Publications Ltd, 1992).

Faldo, Nick, with Simmons, Richard, *Faldo: A Swing for Life* (Phoenix Illustrated/Orion Publishing Group, 1995).

Fazio, Tom, *Golf Course Designs by Fazio* (Paragon Press, 1984).

Finegan, James W., *Where Golf is Great: The Finest Courses of Scotland and Ireland* (Artisan, 2006).

Finsterwald, Dow, *The Wedges: Pitching and Sand* (Sterling Publishing Co., Inc., 1965).

Fodor's Travel Guides, *Scotland* (Hodder & Stoughton, 1983).

Gambaro, Cristina, *Castles of Scotland: Past and Present* (Barnes & Noble Publishing Inc., 2005).

Gilbert, Andy, *The Art of Making a Difference* (Go MAD Books, 2001).

Gummer, Scott, *The Seventh at St Andrews: How Scotsman David McLay Kidd and His Ragtag Band . . .* (Penguin Group USA, 2007).

Hagen, Walter, as told to Heck, Margaret Seaton, *The Walter Hagen Story* (Simon and Schuster, 1956).

Harney, Paul, *How to Putt* (Sterling Publishing Co., Inc., 1965).

Harris, Paul (compiler), *Scotland: An Anthology* (Cadogan Publications Ltd, 1985).

Hotelling, Neal, *Pebble Beach: The Official Golf History* (Triumph Books, 2009).

—— *Pebble Beach Golf Links: The Official History* (Sleeping Bear Press, 1999).

Iooss, Jr., Walter, *Classic Golf* (Harry N. Abrams, Inc., 2004).

Jarrett, Tom, *St Andrews Golf Links: The First 600 Years* (Mainstream Publishing, 1995).

—— and Mason, Peter, *St Andrews Links: Six Centuries of Golf* (Mainstream Publishing, 2009).

Jones, Robert Trent (ed.), *Great Golf Stories* (Galahad Books, 1982).

Joy, David, *St Andrews and the Open Championship*, (Sleeping Bear Press, 2000).

—— and Lowe, Iain Macfarlane, *St Andrews and the Open Championship: The Official History* (Sleeping Bear Press, 1999).

—— —— and Phillips, Kyle, *Scottish Golf Links* (Clock Tower Press, 2004).

—— —— and —— *St Andrews, the Old Course and Open Champions* (St Andrews Press, 2000).

Klein, Naomi, *No Logo* (Picador, 2002).

Lamont-Brown, Raymond, *St Andrews: City by the Northern Sea* (Birlinn Limited, 2006).

—— *St Andrews: Scotland in Old Photographs* (Alan Sutton Publishing Limited, 1996).

—— *Villages of Fife* (John Donald Publishers, 2002).

Lim, Gerrie, *Idol to Icon: The Creation of Celebrity Brands* (Marshall Cavendish Business, 2005).

Lowe, Iain Macfarlane, *Scottish Golf Links: A Photographer's Journey* (Clock Tower Press, 2004).

Lyle, Sandy, *The Championship Courses of Scotland* (The Kingswood Press, 1982).

MacAlindin, Bob *Links with the Past* (Dunfermline Publishing Services, 2000).

Machat, Udo, *The Golf Courses of the Monterey Peninsula* (Simon and Schuster, 1989).

Mackay, Charles, *The Auld Scots Dictionary* (Lang Syne Publishing, 2003).

MacKenzie, Alister, *The Spirit of St. Andrews* (Clock Tower Press, 1998).

Mackenzie, Richard, *A Wee Nip at the 19th Hole* (Sleeping Bear Press, 1997).

Mackie, Keith, *Golf at St Andrews* (Aurum Press, 1995).

MacKinnon, Charles, *Scottish Highlanders: A Personal View* (Marboro Books Corp., 1984).

Matthew, Sidney L., *Wry Stories on the Road Hole* (Sleeping Bear Press, 2000).

McCallen, Brian, *Golf Resorts of the World: The Best Places to Stay and Play* (Harry N. Abrams, 1993).

McCaw, Harry and Henderson, Brum, *Royal County Down Golf Club* (The Royal County Down Golf Club, 1988).

McCord, Robert R., *Golf: An Album of its History* (Burford Books, Inc., 1998).

McGuire, Brenda and McGuire, John, *Golf at the Water's Edge: Scotland's Seaside Links* (Abbeville Press, 1997).

Miller, Dick, *Triumphant Journey: The Saga of Bobby Jones and The Grand Slam of Golf* (Holt, Rinehart and Winston, 1980).

Morris, Tom and Joy, David (compiler), *The Scrapbook of Old Tom Morris* (John Wiley & Sons, Incorporated, 2001).

Nicklaus, Jack with Bowden, Ken, *The Full Swing* (Golf Digest/Tennis Inc., 1984).

—— —— *Jack Nicklaus' Lesson Tee* (Simon and Schuster, 1977).

Peper, George, *Golf Courses of the PGA Tour* (Harry N. Abrams Incorporated, 1986).

—— *Two Years in St. Andrews* (Simon and Schuster, 2006).

Pitkin Guide, *St Andrews: The Royal Burgh* (Pitkin Guides, 2000).

Pride, Glen L., *The Kingdom of Fife* (The Rutland Press, 1999).

Quirin, William, *America's Linksland: A Century of Long Island Golf* (Clock Tower Press, 2002).

Riding, Alan and Dunton-Downer, Leslie, *Opera* (Dorling Kindersley, 2006).

Robinson, Lawrence and Graham, James (eds), *Golfer's Digest: First Anniversary Deluxe Edition* (Golfer's Digest Association, 1966).

Ruskin, Bill with Renfrew, Tom, *The American Golfer's Guide to Scotland* (Author House, 2004).

Santella, Chris, *Fifty Places to Play Golf Before You Die* (Stewart, Tabori & Chang, 2005).

Shapiro, Mel, Dohn, Warren and Berger, Leonard, *Golf: A Turn-of-the-Century Treasury* (Castle, 1986).

Smith, Douglas LaRue, *Winged Foot Story: The Golf, The People, The Friendly Trees* (Winged Foot Golf Club Inc., 1984).

Steel, Donald, *Classic Golf Links of England, Scotland, Wales, and Ireland* (Pelican Publishing Company Inc., 1992).

Stevens, Mark, *Your Marketing Sucks* (Three Rivers Press, 2005).

Tatum, Frank 'Sandy', Jr., *A Love Affair With the Game* (The American Golfer Inc., 2002).

Tillinghast, Albert Warren, *The Course Beautiful: A Collection of Original and Photographs on Golf Course Design* (TreeWolf Productions, 1995).

—— *Gleaning From the Wayside: My Recollections as a Golf Course Architect* (TreeWolf Productions, 2001).

—— *Reminiscences of the Past: A Treasury of Creative Essays and Vintage Photographs on Scottish and Early American Golf* (TreeWolf Productions, 1998).

Updike, John, *Golf Dreams* (Alfred A. Knopf, 1996).

Ward-Thomas, Pat, *The New World Atlas of Golf: The Great Courses and How They are Played* (Gallery Books, 1976).

Wentz, Leon E., *Pebble Beach to Augusta* (Mountain Lion, Inc., 2006).

Wexler, Daniel, *Lost Links: Forgotten Treasures of Golf's Golden Age* (Clock Tower Press, 2003).

—— *The Missing Links: America's Greatest Lost Golf Courses & Holes* (Clock Tower Press, 2000).

Wind, Herbert Warren, *Following Through* (Ticknor & Fields, 1985).

—— *Herbert Warren Wind's Golf Book* (Simon and Schuster, 1981).

Wodehouse, P.G., *Fore! The Best of Wodehouse on Golf* (Ticknor & Fields, 1983).

Zaczek, Iain, *Clans and Tartans of Scotland* (Barnes & Noble, Inc., 2000).

Znamierowski, Alfred, *The World Encyclopedia of Flags* (Hermes House, 2002).

ST ANDREWS LINKS:
SIX CENTURIES OF GOLF
Tom Jarrett and Peter Mason

ISBN 9781845965013

£20.00 (HARDBACK)

AVAILABLE NOW

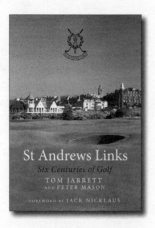

Recognised the world over as the 'Home of Golf', St Andrews Links has borne witness to over 600 years of golfing history. That the game evolved and developed into its final form here has never been in question: St Andrews is the home of the game's most influential ruling body, the Royal and Ancient Golf Club, and it was here in 1764, when the 22-hole Old Course was reduced, that today's standard 18-hole round was established.

One golf course has now become seven, and many of golf's most dramatic moments, affecting the world's greatest players, have occurred here. The Links has played host to the game's greats, among them Allan Robertson and the Morrises in the nineteenth century, Bobby Jones and Jack Nicklaus in the twentieth, and Tiger Woods in the twenty-first, as well as those enthusiastic amateurs for whom the chance to play St Andrews' hallowed turf is a dream come true. As the great Jack Nicklaus remarked: 'If a golfer is to be remembered, he must win the title at St Andrews.'

The worldwide fame of St Andrews is the result of a unique 110-year-old partnership between the town's local government and the R&A, who between them have assured the Links' status, by Act of Parliament, as public courses. This celebratory volume, the official history of golf's most important location, was written by Tom Jarrett, a caddie, journalist, golfer and author who lived all his life in this historic town, and has been updated by Peter Mason, who was involved in managing the Links throughout its most intensive – and controversial – phrase of development.